Wafer, Weltkunst, Wanderlust
Wirtschaftsstandort Dresden

Wafers, World Art, Wanderlust
Business Location Dresden

Herausgegeben in Zusammenarbeit mit der
Industrie- und Handelskammer Dresden

*Published in cooperation with the
Dresden Chamber of Commerce and Industry*

Redaktion / *Editorial work*:
Cornelia Pretzsch
Geschäftsführerin (IHK) / *Executive Officer (CCI)*

Autor / *Author*:
Stefan Frohmader, Dresden
freier Journalist und PR-Berater / *free journalist and PR adviser*

Erste Ausgabe 2012
First edition 2012

Verlag Kommunikation & Wirtschaft GmbH, Oldenburg (Oldb)

Wafer, Weltkunst, Wanderlust
Wirtschaftsstandort Dresden

Wafers, World Art, Wanderlust
Business Location Dresden

Bibliographische Information der
Deutschen Bibliothek
Die Deutsche Bibliothek verzeichnet diese
Publikation in der Deutschen National-
bibliographie; detaillierte bibliographische
Daten sind im Internet über
http://dnb.ddb.de abrufbar.

Das Buch erscheint im Verlagsbereich
Regionalmedien
Alle Rechte bei Kommunikation &
Wirtschaft GmbH, Oldenburg (Oldb)

Printed in Germany 2012

Das Manuskript ist Eigentum des Verlages.
Alle Rechte vorbehalten. Auswahl und
Zusammenstellung sind urheberrechtlich
geschützt. Für die Richtigkeit der im
Inhaltsverzeichnis aufgeführten Autoren-
beiträge und der PR-Texte übernehmen
Verlag und Redaktion keine Haftung.

Übersetzungen:
KERN AG, Sprachendienste, Bremen

Bildbearbeitung:
Kommunikation & Wirtschaft GmbH,
Oldenburg (Oldb)

Druck:
B.o.s.s Druck und Medien GmbH, Goch

Bildquellen: Seite 144

ISBN 978-3-88363-339-8

Bibliographic information of the German
National Library
The German National Library records this
publication in the German National
Bibliography. Detailed bibliographic data
can be called up on the internet via
http://dnb.ddb.de.

This book is published in the division
Regionalmedien
All rights reserved by Kommunikation &
Wirtschaft GmbH, Oldenburg (Oldb)

Printed in Germany 2012

The manuscript is the property of the
publisher. All rights reserved. The selection
and compilation are protected by copy-
right. The publisher and editor accept no
liability for the accuracy of the author
contributions and PR-texts detailed in the
contents.

Translations:
KERN AG, Sprachendienste, Bremen

Image processing:
Kommunikation & Wirtschaft GmbH,
Oldenburg (Oldb)

Printing:
B.o.s.s Druck und Medien GmbH, Goch

Picture sources: page 144

ISBN 978-3-88363-339-8

■ Vorwort	6	■ Foreword	6
Dr. Detlef Hamann, Hauptgeschäftsführer der Industrie- und Handelskammer Dresden		Dr. Detlef Hamann, CEO of the Dresden Chamber of Commerce and Industry	
■ Canaletto-Blick auf Ostsachsen	8	■ Canaletto view of East Saxony	8
Schöne Aussichten		Good views	
■ Wandel, Wachstum, Wunder	18	■ Change, growth, miracles	18
Lebensraum und Wirtschaft in der Zeitmaschine		Living space and business in a time machine	
■ Sechs Richtige im globalen Wettbewerb Schwergewichte und Innovationstreiber	47	■ Six winners in global competition Heavyweights and innovation drivers	47
Genau richtig:		Big winners:	
Ernährungswirtschaft	48	Food industry	48
Maschinen- und Anlagenbau	52	Machine and plant construction	52
Mikroelektronik und Informationstechnologie	59	Microelectronics and information technology	60
Metallerzeugung und -verarbeitung	69	Metal production and processing	70
Energie- und Umwelttechnologie	74	Energy and environment technology	74
Bio- und Nanotechnologie	79	Bio- and nanotechnology	80
■ Sprudelnde Quellen für Spitzenleistungen	86	■ Flourishing sources for top achievements	86
Forschungspool von Weltrang		World ranking research pool	
■ Von Arzneimittel bis Zeitmesser	93	■ Drugs, chronometers and much more besides	93
Neue Chancen mit Tradition, Qualität und Vielfalt		New chances with tradition, quality and diversity	
■ „Der Sachse liebt das Reisen sehr"	117	■ "The Saxons love to travel"	117
Tourismus als Wirtschaftsfaktor		Tourism as an economic factor	
■ Kein schöner Land	124	■ No place more beautiful	124
Ein unverwechselbarer Lebens- und Kulturraum		Unmistakable living space and culture area	
■ Coaching für die Zukunft	134	■ Coaching for the future	134
Die IHK Dresden stärkt Vertrauen und Zuversicht		Dresden CCI reinforces trust and confidence	
■ Verzeichnis der PR-Bildbeiträge	142	■ List of illustrated contributions	142
■ Bildquellen	144	■ Picture sources	144

Vorwort

Sächsischer Erfindergeist und sächsisches Unternehmertum brachten bereits im letzten Drittel des 19. Jahrhunderts eine tragfähige industrielle Produktion und einen florierenden Handel hervor. Glas- und Porzellanindustrie, Feinmechanik und Maschinenbau legten als Wegbereiter einer modernen Industriekultur die Grundsteine wirtschaftlichen Wachstums in Mitteldeutschland. Im Verlauf der Jahrzehnte entwickelte sich der mitteldeutsche Raum so zu einem bedeutenden Industrie- und Handelsstandort in Europa. Sachsen zählt heute technologisch zu den innovativsten und gefragtesten Investitionsstandorten weltweit. Im Zusammenwirken von Wirtschaft, Forschung und Politik avancierte die Region zu einer der wirtschaftlich dynamischsten. Im Fokus liegt vor allem das Dreiländereck Deutschland–Polen–Tschechien, in dem sich der IHK-Bezirk Dresden befindet. Investoren und Touristen schätzen auch andere Vorzüge der Region. Kulturelle Reichtümer, sportliche Traditionen und reizvolle Landschaften machen diesen Landstrich liebens- und lebenswert. Erfolgreich arbeiten, entspannt wohlfühlen – das Verhältnis stimmt. Willkommen in Sachsen. Willkommen im Kammerbezirk. Willkommen in der IHK Dresden – einer Kammer mit 150-jähriger Geschichte!

Der Ballungsraum um die sächsische Landeshauptstadt Dresden gehört heute zu den wirtschaftsstärksten Räumen in Deutschland. Die Region zieht nicht nur mit ihren kulturellen Reichtümern weltweit Aufmerksamkeit auf sich, auch viele der hier ansässigen Unternehmen haben sich international einen ausgezeichneten Ruf erworben. Exzellentes Fachwissen hat die Region zu einem besonders attraktiven Investitionsraum gemacht. Firmen aus den Wachstumsbranchen Mikroelektronik, Bio- oder Nanotechnologie profitieren von der Nähe zur Technischen Universität und den Hochschulen ebenso, wie zu den Helmholtz-, Max-Planck-, Leibniz- und Fraunhofer-Instituten. Firmen wie Siemens, Infineon, GLOBALFOUNDRIES oder VW nutzen dieses Potenzial und binden gut ausgebildete Nachwuchskräfte an ihre Unternehmen. Leistungsstark zeigt sich auch die Infrastruktur. Ob auf der Straße, per Schiene, Schiff oder Flugzeug – Unternehmen bietet die verkehrsgünstige Lage der Region ideale Ausgangsbedingungen zur Erschließung der Märkte sowohl in den benachbarten ost- und südosteuropäischen Ländern als auch weltweit.

Foreword

Saxonian ingenuity and Saxonian entrepreneurship already laid the foundation for sound industrial production and flourishing trade in the last third of the 19th century. The glass and porcelain industry, precision engineering and mechanical engineering succeeded in paving the way for a state-of-the-art industrial culture that has facilitated economic growth in Central Germany. Thus, in the course of the last decades, the Central German region has developed into an industrial and trade location of significant importance within Europe. Today, when considered from a technological vantage point, Saxony is among the most innovative and sought-after investment locations worldwide. In cooperation with the economy, research and politics, the region has advanced to one of the economically most dynamic. In key focus, first and foremost, is the Three-Country Point of Germany, Poland and the Czech Republic, in which the Chamber of Commerce and Industry (CCI) district of Dresden is located. What is more, investors and tourists also appreciate the other regional benefits. A treasure trove of cultural riches, sporting traditions and truly inspiring landscapes all contribute in making this stretch of land particularly endearing and also worthwhile living in. Success at work, and a feeling of well-being during leisure activities – the ratio between the two is attractive. Welcome to Saxony. Welcome to the chamber's district. Welcome to the Dresden Chamber of Commerce and Industry (CCI) – a chamber that can look back at a history spanning 150 years!

Today, the agglomeration area surrounding the Saxonian state capital of Dresden ranks among the strongest economic regions in Germany. The region succeeds in attracting global interest, not only thanks to its vast array of cultural treasures, but also because numerous companies located here have an excellent reputation throughout the world. Outstanding expertise has made this region a particularly attractive area for investing. Companies from the growth industry branches such as microelectronics, bio- or nanotechnology benefit from the proximity to the University of Technology and other universities, as well as the presence of the Helmholtz, Max Planck, Leibniz and Fraunhofer Institutes. Companies such as Siemens, Infineon, GLOBALFOUNDRIES or VW make use of this potential and are successful at binding well-educated junior employees to their companies. On top of this, the infrastructure is also highly efficient. Be it by road, by rail, by ship or aeroplane – the easily accessible location of this region offers companies

Vorwort

Der Bogenschütze am Neustädter Elbufer in Dresden

The archer on the Neustädter bank of the River Elbe in Dresden

Wie es der Titel bereits erahnen lässt, möchte Ihnen das vorliegende Buch möglichst viele Facetten, die den Wirtschaftsstandort Dresden – vom Wafer über Weltkunst bis zur Wanderlust – ausmachen, auf eine unterhaltsame und wissenswerte Weise näher bringen. Es soll aber auch eine ganz praktische Aufgabe erfüllen. Es soll Kooperationen und neue Geschäftskontakte mit den auf den folgenden Seiten präsentierten Firmen und Ihnen als Leser fördern. Und wer weiß, vielleicht ist die Region Dresden ja auch Ihr Unternehmensstandort der Zukunft?!

Dr. Detlef Hamann
Hauptgeschäftsführer der Industrie- und Handelskammer Dresden
CEO of the Dresden Chamber of Commerce and Industry

ideal exit criteria for accessing the neighbouring Eastern- and Southern-European countries and also for opening up new markets worldwide.

As the title has already suggested, this book would like to act as a platform, presenting the numerous facets that make the business location of Dresden to what it is – from wafers to world art, right up to wanderlust. The intention is to present it in an entertaining manner, with many worthwhile facts. Yet, is should also satisfy a very practical purpose. It should promote cooperations and new business contacts with the companies that are to be presented on the following pages, and support you as a reader. And who knows, perhaps the region of Dresden might also become your future company location?!

Canaletto-Blick auf Ostsachsen
Schöne Aussichten

Kursachsen 1748. Ein junger Italiener wandelt am rechten Elbufer stromaufwärts. Er blickt zur Augustusbrücke mit ihren 17 Bögen, schaut zur Stadt am anderen Elbufer. Ja, von hier aus will er Dresden malen. Die sächsische Residenzstadt ist in Europa zu Ansehen und Glanz gekommen. Die Bauweise, die ihre Silhouette prägt, wird man später Barock nennen. Bernardo Bellotto – Mitte zwanzig – ist Hofmaler von August III., Kurfürst von Sachsen und König von Polen.

Der Sohn Augusts des Starken liebt die venezianische Malerei und schätzt den talentierten Künstler, der sich nach seinem berühmten Onkel in Venedig Canaletto nennt. Der junge Canaletto malt die prächtige Stadt wirklichkeitsgetreu bis hin zu ihrem Spiegelbild im Elbwasser. Nur bei der im Bau befindlichen Hofkirche schummelt er ein wenig: Den imposanten Turm fügt er kühn hinzu, obwohl dieser erst Jahre später vollendet sein wird.

Verführung zum eigenen Bildnis

Canaletto hat viele Stadtansichten – Veduten genannt – mit venezianisch feinem Pinselstrich gemalt. Keine ist so berühmt geworden wie die Dresdner von 1748. Kein anderes Gemälde hat zugleich das weltweite Bild von Dresden so geprägt wie der 2,37 Meter breite und 1,33 Meter hohe „Canaletto-Blick", der sich heute in der Gemäldegalerie Alte Meister befindet. Ein Blick, der die Wirklichkeit getreu ins Auge fasst und zugleich die Fantasie beflügelt – könnte man sich auch vorstellen, diesen auf einen ganzen Landstrich zu richten? Lassen Sie uns mit einem Augenzwinkern diesen Blick wagen. Schauen wir auf ein Gebiet, das sich von Dresden aus in alle Himmelsrichtungen über 7931 Quadratkilometer erstreckt und 43 Prozent der Fläche Sachsens einnimmt.

Auf diesem Terrain mit Flach- und Hügelland, Mittelgebirgen, Elbe, Spree und Neiße leben 1,624 Millionen Menschen, fast 40 Prozent aller Einwohner Sachsens. Über 551 000 von ihnen sind sozialversicherungspflichtig beschäftigt, wiederum fast 40 Prozent der Beschäftigten in ganz Sachsen. Reichlich ein Fünftel arbeitet im produzierenden Gewerbe, zwölf Prozent erbringen freiberufliche, wissenschaftliche, technische und sonstige wirtschaftliche Dienstleistungen.

Der Verwaltungsstruktur nach gliedert sich dieses Territorium in die Großstadt Dresden und – von West nach Ost – die Landkreise Meißen, Sächsische Schweiz-Osterzgebirge, Bautzen und Görlitz mit rund 200 Städten und Gemeinden. Aus wirtschaft-

Canaletto view of East Saxony
Good views

Electorate of Saxony, 1748. A young Italian walks up river along the right bank of the river Elbe. He sees the Augustus bridge with its 17 arches and looks across at the city on the other bank. Yes, this is where he will sit to paint Dresden. Saxony's city of residence has acquired prestige and splendour in Europe. The style of architecture that defines its silhouette will become known as late Baroque. In his mid twenties, Bernardo Bellotto is the court painter of August III, Elector of Saxony and King of Poland.

The son of August the Strong loves Venetian painting and esteems the talented artist who calls himself Canaletto after his famous uncle in Venice. The young Canaletto produces a realistic picture of the splendid city right down to its reflection in the river Elbe, cheating just a little with the court church where he cunningly adds the impressive tower which in fact was only completed years later.

Drawing our own portrait

Canaletto painted many cityscapes, called vedutas, with his fine Venetian brush strokes. None has become quite as famous as the picture of Dresden dated 1748. At the same time, no other painting has shaped the world's view of Dresden as the "Canaletto View" measuring 2.37 metres in width and 1.33 metres in height and which can be seen today in the Old Masters Art Gallery. A view which is true to reality while still inspiring the imagination – is it possible to take such a view of the whole region? Let us make a not-quite-serious attempt to do just that: let us look at an area spreading out from Dresden in all the directions of the compass covering 7,931 square kilometres and accounting for 43 percent of the state surface area.

This territory with its plains, hills and mountains together with the rivers Elbe, Spree and Neiße is home to 1,624 million people or nearly 40 percent of Saxony's total population. More than 551,000 of them are gainfully employed, in turn accounting for nearly 40 percent of the workforce in the whole of Saxony. A good fifth work in manufacturing, while 12 percent provide freelance, scientific, technical or other services.

Blick vom Neustädter Elbufer auf die Augustusbrücke und den Stadtkern von Dresden im 18. Jahrhundert, besser bekannt als „Canaletto-Blick".

Seit Jahrhunderten nahezu unverändert, dabei aber lohnenswert wie eh und je: der Blick auf Dresden wie Canaletto (richtiger Name Bernardo Bellotto, 1722–80) ihn sah.

Das obere Bild zeigt das weltbekannte Gemälde des Künstlers aus der Staatlichen Kunstsammlung Dresden, Galerie der Alten Meister.

View from the Neustädter bank of the River Elbe to the Augustus bridge (Augustusbrücke) and the city centre of Dresden in the 18th century, better known as the "Canaletto View".

Virtually unchanged for centuries, yet definitely still worth the visit: the view across the city of Dresden as Canaletto (whose real name is Bernardo Bellotto, 1722–80) saw it.

The image at the top shows the world-famous painting by the artist, from the Dresden State Art Collection, Gallery of Old Masters.

licher Sicht ist die Bezeichnung „Kammerbezirk der Industrie- und Handelskammer Dresden" zutreffend. Hier sind fast 97 000 Mitgliedsunternehmen der IHK Dresden angesiedelt, mehr als jemals in deren 150-jähriger Geschichte.

Frei, demokratisch, sächsisch

Landsmannschaftlich gehört das Gebiet zu Sachsen, zusammen mit den sechs Landkreisen um die Großstädte Leipzig und Chemnitz. 1990 hat das östlichste Bundesland die Zusatzbezeichnung „Freistaat" gewählt. Diese trug Sachsen bereits in der Weimarer Republik, um auf seine neu gewonnene Demokratie aufmerksam zu machen. Freie Bürger gingen auch aus der Friedlichen Revolution 1989 in der DDR hervor. In Sachsen hatte sie mutig ihren Anfang genommen. So lag es nahe, dass die Sachsen erneut den symbolträchtigen Beinamen wählten.

In terms of administration, the territory breaks down into the City of Dresden and (from West to East), the rural districts of Meißen, Sächsische Schweiz-Osterzgebirge (Saxon Switzerland/Eastern Erzgebirge), Bautzen and Görlitz with around 200 towns and municipalities. In business terms, the area is referred to as the "Chamber District of Dresden Chamber of Commerce and Industry", with nearly 97,000 member companies, more than ever before in the 150-year history of the CCI Dresden.

Free, democratic, Saxon

When it comes to state affiliation, the area belongs to Saxony, together with the six rural districts around the cities of Leipzig and Chemnitz. In 1990, the most eastern federal state chose to give itself the attribute of "Free State". Saxony had already used this name during the Weimar Republic to draw attention to its

Die Bastei ist eine der meistbesuchten Touristenattraktionen in der Sächsischen Schweiz.

The bastion is one of the most popular tourist attractions in Saxon Switzerland.

Schaut man auf die Landkarte, so teilt die Linie zwischen der nördlichen Elbestadt Strehla und der südlichen Erzgebirgsgemeinde Hermsdorf Sachsen in einen westlichen und einen östlichen Teil. Liegen die IHK-Bezirke Leipzig und Chemnitz westlich, so ist das östliche Gebiet identisch mit dem Kammerbezirk Dresden.

Tausend Jahre und frischer Geist

Sachsen ist gut 1000 Jahre alt. Als bekanntester Regierungschef ging Kurfürst und Polenkönig August der Starke, dem 365 Kinder nachgesagt werden, in die Geschichte ein. Gefolgt wohl von „König Kurt", so wie die Sachsen ihren ersten Ministerpräsidenten im geeinten Deutschland, Kurt Biedenkopf, scherzhaft und anerkennend zugleich nannten.

Silberfunde im Erzgebirge machten Sachsen einst reich. Mit Textilien, später Maschinen, Glas und Porzellan, Feinmechanik und Automobilen blühte das Land auf. 1839 schnaufte Deutschlands erste Ferneisenbahn in Sachsen. In den 1920er-Jahren schlug das industrielle Herz Deutschlands in diesem Raum. In der DDR erbrachten die sächsischen Bezirke Dresden, Leipzig und Karl-Marx-Stadt (Chemnitz) 40 Prozent der gesamten Industrieproduktion.

Heute ist „Silicon Saxony" zum Synonym für Sachsen als Hightechstandort geworden. Das „Autoland Sachsen" verkörpern

newly acquired democracy. Free citizens also emerged from the Peaceful Revolution of 1989 in the GDR, which had found its courageous beginnings in Saxony. This made it appropriate for Saxony to use the symbolic attribute once more.

On a map, Saxony can be seen to be divided into a western and eastern part by a line between the northern town of Strehla on the river Elbe and the Erzgebirge mountain village of Hermsdorf in the south. While the CCI districts of Leipzig and Chemnitz are in the west, the eastern area is identical with the Dresden chamber district.

A thousand years and fresh minds

Saxony is a good 1,000 years old. The best known head of state in history is August the Strong, Elector and King of Poland, who is said to have had 365 children. He is probably followed in the popularity stakes by "King Kurt", which is the nickname fondly and appreciatively given by the Saxons to Kurt Biedenkopf, their first Minister-President in the united Germany.

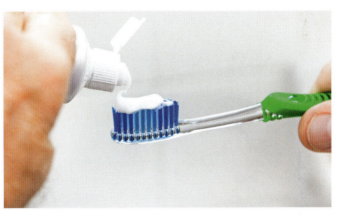

Drei Erfindungen aus Sachsen, die die Welt eroberten: die Spiegelreflex-Kamera, der Teebeutel und die Zahnpasta aus der Tube

Three inventions from Saxony that succeeded in conquering the world: the reflex camera, the teabag and toothpaste out of a tube

Global Player wie VW, BMW und Porsche mit ihren Ansiedlungen sowie Hunderte Zulieferer kreuz und quer durch alle Kammerbezirke. Auf dem Tourismusmarkt gilt Sachsen als deutsches Kulturreiseland Nummer eins.

Seine Stärken verdankt das Bundesland den schönen Landschaften, entstanden durch Launen der Natur, dem Kunst- und Repräsentationssinn einstiger Landesherren und selbstbewusster Bürger, der Leistung und Kreativität vieler Generationen arbeitsamer Menschen. Die erste deutsche Dampflok, das erste europäische Porzellan, der BH, das erste synthetische Feinwaschmittel, die Kaffeefiltertüte, der mechanische Webstuhl, der Bierdeckel, die Kleinbild-Spiegelreflexkamera, das Mundwasser, der Teebeutel, die Nähwirktechnik, Europas erste Gaslaternen, die Zahncreme in Tuben, das erste industriell hergestellte Arzneimittel – was haben sie gemeinsam? Sie wurden in Sachsen erfunden.

The discovery of silver ore in the Erzgebirge mountains was the source of Saxony's prosperity many moons ago. The state then flourished with textiles, followed by machinery, glass and porcelain, precision engineering and the automotive industry. In 1839, Germany's first long-distance railway puffed its way through Saxony, while in the 1920s this region was the industrial heart of the nation. In the GDR, the Saxon districts of Dresden, Leipzig and Karl-Marx-Stadt (Chemnitz) generated 40 percent of total industrial production.

Today, "Silicon Saxony" has become the synonym for Saxony as a high-tech location, while global players such as VW, BMW and Porsche have also settled here, personifying the "Car State Saxony" together with hundreds of supplier firms right across all chamber districts. And on the tourism market, Saxony is deemed to be Germany's Number One destination for cultural trips.

Saxony owes its strengths to the lovely countryside, generated by the whims of nature, together with the appreciation of art and prestige showed by former sovereigns and self-confident citizens, as well as the achievement and creativity of

Wo „fischelant" ein Charakterzug ist

Der Begriff „Innovation", in dem das lateinische Wort „innovatio" für Erneuerung und Veränderung steckt, war in früheren Zeiten noch nicht in aller Munde. Innovativ jedoch sind die Sachsen von alters her. Sie bezeichnen sich selbst als „fischelant". Der Duden schreibt das Wort standardsprachlich so: „vigilant". Im Lateinischen bedeutet „vigilantia" Wachsamkeit. Achtsam, gewandt, pfiffig, lebhaft, klug, clever – so deuten die Sachsen diesen Begriff.

Die Ahnenreihe kluger und kreativer Sachsen ist lang und beachtlich. Die Philosophen Gottfried Wilhelm Leibniz und Johann Gottlieb Fichte, die Schriftsteller Gotthold Ephraim Lessing, Karl May und Erich Kästner, die Komponisten Heinrich Schütz, Carl Maria von Weber, Robert Schumann und Richard Wagner, der Universalgelehrte Georgius Agricola, die Pianistin Clara Wieck (Schumann), der Buchhändler Anton Philipp Reclam – alle waren waschechte Sachsen.

Die Reihe lässt sich mit zugezogenen Koryphäen ergänzen: Rechenmeister Adam Ries(e), Komponist Johann Sebastian Bach, Maler Caspar David Friedrich, Autobauer August Horch – dessen latinisierter Familienname den Markennamen Audi hervorbrachte – und Erfinder Karl August Lingner. Im Sport beeindruckt die Liste der Olympiasieger und Weltmeister allein schon wegen der Wintersportlegenden Jens Weißflog, Katarina Witt und Sylke Otto. Auch der erste Deutsche im All war ein Sachse: Sigmund Jähn. Selbst der „Ur-Berliner" Maler Heinrich Zille hatte sächsische Wurzeln, nämlich in Radeburg.

Asche oder Feuer?

Lorbeeren verführen dazu, sich auf ihnen auszuruhen. Komponist Gustav Mahler, der auch in Sachsen dirigiert hat, formulierte: „Tradition ist die Weitergabe des Feuers und nicht die Anbetung der Asche." Die Sachsen sind stolz auf ihre Traditionen und setzen sie im 21. Jahrhundert auf neue Weise fort. Fast die Hälfte aller Forscher und Entwickler in den neuen Bundesländern arbeitet in Sachsen. 2010 kamen 46 Prozent aller Patentanmeldungen in den neuen Ländern aus Sachsen. Im Freistaat ballen sich Bildungs- und Forschungseinrichtungen.

Ohnehin macht Sachsen seinem einstigen Ruf als Industriehochburg erneut alle Ehre. Ein tiefgreifender, schmerzhafter Strukturwandel hat klassische Branchen wieder wettbewerbsfähig gemacht. Bei Spitzentechnologien mischt Sachsen ganz vorn mit. Der Werbespruch der Baden-Württemberger trifft wohl auch auf die Sachsen zu: „Wir können alles. Außer Hochdeutsch."

„laufen" wird zu „loofen"

Schätzt man überall sächsische Hand- und Kopfarbeit, so trifft Gleiches auf das sächsische Mundwerk nicht zu. Der Dialekt – so

---

many generations of hard-working people. What is the common denominator of Germany's first steam locomotive, Europe's first porcelain, the bra, the first synthetic mild detergent, the coffee filter cone, the mechanical weaving loom, the beer mat, the small-format reflex camera, mouthwash, teabags, stitch bonding, Europe's first gas lamp, toothpaste in tubes and the first industrially produced drugs? They were all invented in Saxony.

Where vigilance is a character trait

In the past, the word "innovation" from the Latin "innovatio" for renewal and change was rarely used. But in Saxony they've always been innovative. With the local accent, they call themselves "fischelant". According to the dictionary, the correct word is "vigilant", from the Latin "vigilantia" for alertness. Alert, skilful, smart, lively, clever – that's what it is taken to mean in Saxony.

There is a long, impressive list of clever, creative Saxons. It includes the philosophers Gottfried Wilhelm Leibniz and Johann Gottlieb Fichte, authors Gotthold Ephraim Lessing, Karl May and Erich Kästner, composers Heinrich Schütz, Carl Maria von Weber, Robert Schumann and Richard Wagner, universal scholar Georgius Agricola, the pianist Clara Wieck (Schumann) and the bookseller Anton Philipp Reclam – all genuine Saxons.

Other experts came to live here by choice: mathematician Adam Ries(e), composer Johann Sebastian Bach, painter Caspar David Friedrich, car maker August Horch – whose family name transposed into Latin produced the brand name Audi – and inventor Karl August Lingner. In terms of sport, Saxony offers an impressive range of Olympic and World Champions, including winter sport legends Jens Weißflog, Katarina Witt and Sylke Otto. And the first German in outer space was also a Saxon: Sigmund Jähn. Even the Berlin painter Heinrich Zille had Saxon roots, namely in Radeburg.

Ash or fire?

Laurels tend to be used for resting. Composer Gustav Mahler, who also conducted orchestras in Saxony, once said: "Tradition consists in passing on the fire, not worshipping the ashes." The Saxons are proud of their traditions which they continue in the 21st century with a new approach. Nearly half of all researchers and developers in Germany's new states work in Saxony. In 2010, 46 percent of all patent applications in the new states came from Saxony. The Free State offers a rich accumulation of education and research institutions.

Indeed, Saxony truly lives up to its former reputation as a stronghold of industry. A painful, in-depth process of structural change has made classic branches competitive once again. Saxony finds itself right up there at the cutting edge of advanced technologies. Saxony could also adopt the advertising

Einer der insgesamt neun historischen Raddampfer: Die Sächsische Dampfschiffahrt verfügt damit über die älteste und größte Raddampferflotte der Welt.

One of a total of nine historical paddle steamers: Saxonian steam navigation thus has the oldest and largest fleet of steamers on earth.

claim used by the state of Baden-Württemberg: "We can do everything. Apart from speak proper German."

Local dialect

While Saxon workmanship and brainwork enjoys high esteem, the same cannot be said for the Saxon accent, which surveys show to be not very popular with almost half of the German population. Imitating the Saxon accent is a quick way to get a laugh. The Saxons join in too – there's no denying their sense of humour. However, Dresden-born author Erich Kästner did issue a warning about too much ridicule, saying that the locals are not as cute as they sound.

Those who like the accent hear its warmth and humour. It makes the words softer: "P" becomes a "B", "T" becomes a "D". Vowels get modified and lengthened. The ends of words get swallowed and whole words are compacted together. The Saxon dialect also has its own vocabulary: heat is called "Dämmse", while "Gusche" means mouth.

Once upon a time, the mocked dialect was highly regarded. In the late Middle Ages, Meißen officialese from the flourishing Electorate of Saxony became the official German language. Luther used it for his translation of the Bible. But Saxony gradually took a back seat with the rise of Prussia. North German

belegen Umfragen – ist bei fast der Hälfte der Deutschen unbeliebt. Wer Sächsisch nachahmt, hat schnell die Lacher auf seiner Seite. Auch die der Sachsen. Sie haben Humor. Der gebürtige Dresdner Erich Kästner warnte allerdings jene, die sie „verhohnebiebeln" (verhöhnen) wollen: „Wir sinn nich so gemiedlich, wie wir schbrechen."

Ist man dem Dialekt gewogen, hört man Wärme und Witz daraus. Die Worte werden weicher, das „P" verwandelt sich in ein „B", das „T" in ein „D". Vokale verändern und dehnen sich: „laufen" wird zu „loofen", „kaufen" zu „koofen". Endungen werden verschluckt, Wörter zusammengezogen. „Haben wir" wird zu „hammer" verkürzt. Hinzu kommt ein eigener Wortschatz: Hitze heißt „Dämmse" und „Gusche" Mund. Schillers „Handschuh" klingt in den Worten von Mundartdichterin Lene Voigt so: „Dr Geenich Franz, das war ä Freind / Von Bandern, Lem un Diechern..."

Der belächelte Dialekt stand in der Geschichte einmal hoch im Kurs: Im Spätmittelalter hatte sich die Meißner Kanzleisprache aus dem florierenden Kurfürstentum Sachsen als deutsche Verkehrssprache durchgesetzt. Luther nutzte sie für seine Bibelübersetzung. Mit dem Aufstieg Preußens zur Großmacht geriet Sachsen ins Hintertreffen. Maßgeblich für „richtiges" Deutsch wurde die nördliche Aussprache. Im heutigen Sachsen vernimmt man die sächsische Sprachfärbung ebenso wie Erzgebirgisch und das Oberlausitzische mit dem rollenden R. Mit dem Sorbischen ist sogar eine slawische Sprache vertreten. Geschichte, Mentalität und Dialekt aller Sachsen sind Farben, die unser Bild grundieren.

Gleich dreimal hoch hinauf

Das Osterzgebirge prägt unser Panorama mit Erhebungen zwischen 600 und 900 Metern. Höchster Gipfel ist der Kahleberg (905 Meter). Im benachbarten Zittauer Gebirge – Deutschlands kleinstem Mittelgebirge – streckt sich die Lausche (792 Meter) am höchsten empor. Über den Berg verläuft die Grenze zwischen Deutschland und Tschechien. Ein Naturwunder verbindet die zwei Mittelgebirge – das 700 Quadratkilometer große Elbsandsteingebirge. Der deutsche Teil heißt Sächsische, der tschechische Teil Böhmische Schweiz.

Alle drei Gebirge eint eigenwillige Schönheit und touristische Anziehungskraft. Allein die Sächsische Schweiz zählt jährlich sieben Millionen Touristen. Wanderer, Radler, Kletterer und Wintersportler fühlen sich an allen drei Höhenzügen wohl. Der Malerweg, der Oberlausitzer Bergweg und der Kammweg Erzgebirge-Vogtland sind die Stars unter den Wanderstrecken.

Radlerfreuden und Stadtschönheiten

Die Natur hat Sachsen mit einem schönen Wasserlauf bevorzugt: Auf rund 150 Kilometern schlängelt sich die Elbe durch den östlichen Teil. Sie entspringt im tschechischen Riesengebirge und tritt bei Schmilka über die Grenze. Bei Torgau verlässt sie Sachsen. Schon seit 1835 fahren Dampfschiffe auf dem Strom. Bis heute ist er eine wichtige Verkehrsader. Der Elberadweg – Deutschlands beliebtester Radwanderweg – begleitet ihn.

In Sachsen schmückt sich die Elbe mit Perlen wie Bad Schandau, Pirna, Dresden, Meißen und Riesa. Dresden – das Elbflorenz – ist die glanzvollste. August der Starke prägte ihr Image als Barockstadt, so wie sie Canaletto verewigt hat. Zu Synonymen für die Kulturmetropole sind Zwinger, Frauenkirche, Semperoper und Grünes Gewölbe geworden. Die futuristische Gläserne Manufaktur von Volkswagen signalisiert: Dresden ist ebenso ein Platz der Hochtechnologien von europäischem Format.

Die Stadt ist erst seit dem 16. Jahrhundert Zentrum sächsischen Lebens, Wirtschaftens und Regierens. Die Wiege Sachsens stand im 25 Kilometer entfernten Meißen: 929 gründete der deutsche König Heinrich I. die Mark Meißen mit einer

pronunciation grew to be the accepted "correct" German. In Saxony today, you can hear the Saxon dialect together with the dialect from the Erzgebirge mountains and from Oberlausitz where they roll their "Rs". The Slavic Sorbian language also abounds. The history, mentality and dialect of all Saxons are the colours that paint our picture.

Three mountain ranges

The eastern Erzgebirge mountains provide a fine backdrop to our panorama with peaks between 600 and 900 metres. The highest summit is the Kahleberg (905 metres). The highest peak in the neighbouring Zittauer Gebirge mountains is the Lausche (792 metres) and is at the same time the frontier between Germany and the Czech Republic. The two mountain ranges are connected by a true miracle of nature – the Elbsandstein mountains covering 700 square kilometres, with the German area called Saxon Switzerland and the Czech area Bohemian Switzerland.

All three mountain ranges offer their own special beauty and are a tourist attraction in their own right. Saxon Switzerland alone attracts seven million tourists each year. Walkers, cyclists, climbers and winter athletes feel equally at home in all three ranges. The "Painter's Footpath", the "Oberlausitz Mountain Path" and the "Erzgebirge-Vogtland Ridge Path" are the most popular walking routes.

Cycling pleasure and attractive towns

Nature has blessed Saxony with a lovely river: the Elbe curves its way along 150 kilometres through the east of the state, after rising from its source in the Czech Riesengebirge mountains and crossing the frontier at Schmilka. Torgau is the point where the Elbe leaves Saxony again. Steam ships have operated on the river since 1835. Today it is an important traffic route. Germany's most popular cycling path runs along its banks.

Lovely towns decorate the banks of the river Elbe in Saxony, including Bad Schandau, Pirna, Dresden, Meißen and Riesa. Dresden, known as Florence of the North, is the most splendid. The city owes its image as a Baroque city to August the Strong and is immortalised in Canaletto's painting. Buildings such as the Zwinger, Frauenkirche, Semperoper and Grünes Gewölbe have become synonymous for the cultural metropolis. On the other hand, Volkswagen's futuristic Gläserne Manufaktur (glass car factory) indicates that Dresden is equally the home for hightech of European format.

It is only since the 16th century that Dresden has been the centre of life, business and government in Saxony. Saxony's cradle is to be found in Meißen, 25 kilometres away. Here in 929, German King Heinrich I founded the Mark Meißen with a castle built on a cliff overlooking the river Elbe. Soon after-

Die Albrechtsburg aus dem 15. Jahrhundert bestimmt das Stadtbild von Meißen.

The Albrechtsburg, which dates back to the 15th century, is a dominant feature of the cityscape of Meißen.

Burg auf einem Elbefelsen. Bald darauf residierten die Wettiner dort, das spätere sächsische Fürsten- und Königsgeschlecht.

Weiter flussabwärts soll einst ein Riese am Ufer gerastet haben. So erklären die Riesaer Einwohner Entstehung und Namen ihrer Stadt. Die Sagengestalt hat sich im Stadtwappen verewigt. Riesig war das Stahlwerk zu DDR-Zeiten, nicht mehr konkurrenzfähig nach der Wende. Die Stahlproduktion ist – kleiner, aber leistungsfähig – heimisch geblieben. Als Sportstadt setzt Riesa neue Akzente.

Brücken zu den Nachbarn

Vervollständigen wir unser Panorama östlich. Dort, wo die geschichtsträchtige Neiße fließt und Berlins Hausfluss, die Spree, entspringt. Die Oberlausitz ist erst 1635 zu Sachsen gekommen. Zuvor hatte sie als eigenständiges Markgrafentum zur Böhmischen Krone gehört, zeitweilig sogar zum Habsburger Weltreich. Nach der Reformation konnten sich im evangelischen Umfeld katholische Inseln behaupten, so die bis heute bestehenden Zisterzienserinnenklöster St. Marienstern und St. Marienthal aus dem 13. Jahrhundert.

Gleichfalls Tupfen auf unserem Bild sind die einstigen Handelsstädte Bautzen, Görlitz, Kamenz, Löbau und Zittau mit

wards, this became home to the House of Wettin with its future princes and kings.

Further down river, a giant (Riese in German) was supposed to have rested on the river banks. This is at least how the people of Riesa explain the name and origins of their town. The legendary figure has been perpetuated in the town's coat of arms. Gigantic was also the steel mill in the GDR era, but no longer competitive after reunification. On a smaller but more efficient scale, the steel industry has remained loyal to the town, which now sets new accents in sport.

Die historische Altstadt von Görlitz besteht aus Hunderten von denkmalgeschützten Häusern.

The historic city centre of Görlitz has hundreds of heritage-protected houses.

Bridges to the neighbours

Let us turn to the east to complete our panorama, where the historically portentous river Neiße flows and where Berlin's very own river, the Spree, rises from its source. It was not until 1635 that the Oberlausitz became part of Saxony. Before then, it had been an autonomous margraviate under the Bohemian crown and even at times part of the Habsburg empire. After the Reformation, individual islands of Roman Catholics managed to survive in the protestant surroundings, including the 13th century Cistercian convents of St. Marienstern and St. Marienthal, which still exist today.

Other spots in our picture include the former trading towns of Bautzen, Görlitz, Kamenz, Löbau and Zittau with lovely old town centres. Together with the town of Lauban – now Lubań in Poland – they formed the "six town alliance" keeping peace in Oberlausitz for centuries. In 1991, they restored their association with a present-day focus on art, culture, sport and tourism. Görlitz, with its bridge over the river Neiße to Zgorzelec in Poland, offers 4,000 listed buildings, more than any other town in Germany. The film world has discovered the town as an ideal backdrop: this is where Quentin Tarantino filmed parts of the "Inglorious Basterds".

A referendum in 1990 brought the areas around Hoyerswerda and Weißwasser back into Saxon Oberlausitz, after belonging to Cottbus, now part of Brandenburg, during the GDR regime. The lignite mining landscape around both towns is turning into a lake district with flooded quarries. The adjoining heath and pool landscape – now a UNESCO biosphere reserve – was created by nature; with 30,102 hectares of water, this is one of Germany's largest pool areas.

In the south, the old regions of Oberlausitz, Bohemia and Silesia merge into each other. Here our panorama extends to Poland and the Czech Republic, where the old Via Regia trading route used to link East and West Europe. The frontier region's bridge function was restored by the enlargement of the EU in 2004. Attention once again turns to common ground in history, culture and business. Good neighbourly relations are just one of the achievements of more recent history, providing strong contours for our picture.

Common sense and gut feeling

There's still a lot missing in our picture. But our very own Canaletto view is already worth looking at. Art connoisseurs praise the original for its balance of water, landscape, people,

schönen Altstadtkernen. Zusammen mit Lauban – heute Lubań in Polen – schützten sie als „Sechsstädtebund" über Jahrhunderte den Landfrieden in der Oberlausitz. 1991 haben sie ihre Gemeinschaft neu belebt – mit Kunst, Kultur, Sport und Tourismus als heutigem Bündniszweck. Görlitz – mit einer Neißebrücke ins polnische Zgorzelec – ist mit 4000 Baudenkmalen Deutschlands größtes Flächendenkmal. Die Filmwelt hat die Stadt als Kulisse entdeckt. Quentin Tarantino drehte dort Teile seines Films „Inglorious Bastards".

Ein Volksentscheid 1990 brachte die Gebiete um Hoyerswerda und Weißwasser zurück in die sächsische Oberlausitz. Die künstliche DDR-Bezirksstruktur hatte sie 1952 dem Bezirk Cottbus – heute Teil Brandenburgs – zugeschlagen. Die Braunkohlenlandschaft um beide Städte verwandelt sich mit gefluteten Tagebauen in ein Seenland. Die angrenzende Oberlausitzer Heide- und Teichlandschaft – ein UNESCO-Biosphärenreservat – hat die Natur geschaffen. Mit 30 102 Hektar Wasserfläche gehört sie zu den größten Teichgebieten Deutschlands.

Im Süden gehen die alten Regionen Oberlausitz, Böhmen und Schlesien ineinander über. Unser Panorama weitet sich dort nach Polen und Tschechien. Einst verband die Handelsstraße Via Regia Ost- mit Westeuropa. Die EU-Erweiterung 2004 hat der Grenzregion ihre Brückenfunktion zurückgegeben. Gemeinsamkeiten

Eindrucksvolles Wintermärchen aus Licht und Farben: die Silhouette des 1000-jährigen Bautzen mit ihrem historischen Stadtkern

A truly impressive winter fairy tale of light and colours: the silhouette of 1000-year old Bautzen, with its historical city centre

in Geschichte, Kultur und Wirtschaft treten neu hervor. Gute Nachbarschaft gehört zu den Errungenschaften der jüngeren Geschichte. Sie gibt unserem Bild kräftige Konturen.

Vernunft und Bauchgefühl

Viele Pinselstriche fehlen noch. Doch unser Canaletto-Blick kann sich schon sehen lassen. Kunstkenner rühmen das Original für die Ausgewogenheit von Wasser, Landschaft, Menschen, Gebäuden und Himmel. Auch unser Bild zeigt das östliche Sachsen als Landstrich mit innerer Balance. Vielfalt der Natur harmoniert mit urbanem und ländlichem Leben, eine lange Geschichte und reiche Traditionen verbinden sich mit fleißigen und klugen Menschen, nicht nur sächsischer Zunge.

Standortqualität. Dieser unromantische Begriff beschreibt, wie förderlich Regionen für Unternehmen sind. Unser Canaletto-Blick charakterisiert weiche Faktoren. Jene Gegebenheiten, die immer wichtiger werden für Ansiedlungsentscheidungen. Merkmale wie Image und innovatives Milieu, Umweltqualität und Freizeitwert entscheiden zunehmend darüber, ob sich ein Unternehmen und seine Beschäftigten wirklich wohlfühlen. Der Mensch lebt – so weiß die Bibel – nicht vom Brot allein. Auch nicht allein von der Arbeit. Er braucht ein lebens- und liebenswertes Umfeld, neben der richtigen Kopfentscheidung ein gutes Bauchgefühl. Eine Empfehlung für den Kammerbezirk Dresden.

buildings and sky. Our picture also portrays East Saxony as a balanced region, where the diversity of nature harmonises with urban and rural life, a long history and rich traditions combine with hardworking, clever people, speaking not just the local dialect.

Location quality. This prosaic phrase describes how regions can help companies. Our Canaletto view characterises the soft factors – those aspects that play an ever increasing role in decisions to relocate. Features such as image and innovative milieu, environmental quality and leisure value increasingly decide whether a company and its employees really feel at home. As it says in the Bible, man does not live on bread alone. Nor from work alone. Man needs a lovable setting worth living in, with a good gut feeling as well as common sense. Just one recommendation for the Dresden chamber district.

Wandel, Wachstum, Wunder
Lebensraum und Wirtschaft in der Zeitmaschine

Als Erster schickte der englische Schriftsteller H. G. Wells 1895 einen Menschen in die Zukunft. Der Roman „Die Zeitmaschine" begründete das Science-Fiction-Genre der Zeitreisen. Ein Sprung in die Zukunft, die plötzliche Konfrontation mit neuen Anforderungen, eine grundlegende Veränderung in kürzester Zeit – versteht man eine Zeitreise so, dann haben die Ostdeutschen eine solche Reise erlebt. Sie fegten 1989 das kommunistische Herrschaftssystem hinweg und organisierten ihr Leben auf ungewohnter, weil freier, demokratischer Grundlage völlig neu.

Symbol Frauenkirche Dresden

Der herbeigesehnte, doch in seiner Dramatik und Dynamik unterschätzte Wandel vollzog sich rasend schnell. Ein Crashkurs, der mit einer emotionalen Achterbahnfahrt verbunden war: Hoffnung und Enttäuschung, Aufbruchstimmung und Verzagtheit wechselten einander ab. Trotz aller Widersprüche und Verwerfungen setzte die „Zeitmaschine" zugleich Kreativität, Mut zum Risiko und Tatendrang frei. Etwas unternehmen – das war plötzlich möglich geworden. Die politische Wende befreite von alten Zwängen und Denkschablonen.

Gibt es im Kammerbezirk Dresden ein Symbol für die Veränderungen? Für viele Menschen ist es die Frauenkirche, das auferstandene Zeugnis barocker Sakralbaukunst im Herzen der Landeshauptstadt. Der Bombenangriff am 13. Februar 1945 hatte das über 91 Meter hohe Gotteshaus zerstört. In 40 Jahren DDR bot die Ruine einen trostlosen Anblick. Kühne Visionäre brachten 1990 den Wiederaufbau ins Spiel. Das war damals eine utopische Vorstellung. Doch in elf Jahren wurde die Kirche neu errichtet – dank der mobilisierenden Idee, vielen Bürgerinitiativen und zahlreichen Spenden aus aller Welt. Die dunklen Steine des Originals in der hellen Sandsteinfassade erzählen die Geschichte nach.

Das offene und lebendige Bauwerk ist ein Sinnbild für erneuerte Kultur und Urbanität, aber auch für den wirtschaftlichen Aufschwung im Zeitraffer. Diesen brachte eine neue, selbstständige Kraft mit voran: Ab Frühjahr 1990 bauten engagierte Männer und Frauen die Industrie- und Handelskammer im Dresdner Raum auf. Sie konnten ihre berufsständige Körperschaft ebenso auf historischem Fundament errichten, der 1862 gegründeten Handels- und Gewerbekammer zu Dresden. Die erste Statistik der IHK Dresden wies 1991 etwa 36 000 Mitgliedsbetriebe aus. Heute sind es beinahe dreimal so viele.

Change, growth, miracles
Living space and business in a time machine

The English author H. G. Wells was the first to send man into the future, back in 1895. "The Time Machine" triggered the science-fiction genre of travelling through time. A leap into the future, sudden confrontation with new challenges, fundamental change in next-to-no time – if that's what travelling in time means, then the East Germans have been there, done that. In 1989, they turned out the communist regime and reorganised their life along completely new, democratic lines based on what for them was the unusual attribute of freedom.

Dresden's Frauenkirche

The much yearned-for change, with all its underestimated dramatic and dynamic effects, came about at high speed: a crash course, accompanied by an emotional roller coaster ride. Hope alternated with disappointment, euphoria with despondency. Despite all contradictions and problems, at the same time the "time machine" released pent-up creativity, drive and the willingness to take risks. All of a sudden, it was possible to undertake something. Political change released the old bonds, restraints and imposed thought patterns.

Does the Dresden chamber district have a symbol for change? For many it is the Frauenkirche, the resurrected witness of Baroque church architecture right at the heart of the state capital. The bomb raid on 13 February 1945 had destroyed the 91 metres high place of worship, leaving ruins that remained in a sorry state throughout 40 years of GDR rule. In 1990, daring visionaries started thinking and talking about reconstruction, a utopian idea at the time. But eleven years later, the new church was completed – thanks to the mobilising idea, many citizens' initiatives and countless donations from all over the world. The dark stones of the original building in the pale sandstone façade have their own story to tell.

The open, living building symbolises renewed culture and urbanity, while personifying economic recovery in a time lapse. This was driven by a new, independent force: from the spring of 1990, committed men and women set out to establish the

Wandel, Wachstum, Wunder

Dresden bietet seinen Besuchern aus der ganzen Welt ein Füllhorn an Sehenswürdigkeiten – die Frauenkirche ist die bedeutendste von allen.

Dresden offers visitors from across the world a cornucopia of tourist attractions – the Frauenkirche being the most noteworthy of all.

Neue Stärke und Dynamik

Nahezu 40 Prozent des sächsischen Bruttoinlandsproduktes werden im Kammerbezirk Dresden erwirtschaftet. Das waren 2010 rund 95 Mrd. Euro. Insbesondere die Industrie ist heute breit aufgestellt und trotz drastischer Einschnitte nach der Wende in die neue Welt hineingewachsen. Selbst die Textilindustrie – einst ein Riese mit 300 000 Beschäftigten – hat mit intelligenten Nischenprodukten überlebt. Zahlreiche Marken aus DDR-Zeiten, die klug weitergeführt wurden, haben inzwischen im harten Wettbewerb ihre marktwirtschaftliche Taufe erhalten. Ganz neue Zeichen werden hingegen mit Zukunftstechnologien wie der Mikroelektronik, der Nano- und der Biotechnologie gesetzt.

Sachsen wiederum ist eine dynamische Kraft in Deutschland. Hier lebt ein Viertel aller Ostdeutschen. Die Arbeitsplatzdichte liegt bei 470 Erwerbstätigen je 1000 Einwohnern. Das ist die höchste Quote in den neuen Ländern und Platz 6 unter den deutschen Flächenländern. Auf 1000 Einwohner kommen im Freistaat 57 IHK-zugehörige Firmen, im Kammerbezirk Dresden 53. Vergleichszahlen: In Bayern sind es 74, in Sachsen-Anhalt 46.

Respektabel auch das Tempo: Die sächsische Wirtschaft ist von 2000 bis 2011 um mehr als 20 Prozent gewachsen. Kein anderes Bundesland hat so viel Fahrt aufgenommen. Dem deutschen Bruttoinlandsprodukt fügt es 3,8 Prozent bei, etwas mehr als die Bundeshauptstadt Berlin oder der Stadtstaat Hamburg. Sächsische Spitzenprodukte stürmen zunehmend den Weltmarkt. Seit 2000 hat die Industrie ihren Export verdreifacht. Sachsen ist wieder – um seine touristische Eigenwerbung aufzugreifen – ein „Land von Welt".

Lob dem Mittelstand

Der Mittelstand treibt die Wirtschaft voran. Kleine und mittlere Betriebe prägen die Struktur im Kammerbezirk Dresden: 94,5 Prozent der Firmen beschäftigen weniger als zehn Mitarbeiter, rund 4,2 Prozent zwischen zehn und 49 sowie 1,1 Prozent zwischen 50 und 249. Zu den großen Firmen ab 250 Mitarbeitern zählen 0,2 Prozent der Betriebe. Das Unternehmertum gedeiht: Über elf Prozent der Erwerbstätigen in Sachsen sind selbstständig – eine Spitzenposition in den neuen Flächenländern.

Der Arbeitsmarkt profitiert vom sächsischen Aufschwung. Die Erwerbstätigenzahl erreichte 2010 mit 1,951 Millionen den bisher höchsten Stand seit 2000, die Arbeitslosigkeit sank auf den niedrigsten Wert seit 1991. 2011 lag die Arbeitslosenquote noch etwas niedriger bei 10,6 Prozent, jedoch deutlich über dem deutschen Durchschnitt. Dass noch nicht alle Bäume in den Himmel gewachsen sind, verdeutlicht die Arbeitsproduktivität: Sachsen fehlt ein Fünftel der Leistungskraft des deutschen Durchschnitts. Thüringen liegt etwa gleichauf, Bayern mit sieben Prozent über dem Mittelwert.

Fortsetzung Seite 26

Chamber of Commerce and Industry in the Dresden region. They too were able to build their professional organisation on historic foundations – those of the Dresden Chamber of Trade, founded in 1862. The first statistics kept by the CCI Dresden in 1991 revealed 36,000 member firms. Today there are nearly three times as many.

New dynamic strength

Nearly 40 percent of Saxony's gross domestic product is generated in the Dresden chamber district. In 2010, this amounted to 95 billion Euro. Especially the industry has a broad basis, and despite of drastic cuts, all traditional branches have grown into the new world. Even the textile industry, formerly a giant sector with 300,000 employees, has survived with intelligent niche products. Numerous GDR brands have been continued along clever strategic lines, meanwhile standing their ground in the face of tough competition. At the same time, new signs will be set with future technologies such as microelectronics, nanotechnology and biotechnology."

In turn, Saxony is a dynamic force to be reckoned with in Germany. It is home to one quarter of all East Germans and offers an employment density of 470 gainfully employed per 1,000 citizens. That is the highest rate in the new German states and sixth position among Germany's non-city states. The whole Free State has 57 companies per 1,000 citizens that belong to the CCI, with 53 in Dresden chamber district. By comparison, Bavaria has 74 and Saxony-Anhalt 46.

The tempo is also respectable: between 2000 and 2011, Saxony's economy grew by more than 20 percent. No other federal state picked up pace in this way. It contributes 3.8 percent to Germany's gross domestic product, a little more than the capital of Berlin or the city state of Hamburg. First-rate products from Saxony are increasingly storming onto the world market. Since 2000, industry has tripled its exports. To use its tourism claim, Saxony is once more "a country of the world".

Praise for the SME sector

The SME sector is the driving force behind the economy. Small and medium-sized businesses define the structure of Dresden chamber district. 94.5 percent of the firms have less than ten employees, around 4.2 percent between ten and 49 and 1.1 percent between 50 and 249. Only 0.2 percent of the companies are on a really large scale with more than 250 employees. Entrepreneurship is flourishing: more than eleven percent of the gainfully employed in Saxony are self-employed, putting it in the lead above the other new non-city states.

The job market has benefited from Saxony's recovery. In 2010, employment figures reached the highest level since 2000 with 1.951 million gainfully employed, while unemployment fell to the lowest rate since 1991. In 2011, the unemployment

Continued on page 26

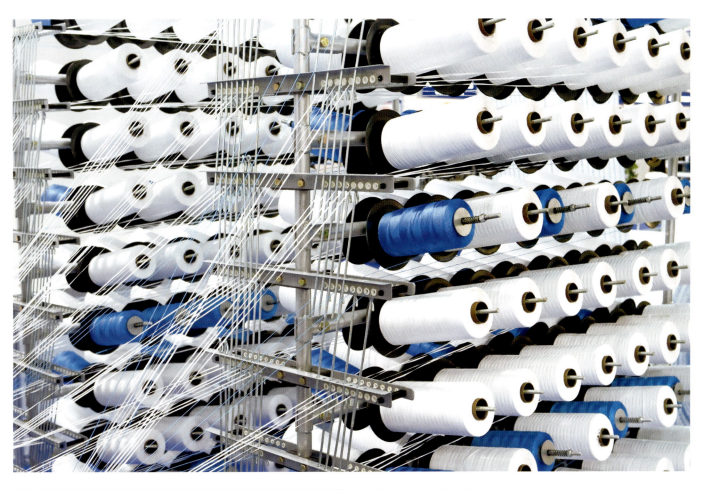

Textilindustrie und Maschinenbau: zwei Branchen mit einer langen Tradition in Ostsachsen – und mit glänzenden Zukunftsperspektiven

Textile industry and engineering: two branches that can look back at a long tradition in East Saxony – and with excellent future prospects

Information

Gründungsjahr:
SICK (Stammhaus): 1946,
SICK Engineering GmbH: 1991

Mitarbeiter: weltweit rund 6000, davon rund 200 bei der SICK Engineering GmbH

Produkte:
· Gaszähler
· Volumenstrom-Messgeräte
· Staubmessgeräte

Year founded:
SICK (headquarters): 1946,
SICK Engineering GmbH: 1991

Employees: around 6,000 worldwide, including around 200 at SICK Engineering GmbH

Products:
· gas meters
· volume flow measuring devices
· dust measuring devices

SICK Engineering GmbH
Ottendorf-Okrilla

SICK Engineering GmbH

Viele der weltbesten Gaszähler für Erdgas-Pipelines kommen aus Ottendorf-Okrilla in der Nähe von Dresden: von der SICK Engineering GmbH. Die kleinsten Zähler passen gerade noch in eine Aktentasche; durch die größten hingegen könnte man hindurchlaufen. Was auch damit zu tun hat, dass die Geräte innen leer sind – denn sie arbeiten mit Ultraschall. In Ottendorf-Okrilla paart sich modernste Sensorik, das Herzstück der Gaszähler, mit dem Wachstumsmarkt Erdgasindustrie und lässt die Dresdner hoffnungsvoll in die Zukunft blicken.

Die SICK Engineering GmbH ist Teil des weltweit agierenden SICK-Konzerns (Umsatz 2011: über 900 Mio. Euro), der intelligente Sensorlösungen für die Fabrik-, Logistik- und Prozessautomation anbietet. Das Unternehmen wurde 1946 von Erwin Sick gegründet, einem begnadeten Erfinder und Unternehmer. „Wir brauchen zweifellos nicht mehr, sondern bessere und sinnvollere Technik", lautete dessen Motto. Die herausragende Anwendungsfreundlichkeit und Haltbarkeit der Produkte von SICK ist bis heute Teil ihres weltweiten Erfolges.

Extreme Sorgfalt in der Fertigung zeichnet die Gaszähler von SICK aus.

Extremely meticulous production makes gas meters by SICK stand out.

Gaszähler von SICK arbeiten mit Ultraschall und werden für hochgenaue Messungen, beispielsweise bei der Erdgasabrechnung, eingesetzt.

Gas meters by SICK work with ultrasound and are used for high-precision measurements, for example in custody transfer.

SICK Engineering GmbH

Gaszähler von SICK sind begehrt in aller Welt.

Gas meters by SICK are in demand all over the world.

SICK Engineering GmbH

Many of the world's best gas meters for natural gas pipelines come from SICK Engineering GmbH in Ottendorf-Okrilla near Dresden. The tiniest meters just fit in a brief case, while you could walk right through the largest. This all has to do with the fact that the devices are empty inside, as they work with ultrasound. In Ottendorf-Okrilla, ultra-modern sensors at the heart of the gas meters are paired with the natural gas industry as a key growth market, so that the future is viewed in optimistic terms.

SICK Engineering GmbH is part of the global SICK Group (turnover of more than 900 million Euro in 2011), which offers intelligent sensor solutions for factory, logistics and process automation. The company was founded in 1946 by Erwin Sick, a talented inventor and business man. His motto is: "Without doubt, what we need is not more technology, but better and more appropriate technology." SICK products are outstandingly easy to use with long service lives, just two aspects that have led to their global success today.

Spezialtechnik Dresden GmbH

Die Spezialtechnik Dresden GmbH steht an der Spitze der Spezialtechnik-Gruppe Dresden, die dem privaten amerikanischen Technologiekonzern General Atomics nahe steht. Der Schwerpunkt ihrer Geschäftstätigkeit liegt in der Bereitstellung kaufmännisch geprägter und vertriebsorientierter Dienstleistungen bei gleichzeitiger Organisation und Koordination der langfristig orientierten Geschäftsaktivitäten der Spezialtechnik-Gruppe Dresden, die im interaktiven Wirken sowohl mit dem General Atomics-Konzern als auch den einzelnen Unternehmen zuverlässig und flexibel entwickelt werden.

Damit wird einerseits den Unternehmen der Spezialtechnik-Gruppe Dresden die Möglichkeit gegeben, an unternehmensübergreifenden Erkenntnissen zu partizipieren und andererseits deren strategische Entwicklung bei Schwerpunktkomplexen profiliert.

Ursprünglich ein Werk der Deutschen Reichsbahn bzw. der Deutschen Bahn AG gehört die GBM Gleisbaumechanik Brandenburg/H. GmbH (GBM) seit 2002 zur Spezialtechnik-Gruppe Dresden. Aufbauend auf Schienenkraftlastwagen wurden mehrere Generationen von Gleisarbeitsfahrzeugen entwickelt und in größerer Stückzahl gefertigt. Heute werden die Bereiche Instandhaltung/Service sowie Modernisierung/Umbau kontinuierlich ausgebaut.

Die Spreewerk Lübben GmbH (ISL) ist ein zuverlässiger Partner in den Bereichen Munitionszerlegung und Explosivstoffverwertung. Dazu gehören konventionelle Munition, Pyrotechnik, Raketen, Sprengmittel und die Rückführung der dabei anfallenden Komponenten in den Wirtschaftskreislauf. Weit über 90 Prozent der eingehenden Materialien werden dem zivilen Markt wieder bereitgestellt.

Die EST Energetics GmbH (EST) verwertet und vernichtet Explosivstoffe und Munition auf umweltgerechte Art und Weise. Die hochinnovativen Anlagen wandeln die Wärme, die bei der Behandlung der Munition und Explosivstoffe freigesetzt wird, in wertvolle Elektroenergie um, die dann in das öffentliche Stromnetz eingespeist wird.

Zur Unternehmensgruppe gehört außerdem die SGL Spezial- und Bergbau-Servicegesellschaft Lauchhammer mbH (SGL), deren Aufgabe es ist, umweltgerechte Sanierungen von Industrieanlagen durchzuführen. Darüber hinaus bietet die SGL eine breite Palette von Bauleistungen an.

Die Umwelt- und Ingenieurtechnik GmbH Dresden (UIT) ist Spezialist für die Realisierung von Projekten in den Geschäftsbereichen Wassertechnologie und Umweltüberwachung.

Fertigung und Instandhaltung schienengebundener Spezialfahrzeuge in der GBM Gleisbaumechanik Brandenburg/H. GmbH (GBM)

Production and maintenance of special rail vehicles at GBM Gleisbaumechanik Brandenburg/H. GmbH (GBM)

Ein weiteres Gruppenunternehmen ist die B+F Beton- und Fertigteilgesellschaft mbH Lauchhammer (BFL). Sie ist ein zuverlässiger Partner, bei der Fertigung und Montage hochwertiger Stahlbeton-Fertigteile.

Abgerundet wird das Spektrum durch die Spezialtechnik Dresden Service GmbH (SDS). Sie ist im Immobilienbereich aktiv und bewirtschaftet und entwickelt die Immobilien der Unternehmen der STD-Gruppe. Darüber hinaus vermittelt sie Vermietungsobjekte (Büro- und Gewerbeflächen) in Dresden-Klotzsche und an den Standorten der Schwesterunternehmen.

Spezialtechnik Dresden GmbH

Spezialtechnik Dresden GmbH stands at the head of the Spezialtechnik-Group Dresden, which has close connections with the private American technology group General Atomics. The main focus of its business activity consists in providing commercial and sales-related services. At the same time it organises and coordinates the long-term business activities of the Spezialtechnik-Group Dresden, which are developed reliably and flexibly in interactive work with the General Atomics group and also with the individual companies.

This gives the companies of the Spezialtechnik-Group Dresden on the one hand the possibility of sharing inter-company knowledge, while on the other hand clearly defining the strategic development of the companies regarding main topics.

Originally part of Deutsche Reichsbahn respectively Deutsche Bahn AG, since 2002 GBM Gleisbaumechanik Brandenburg/H. GmbH (GBM) has been part of the Spezialtechnik-Group Dresden. Several generations of track working vehicles were developed and mass-produced on the basis of rail goods trucks. Today, the fields

Entwicklung und Fertigung u. a. biotechnologischer Anlagen in der Umwelt- und Ingenieurtechnik GmbH Dresden (UIT)

Development and production among others of biotechnological units at Umwelt- und Ingenieurtechnik GmbH Dresden (UIT)

of maintenance/servicing and modernisation/conversion are expanding constantly.

Spreewerk Lübben GmbH (ISL) is a reliable partner specialising in demilitarisation and recycling of munitions and explosives. This includes conventional munitions, pyrotechnics, rockets and exploders, together with the recycling of the resulting components. Way over 90 percent of the resulting materials are returned to civilian use.

EST Energetics GmbH (EST) recycles and destroys explosives and munitions with an environmentally friendly approach. The highly innovative machines convert the heat released during the treatment of munitions and explosives into valuable electricity which is then fed into the public grid.

The Group also includes SGL Spezial- und Bergbau-Servicegesellschaft Lauchhammer mbH (SGL), whose remit entails the environmentally friendly refurbishment of industrial plants and facilities. In addition, SGL also offers a wide range of construction services.

Umwelt- und Ingenieurtechnik GmbH Dresden (UIT) specialises in water technology and environmental monitoring projects.

Another Group company is B+F Beton- und Fertigteilgesellschaft mbH Lauchhammer (BFL), a reliable partner for the production and installation of top quality prefabricated concrete elements.

The range offered by the Group is rounded off by Spezialtechnik Dresden Service GmbH (SDS). This company operates on the property sector and is responsible for facility management and development of real estate belonging to the companies in the STD Group. It also acts as letting agent for office and commercial properties in Dresden-Klotzsche and at the sites of the affiliated companies.

Information

Gründungsjahr: 1992 Privatisierung eines Teils des ehemaligen staatseigenen Kombinats und Übernahme in den General Atomics-Konzern, San Diego (USA)

Mitarbeiter: ca. 600

Leistungsspektrum der Unternehmensgruppe:
Die Spezialtechnik Dresden GmbH steht an der Spitze einer Unternehmensgruppe, deren Unternehmen auf folgenden Gebieten tätig sind:
· Instandhaltung/Fertigung, Service und Modernisierung/Umbau von Schienenfahrzeugen
· Demilitarisierung und Verwertung von konventioneller Munition, Raketen und Sprengmitteln
· Demilitarisierung und Verwertung von Explosivstoffen
· Tief- und Wasserbau
· Baugrund- und Böschungsstabilisierung
· Erd- und Landschaftsbau
· Altlastsanierung und Industrierückbau
· Umweltüberwachung und Laborleistungen
· Entwicklung und Realisierung von physikalischen und chemischen Verfahren zur Wasseraufbereitung und Wertstoffgewinnung
· Herstellung von großvolumigen Betonfertigteilen
· Immobilienbewirtschaftung und -entwicklung

Year founded: 1992 privatisation of part of the former state-owned collective combine and takeover by the General Atomics Group, San Diego (USA)

Employees: approx. 600

Range of services offered by the Group:
Spezialtechnik Dresden GmbH stands at the head of a Group made of companies operating in the following fields:
· maintenance/production, servicing and modernisation/conversion of rail vehicles
· demilitarisation and recycling of conventional munitions, rockets and exploders
· demilitarisation and recycling of explosives
· civil engineering and water engineering
· subsoil and embankment stabilisation
· earthworks and landscape engineering
· remediation of inherited pollution and the dismantling of industrial facilities
· environmental monitoring and laboratory services
· development and implementation of physical and chemical processes for water treatment and material recovery
· production of large-scale prefabricated concrete elements
· facility management and property development

Spezialtechnik Dresden GmbH
Dresden

Niedergang vor dem Umbruch

3. Oktober 1990. Mit diesem Tag wurde das jahrhundertealte Sachsen zum neuen Bundesland. Die wirtschaftliche Erneuerung begann ebenfalls im Einheitsjahr und dauert bis heute an. Vor den Erfolg – so sagt das Sprichwort – haben die Götter den Schweiß gesetzt. Dem können die Sachsen beipflichten. Der „real existierende Sozialismus" hatte ihnen ein desolates Wirtschaftssystem hinterlassen. Nach der Friedlichen Revolution wälzte sich die gesamte gesellschaftliche, politische, wirtschaftliche und kulturelle Struktur um. Die Planwirtschaft wich der Marktwirtschaft. Sozialistisch organisierte, zentral gesteuerte Betriebe mutierten zu frei am Markt agierenden Unternehmen.

Das war kein leichter Übergang. Ein Blick zurück: Historiker setzen den wirtschaftlichen Niedergang der DDR spätestens mit der Ära Honecker ab 1971 an. Die propagierte „Einheit von Wirtschafts- und Sozialpolitik" sollte die SED-Herrschaft erhalten helfen. Schnell offenbarte sie ihre Tücken: Das Geld reichte nicht. Westschulden wurden zum Dauerproblem. Um das Volk bei Laune zu halten, mussten begehrte Konsumgüter aus dem Westen importiert werden. Der Warenvielfalt aus eigener Kraft hatte die Staatsführung selbst den Todesstoß versetzt – mit der Enteignung der privaten und halbprivaten Betriebe im Jahr 1972. Industriekombinate mussten mit unwirtschaftlichen Kleinproduktionen in die Bresche springen.

Überall herrschte Mangel: bei Waren, Wohnungen, Maschinen, Arbeitskräften. Lebensbereiche wie Altbauzentren oder Umweltschutz wurden vernachlässigt. Prestigeobjekte traten in den Vordergrund, etwa der erste 1-Megabit-Speicher der DDR 1988. Eine erstaunliche Leistung aus Dresden unter schwierigen Bedingungen. Der Aufbau einer eigenen Mikroelektronik erwies sich jedoch als staatliche Fehlentscheidung, weil zugleich andere notwendige Investitionen unterblieben. Auch Exporte westwärts um jeden Preis brachten keine Rettung. 1989 betrug die Netto-Auslandsverschuldung der DDR 19,9 Mrd. Valutamark. Nach Honeckers Rücktritt stellte ein internes Papier fest: „Ein Stoppen der Verschuldung würde 1990 eine Senkung des Lebensstandards um 25 bis 30 Prozent erfordern und die DDR unregierbar machen." Es kam ohnehin anders.

Wir sind das Volk und ein Volk!

Ausreisewelle, Botschaftsbesetzungen, Montagsdemonstrationen, Maueröffnung – Stichworte zu einem atemberaubenden Prozess im Jahr 1989. Mit dem Ruf „Wir sind das Volk!" entzogen die Menschen den kommunistischen Machthabern die Legitimation. Sie forderten Freiheit und Demokratie, bald darauf die deutsche Einheit. Dresden gehörte zu den Brennpunkten: Gewaltsam ging die alte Macht Anfang Oktober gegen Ausreisewillige am Dresdner Hauptbahnhof vor, durch den die Züge der Ausreisenden aus der Prager Botschaft fuhren. Am 8. Oktober erzwangen friedliche Demonstranten in der Innenstadt einen

rate was even slightly lower at 10.6 percent, although this is still clearly above the German average. The productivity rate shows that not all trees will reach the sky, with Saxony one fifth below the average German output. Thuringia is on about the same level, compared to Bavaria with about seven percent above the mean value.

Decline before revival

3 October 1990. This was the date on which the centuries-old Saxony became a new federal state. Economic renewal also began in the same year and is still continuing today. As the saying goes, success is the fruit of hard work, and they've really had to work hard in Saxony. "Really existing socialism" had left them with a desolate economic system. The aftermath of the peaceful revolution brought complete upheaval of the entire social, political, economic and cultural structure. Planned economy made way for market economy. Centrally controlled companies organised on socialist lines changed into business undertakings acting freely on the market place.

This was no easy transformation. A look back in time highlights the year 1971 in which historians say the economic decline of the GDR began with the Honecker era. The propagated "unity of economic and social policy" was supposed to help preserve the SED rule. But it soon revealed its pitfalls. There simply wasn't enough money. Debts with the west became a permanent problem. To keep the people happy, coveted goods had to be imported from the west. It was the state leadership itself that destroyed the country's own diversity of goods – with the expropriation of private and semi-private companies in 1972. State industrial collectives had to step into the breach with unprofitable small-scale production.

There was a shortage of everything – goods, housing, machines and skilled labour. Aspects such as old town centres or environment protection were neglected completely. The focus turned to prestige projects, such as the GDR's first 1-megabit memory in 1988. An amazing achievement from Dresden, given the difficult conditions. But the attempt to set up the country's own microelectronics industry proved to a real mistake, as there was no possibility of making other simultaneously necessary investments. Exports to the west at all cost also failed to produce any salutary effect. In 1989, the net foreign debt of the GDR amounted to 19.9 billion "Valuta Marks". After Honecker resigned, an internal paper came to the following conclusion: "Stopping the debts in 1990 would cut the standard of living by 25 to 30 percent and make the GDR ungovernable." As it was, things turned out differently anyway.

We are the people and one people!

An unprecedented wave of emigration, occupation of embassies, Monday demonstrations, the opening of the Berlin Wall

Eine Deutsche Mark aus dem geschichtsträchtigen Jahr 1990

A Deutsche Mark from 1990, a year steeped in history

Dialog mit Staatsvertretern, den ersten in der damaligen DDR. Am 23. Oktober demonstrierten 250 000 Menschen in Dresden. Die Revolution nahm ihren Lauf ...

Kalenderblatt 19. Dezember 1989: Die Ruine der Frauenkirche in Dresden wird zum Schauplatz deutscher Geschichte. Milde zehn Grad plus, kurz nach 16 Uhr. Bundeskanzler Helmut Kohl spricht zu 20 000 Zuhörern. Unter ihrem stürmischen Applaus sagt er: „Mein Ziel bleibt – wenn die geschichtliche Stunde es zulässt – die Einheit unserer Nation."

Keine elf Monate später war sie erreicht. Der „Kanzler der Einheit" bezeichnete später den Dezembertag als sein Schlüsselerlebnis auf dem Weg dahin. Zu den Transparentsprüchen der Übergangszeit gehörte die Botschaft: „Kommt die D-Mark, bleiben wir, kommt sie nicht, geh'n wir zu ihr!" Die ersten freien Wahlen im März 1990 besiegelten das Ende des kommunistischen Experiments auf deutschem Boden. Die Währungs-, Wirtschafts- und Sozialunion ab 1. Juli stellte die Weichen in die gemeinsame deutsche Zukunft.

Modewort „marode"

Transformation übersetzt der Duden mit Umformung, Umwandlung, Umgestaltung. Gesellschaftliche Transformationsprozesse greifen tief in das Leben der Menschen ein. D-Mark und

– just a few of the catch phrases describing the breathtaking happenings of 1989. The slogan "Wir sind das Volk" (We are the people) brought crowds flocking to the streets, depriving the powers-that-be of their legitimation. They demanded freedom and democracy, and very soon also German unity. Dresden was one of the flashpoints: in early October, the old regime tried to use violence to prevent people from emigrating at Dresden central station, where trains from Prague were passing through with emigrants from the embassy. On 8 October, demonstrators in the city centre forced the state representatives to enter into dialogue with them, the first ever in the GDR. On 23 October, 250,000 people demonstrated in Dresden. The revolution took its course ...

The calendar says 19 December 1989. The ruins of Dresden's Frauenkirche provide the backdrop for a historical moment in German history. It's just after 4 p.m., the temperature a mild 10 °C. Federal Chancellor Helmut Kohl speaks to an audience of 20,000. Earning tumultuous applause, he says: "If history permits, my objective is to reunify our nation."

Just eleven months later, it was accomplished. Later, the "Chancellor of Unity" referred to that day in December as his key experience on the path to reunification. Banner slogans to be seen during the transition period included: "If the Deutschmark comes to us, then we'll stay. Otherwise, we'll go to the

deutsche Einheit veränderten Ostdeutschland fundamental. Aus für die Kommandowirtschaft. Reprivatisierung, freier Wettbewerb, Marktmechanismen. Endlich im Konsumparadies – das westliche Wirtschaftssystem brachte die erhofften Segnungen, aber auch unerwartete, unerfreuliche Härten.

Die Betriebe verkrafteten die plötzliche D-Mark-Aufwertung ihrer Produkte nicht, ihre östlichen Märkte brachen weg, gegenüber dem Westen offenbarte sich eine technologische Lücke. „Marode" wurde zur geläufigen Kennzeichnung der Volkseigenen Betriebe (VEB). Produktionsrückgang, Betriebsschließungen, Massenentlassungen, Arbeitslosigkeit. In Sachsen sank die Erwerbstätigkeit von 1989 bis 1993 um ein Drittel. Das Wort vom „Manchesterkapitalismus" machte die Runde. Die Euphorie wich der Ernüchterung. Frust und Leid, Unsicherheit und Überforderung belasteten die Menschen.

Die schnelle Einheit hatte alle überrascht. Der Politik fehlten ausgereifte Anpassungskonzepte für den Sprung von einer Wirtschaftsform in die andere. Die 1990 gegründete Treuhandanstalt wickelte die DDR ab. Sie privatisierte das Volkseigentum vor allem zugunsten kapitalkräftiger Investoren aus dem Westen. Auch Glücksritter, Spekulanten und Betrüger traten in Goldgräberstimmung auf den Plan. Neben Schatten auch viel Licht: Engagierte Manager und Investoren aus den alten Bundesländern halfen den Ostdeutschen.

Bereit zu Risiko und Neuanfang

Bald regte sich neues Leben. „Management-Buy-out" wurde zur Zauberformel. Betriebszugehörige „Leitungskräfte" und Managertypen kauften ihre Betriebe, um Tradition, Stammbelegschaft und eigene berufliche Zukunft zu retten. Frühere Eigentümer erhielten ihre enteigneten Firmen zurück und begannen neu. Zudem trat eine Generation junger Unternehmer an. Sie nutzte die gewonnene Freiheit, um etwas zu bewegen. Kapitalknappheit erschwerte oft das Durchhaltevermögen. Bei Konzentration auf das Tagesgeschäft – aufs unmittelbare Überleben – blieben zu wenig Mittel für die Forschung und Entwicklung und damit für die Perspektive. Marketing – in der überwundenen Mangelwirtschaft abwegig – musste erst erlernt werden. Selbst hohe Qualität verkaufte sich nicht von selbst.

„Besserwessi" und „Jammerossi" – diese Typisierung traf einen Nerv der Anfangszeit. Ohne Beinamen blieben all jene, die sich beherzt, kräftezehrend und auf gleicher Augenhöhe für die Veränderungen einsetzten. Neue Kooperationen entwickelten sich. Im Alltag traf der Ostdeutsche auf den gewandten Westdeutschen, der sich dank seiner Sozialisation „besser verkaufen" konnte. Der Westdeutsche traf auf den Ostdeutschen, der – zwar weniger eloquent – sein Handwerk dennoch verstand.

Um 1992 die Trendwende: Der „Aufbau Ost" wurde zunehmend erlebbar. Zugpferd der Konjunktur in den 1990er-Jahren war die Bauwirtschaft. Ihr Boom überdeckte die schwierige Anpassung in anderen Branchen. Doch das verarbeitende

Fortsetzung Seite 30

Deutschmark!" The first free elections in March 1990 finally put an end to the communist experiment on German soil. The currency, economy and social union implemented on 1 July set the points for a shared German future.

"Ailing" is the buzzword

Transformation means conversion, commutation, redesigning. Social transformation processes have an in-depth impact on people's lives. The Deutschmark and German unity made fundamental changes to East Germany, bringing the end of the command economy, introducing reprivatisation, free competition and market mechanisms. Consumer paradise, at long, long last – the western economic system brought the hoped-for blessings, but also unexpected, less pleasant hardship.

The companies couldn't cope with the sudden Deutschmark revaluation of their products. Their markets to the east started to dissolve, while a technological gap emerged compared to the west. "Ailing" became a much-used expression for the state-owned companies. Production started to decline, accompanied by works closures, mass redundancies and unemployment. Between 1989 and 1993, employment in Saxony fell by one third. People started to speak of "Manchester Capitalism". The initial euphoria gave way to disillusion. The population was frustrated and suffering, plagued by uncertainty and simply out of its depth.

Everyone was surprised at the speed with which reunification came about. The political sector simply did not have the right kind of concepts to adapt to the sudden leap from one economic form to another. A trust agency ("Treuhandanstalt") was set up in 1990 to wind up the GDR. It privatised the state-owned assets, mainly in favour of financially well-endowed investors from the west. Adventurers, speculators and swindlers also joined in the general "gold rush". Which had not only shadows, but also lighter patches: committed managers from the rest of Germany came forward to help the East Germans.

Willing to take risks and make a new start

Business soon came alive again, with management buy-outs being one of the magic formulas. Senior executives and managers started to buy up their companies to rescue the traditions, the workforce and their own professional future. Expropriated companies were restored to their former proprietors who took this opportunity to make a new start. In addition, a new generation of young entrepreneurs came on the scene, using the newly gained freedom to actually move something. A lack of capital often made it difficult to stay the course. The need to concentrate on day-to-day business – on direct survival – left inadequate resources for research and development and thus for the longer term outlook. Marketing, an absurd concept in the now overcome deficit economy, had to be learnt from scratch. Even top quality doesn't sell itself.

Continued on page 30

STRABAG AG

Information

Gründungsjahr:
1992 in Dresden

Mitarbeiter: ca. 250 in Dresden

Leistungsspektrum:
- Straßen- und Tiefbau
- Kanal- und Rohrleitungsbau
- Erd- und Wasserbau

Year founded:
1992 in Dresden

Employees: approx. 250 in Dresden

Range of services:
- road construction and underground works
- sewer and pipeline construction
- earthworks and hydraulic engineering

STRABAG AG
Direktion Sachsen

STRABAG AG

Die STRABAG AG blickt als Marktführer im deutschen Verkehrswegebau mit etwa 11 500 Mitarbeitern auf über 80 Jahre Tradition zurück und ist Teil eines der größten Baukonzerne Europas. In Dresden ist STRABAG seit 1992 vertreten und mit rund 250 Mitarbeitern im Straßen- und Tiefbau, Kanal- und Rohrleitungsbau sowie im Erd- und Wasserbau tätig.

Zu den anspruchsvollsten STRABAG-Projekten in Dresden zählt die Sanierung des Großen Gartens. In der zentral auf Altstädter Elbseite gelegenen Parkanlage, in der auch Zoologischer Garten, Parkeisenbahn (ehemalige Pioniereisenbahn), Botanischer Garten der TU Dresden und Carolasee liegen, hat STRABAG die bislang ungebundenen Wege entlang von Palais, Palaisteich und Fürstenallee durch eine sandfarbene Asphaltdeckschicht ersetzt. So gelang es, Funktion und Ästhetik im Sinne des Denkmalschutzes zu verbinden.

Auch andernorts in Dresden war STRABAG in den letzten Jahren mehrfach aktiv: Im Alberthafen Dresden-Friedrichstadt, der 1895 als größter sächsischer Eisenbahnverkehrshafen eröffnet wurde, verkleinerte sie von 1997 bis 1998 das Hafenbecken, um zusätzliche Ansiedlungsflächen zu schaffen, und erneuerte anschließend die Straßen- und Eisenbahnanbindung. 2007 errichtete STRABAG vor der Hafeneinfahrt eine Roll-on-/Roll-off-Anlage (RoRo). Auch am Ausbau der südlichen Hafenstraße, die als Zufahrt von der Schwerlastmontagehalle zur RoRo-Anlage dient, war STRABAG beteiligt: Im März 2012 hat das Unternehmen die Straße auf einer Länge von etwa 680 Metern auf fast sieben Meter verbreitert.

STRABAG AG

STRABAG AG is the market leader in the transportation infrastructures business in Germany and has a workforce of about 11,500 employees. Looking back on more than 80 years of tradition, the company belongs to one of Europe's largest construction groups. STRABAG has been present in Dresden since 1992 with around 250 employees working on road construction and underground works, sewer and pipeline construction, earthworks and hydraulic engineering.

STRABAG's most demanding projects in Dresden include refurbishment of the Grosser Garten. In this baroque-style central park located near the river Elbe in the Old Town, which also includes Dresden Zoo, the park railway (formerly pioneer railway), the Botanical Gardens of the Technical University of Dresden and Carolasee Lake, STRABAG has replaced the unpaved paths alongside the palace, palace pond and Fürstenallee with a sand-coloured asphalt surface. This solution combined functional and aesthetic aspects with the stipulations made by the preservation order for the historical monuments.

In recent years, STRABAG has also been very busy at other sites in Dresden. From 1997 to 1998, the company reduced the size of the harbour basin in Alberthafen Dresden-Friedrichstadt, which had been opened in 1895 as Saxony's largest railway harbour, thus creating additional settlement areas. Subsequently, the company also upgraded the road and rail connection. In 2007, STRABAG constructed a roll-on/roll-off (ro-ro) facility at the harbour entrance. The company was also involved in upgrading the southern harbour road acting as access from the heavy load assembly building to the ro-ro facility: here in March 2012, STRABAG widened the road to a width of nearly seven metres across a length of about 680 metres.

Die Wege im Großen Garten bekommen eine Asphaltdeckschicht.

Giving the paths in Grosser Garten an asphalt surface.

Der Alberthafen Dresden-Friedrichstadt mit verkleinertem Hafenbecken

Alberthafen Dresden-Friedrichstadt with smaller harbour basin

www.strabag.de

Kurt Biedenkopf, Sachsens erster Ministerpräsident (1990–2002) nach der Wiedervereinigung, machte aus Sachsen ein kleines Wirtschaftswunderland.

Kurt Biedenkopf, Saxony's first Minister-President (1990–2002) after the German reunification, turned the federal state of Saxony into a true economic miracle.

Gewerbe und die unternehmerischen Dienstleistungen zogen nach. In den 2000er-Jahren wuchsen einzelne Zweige in Sachsen jährlich zwischen acht und zehn Prozent – Spitzenwerte in Deutschland. Inzwischen liegt der Anteil der Industrie an der Bruttowertschöpfung im Freistaat bei 48 Prozent und damit höher als in allen anderen neuen Ländern.

Im Spiegel der Konjunkturberichte

Die IHK Dresden begleitet die Auferstehung seit 1991 auch aus statistischer Sicht. Im Frühjahr 2012 führte sie die mittlerweile 52. Konjunkturumfrage im Kammerbezirk durch. Diese Stimmungsbilder der Unternehmen widerspiegeln nicht nur temporäre Auf- und Abschwünge, sie sind auch Zeitbilder. In den 1990er-Jahren kreisten die Wünsche der Unternehmer vor allem um die Fördermittel. Damals sorgten sie sich in ihren Berichten darum, bei Ausschreibungen leer auszugehen. Auch die schlechte Zahlungsmoral hat sie stark beunruhigt. Heute hingegen verunsichern steigende Energie-, Rohstoff- und Kraftstoffpreise sowie die Euro-Schuldenkrise die Unternehmen.

Die gegenwärtigen Konjunkturbarometer dokumentieren vor allem aber eins: Solidität, Konstanz und Vorwärtsdrang der Unternehmen. Der Wettbewerb hat die Firmen gestärkt, sie haben ihren Platz im „Revier" gefunden, ihr Eigenkapital ist gestiegen, sie investieren in die Rationalisierung und betriebliche Erweiterungen. Außerdem beweist die Entwicklung: Wer sich am Markt behaupten konnte, den werfen auch finanzielle Unwägbarkeiten nicht mehr so schnell um.

Von 2000 bis 2011 sank die Zahl der Unternehmensinsolvenzen im Kammerbezirk Dresden von 891 auf 488. Dass es auch Große treffen kann, bewies 2009 die Schließung des Halbleiterherstellers Qimonda in Dresden. Neue Giganten rücken so schnell nicht nach, aber kleine und mittlere Spezialisten. Jährlich kommen im Kammerbezirk Dresden 2000 bis 3000 Gewerbetreibende hinzu. Wie die schon bestehenden Mittelständler suchen und finden sie ihren Platz als Zulieferer, mit Nischenproduktionen oder im stark gefächerten Dienstleistungsbereich.

"Besserwessi" (know-alls from the West) and "Jammerossi" (moaners from the East) are just a couple of words used to describe the feelings that prevailed in the initial phase. Meanwhile, all those who met on eye level to get down to the hard work involved in implementing the changes remained without any nicknames. New cooperation ventures started to develop. In everyday situations, the East German met the savvy West German who was better at selling thanks to his socialisation. The West German met the East German who, while being less eloquent, was still well skilled at his trade.

It was around 1992 that things started to improve, with economic recovery gradually making itself felt. The locomotive driving the economy during the 1990s was in fact the building trade. The boom in this industry helped to conceal the more difficult adjustments necessary in the other branches. But manufacturing and the services sector started to catch up. In the early years of the new millennium, some branches in Saxony grew by annual rates of between eight and ten percent – top values in Germany. Industry meanwhile accounts for 48 percent of gross value added in the Free State, which is higher than in all other new states.

Reflected in business reports

Since 1991, Dresden CCI has also been monitoring the economic revival in terms of statistics. In spring 2012 it conducted what was meanwhile the 52nd business survey in the chamber district. These impressions given by the companies reflect not just temporary recovery and decline phases, they are also pictures of their time. During the 1990s, the wishes of the entrepreneurs focused primarily on funds. Their reports were full of concerns about failing to win tenders. Poor payment behaviour

Der Aufbau in Sachsen vollzog sich nicht nur symbolisch.

The development in Saxony was not only symbolic in its nature.

Leuchttürme in stürmischer Zeit

Ein Leuchtturm steht auf stabilem Grund, ragt hoch empor, bietet weithin Navigationshilfe. Sachsen hat ab 1990 solche Leuchttürme geschaffen. Ja, es hat sich mit seiner „Leuchtturm-Politik" geradezu als Musterknabe des „Aufbaus Ost" erwiesen. Die Grundidee des Strukturwandels war, mit modernen Kerngebieten Vorbilder zu schaffen, die weithin ins Land wirken. Diese Politik ist mit Kurt Biedenkopf verbunden, Ministerpräsident von 1990 bis 2002. Die „Süddeutsche Zeitung" schrieb 2010 zu seinem 80. Geburtstag: „Er wurde eine der wichtigsten Symbolfiguren beim Zusammenwachsen von Ost und West, machte aus Sachsen ein kleines Wirtschaftswunderland, er reüssierte mit seiner ‚Leuchtturmpolitik', deren Konzept es ist, sich bei der Wirtschaftsförderung auf einige wenige zukunftsorientierte Branchen zu konzentrieren."

Von Dresden ging – neben den Ballungsräumen Leipzig–Halle und Chemnitz–Zwickau – bald diese Strahlkraft aus. Sachsens größte Stadt wurde zu einem kräftig in Schwung gebrachten Motor. Wer im Land am Rande lebte, den freute die konzentrierte Förderung weniger. Die Regionen monierten eine Bevor-

Fortsetzung Seite 34

was another worry. Today by contrast, it is the increasing prices for energy, fuel and raw materials that give companies cause for anxiety, together with the Euro debt crisis.

But current business barometers bear witness above all to one thing: the solidarity, constancy and forward drive of the companies. Competition has made the firms stronger, they have found their place on the "hunting ground", their equity has increased, they are investing in rationalisation and business expansion. Furthermore, developments show that those who hold their own on the market place are more able to withstand financial difficulties.

Between 2000 and 2011, the number of companies going bankrupt in the Dresden chamber district fell from 891 to 488. Big names are also sometimes affected, as illustrated in 2009 when semiconductor manufacturer Qimonda closed down in Dresden. Instead of new big names, it tends to be SME specialists that now come on the scene. Every year, the Dresden chamber district is joined by another 2,000 to 3,000 traders and businessmen. Like the existing SME sector, they also search for and find their place as suppliers with niche products or in the highly diversified services branch.

Continued on page 34

Führungskreis (von links nach rechts): Edgar Winter, (Geschäftsführer); Michael Herrmann, (QMB); Ronny Epperlein, (Bereichsleiter Technische Teile); Sven Baier, (Bereichsleiter Verschlüsse); Jana Roßmej, (Leitung Qualitätsmanagement); Heiko Rösner, (Leitung Werkzeugbau); Hans-Releff Riege, (Leitung Auftragsmanagement); David Schreiber, (Leitung Technik)

Management team (from left to right): Edgar Winter, (Managing Director); Michael Herrmann, (Quality Officer); Ronny Epperlein, (Head of Technical Components); Sven Baier, (Head of Closures); Jana Roßmej, (Head of Quality Management); Heiko Rösner, (Head of Tool Making); Hans-Releff Riege, (Head of Order Management); David Schreiber, (Head of Engineering)

Bergi-Plast GmbH – mehr als nur Spritzguss

Die Firma Bergi-Plast ist ein mittelständisches sächsisches Traditionsunternehmen. Bereits 1875 wurde am heutigen Stammsitz im Kurort Berggießhübel bei Dresden die Produktion von Knöpfen, Reißverschlüssen und Bijouterieware aufgenommen. Seit 1962 liegt der Produktionsschwerpunkt in der Spritzgussverarbeitung von Thermoplasten. Nach Wiedervereinigung und erfolgreicher Privatisierung 1990 konnte Bergi-Plast ein stetiges nachhaltiges Wachstum erzielen.

Heute ist die Kernkompetenz der Bergi-Plast GmbH die Realisierung anspruchsvoller Spritzgussprojekte. Die langjährige Erfahrung und hohe fachliche Kompetenz in den Bereichen Kunststoffspritzguss und Formenbau bildet dabei die Grundlage für das ganzheitliche Leistungsangebot inkl. Entwicklung, Konstruktion, Werkzeugbau und Serienproduktion.

Zielmärkte sind insbesondere die Verpackungs- und Automobilindustrie. Für die Verpackungsindustrie werden Hochleistungswerkzeuge und kosten-/nutzenoptimale Verschlüsse für das eigene Standardprogramm sowie kundenspezifische Anwendungen hergestellt. Die Automobilindustrie wird mit Präzisionswerkzeugen und technisch hochwertigen Konstruktionsteilen beliefert. Die Produktion erfolgt auf modernsten Fertigungseinrichtungen an zwei auf den jeweiligen Produktbereich spezialisierten Standorten.

Ganzheitlich wie das Leistungsangebot ist auch das gelebte Qualitätsverständnis. Das dadurch erreichte hohe Qualitätsniveau, eine ausgeprägte Kundenorientierung und die enge Zusammenarbeit auf allen Leistungsebenen resultiert in der angestrebten langfristigen Verbindung zu Kunden und Lieferanten. Dies ist gleichsam Basis der guten, international erarbeiteten Marktposition wie Garant für die prosperierende weitere Entwicklung.

Modernste Produktionseinrichtungen: 50 Spritzgießmaschinen (inkl. 2-K), zentrale Materialversorgung, 10 Montageautomaten etc.

State-of-the-art production equipment: 50 injection moulding machines (incl. 2C), central material supply, 10 automatic assembly machines, etc.

Bergi-Plast GmbH

Oben: Einsatz von Präzisionshochleistungswerkzeugen, hergestellt im eigenen Werkzeugbau

Top: Using high-performance precision tools, made in the company's own tool making department

Gelebte Qualität in der gesamten Prozesskette – von der Entwicklung bis zur Serie

Quality throughout the whole process chain – from development through to series production

Information

Gründungsjahr: 1875

Mitarbeiter: 160

Produktspektrum:
· Verschlüsse für alle Anwendungsbereiche, als Standardprodukte oder Entwicklung nach Kundenwunsch
· technische Kunststoffteile und Baugruppen, mit hohen Qualitätsanforderungen

Kundenspektrum:
· Flaschen- und Kanisterhersteller, Abfüller, Händler
· Industrieunternehmen und Zulieferer, insbesondere aus der Verpackungs- und Automobilindustrie

Year founded: 1875

Employees: 160

Product range:
· closures for all applications, as standard products or customised developments
· technical plastic parts and assemblies, with high quality requirements

Customer base:
· manufacturers of bottles and canisters, bottling and filling companies, traders
· industrial companies and suppliers, particularly in the packaging and automotive industry

Bergi-Plast GmbH
Berggießhübel

Bergi-Plast GmbH – more than molding

Bergi-Plast is a medium-sized company with a long tradition in Saxony. The production of buttons, zip fasteners and jewellery at the company's present site in Berggießhübel near Dresden began already in 1875. Since 1962, production activities have concentrated primarily on the injection moulding of plastic parts. Following German reunification and successful privatisation in 1990, Bergi-Plast has generated constantly sustainable growth.

Today, Bergi-Plast's core area of expertise consists in sophisticated injection moulding projects. Many years of experience combined with a high level of professional skills in plastic injection moulding and die production form the basis for the company's comprehensive range of services, including development, design, tool making and series production.

Target markets include in particular the packaging and automotive industries. The company serves the packaging industry with high-performance tools and cost/use-optimised closures for proprietary standard programmes and customised applications. The automotive industry is supplied with precision tools and top quality engineering components. Production takes place on state-of-the-art production machinery at two sites specialised for the specific product range.

The implemented quality policy is as comprehensive as the range of products. The high quality standard, pronounced customer focus with close cooperation on all levels results in the sought-after long-term relationships with customers and suppliers. At the same time, this provides the basis for the good position that the company has achieved on the international market, while guaranteeing prosperous further development.

www.bergi-plast.de

zugung der Landeshauptstadt. Gleichwohl reifte die Einsicht, dass ein Flächenland wie Ostsachsen nicht überall gleichermaßen wettbewerbsfähig sein konnte. Inzwischen haben die Regionen im Kammerbezirk Dresden ihre eigenen Wirtschaftsprofile herausgebildet. Viele Unternehmen sind dabei eng mit dem Ballungsraum Dresden verbunden.

Wertschöpfung im „Schwarm"

Der Begriff „Cluster" hat die Metapher „Leuchtturm" abgelöst. Das Langenscheidt Taschenwörterbuch übersetzt ihn mit Büschel, Traube, Schwarm. Wirtschaftlich bezeichnet er regionale Netzwerke von Produzenten, Zulieferern, Forschungseinrichtungen, Dienstleistern, Handwerkern und Institutionen. Eine gemeinsame Wertschöpfungskette bündelt die Interessen aller Beteiligten. Füreinander werden sie günstige Standortfaktoren und Innovationstreiber.

Die Sachsen bilden solche Gemeinschaften bis hin zu Exzellenzclustern bei Schlüsseltechnologien. Mit diesen setzen sie Forschungsergebnisse schnell und erfolgreich am Markt um und sichern am Standort dauerhaft Wachstum und Beschäftigung. Hinter solchen Zukunftsinitiativen steht die Kreativität der Akteure, aber auch staatlicher Wille. Der Freistaat hat ein innovatives Klima geschaffen. Er konzentriert in der Förderperiode bis 2013 fast 43 Prozent der EU-Strukturfonds für Regionale Entwicklung (EFRE) auf Wissenschaft, Forschung, Bildung und Innovation, zwölf Prozent mehr als von 2000 bis 2006.

Seit 1991 unterstützt die Wirtschaftsförderung Sachsen (WFS) in Dresden in- und ausländische Investoren. Die Sächsische Aufbaubank hilft, die Vorhaben finanziell zu schultern. Beim Start und der Konsolidierung können neue Unternehmen online eine Fördermitteldatenbank des Freistaates und den „Wirtschaftsatlas Sachsen" der drei sächsischen IHKs und ihrer Partner nutzen.

Lachendes und weinendes Auge

Als Westkonzerne Ostbetriebe kauften, gliederten sie diese in der Regel als „verlängerte Werkbänke" ins eigene Imperium ein. Der metaphorische Begriff bezeichnet Fertigungsbetriebe ohne komplette Wertschöpfungskette. Die meisten Betriebe ab 500 Beschäftigte im Kammerbezirk Dresden haben diesen Status. Die Produktion am Standort beschränkt sich auf bestimmte Komponenten. Diese für die Globalisierung typische Arbeitsteilung bietet beiden Seiten Vorteile: Der Stammbetrieb investiert mit seiner Ansiedlung in einem gediegenen Umfeld. Die jeweilige Region lebt auf. Industrie bleibt erhalten, Arbeitsplätze werden gerettet oder geschaffen.

Zum lachenden kommt das weinende Auge: Beim Stammbetrieb verbleiben die entscheidenden Unternehmensfunktionen. Der Filialbetrieb bestimmt nicht selbst über die Investitionen. Eigenentwicklung bleibt aus. Die Dichte von Bildung und

Fortsetzung Seite 36

Lighthouses in turbulent times

A lighthouse stands on firm ground, towers high into the sky and is a clearly visible navigation aid. Saxony has created a number of lighthouses since 1990, with a lighthouse strategy that has become exemplary for successful economic recovery in the east. The basic idea of structural change here entailed taking modern key areas to create role models which would then have an extensive effect on the region at large. This policy is closely associated with Kurt Biedenkopf, Minister-President from 1990 to 2002. On his 80th birthday in 2010, the "Süddeutsche Zeitung" wrote: "He became one of the key symbol figures in helping east and west grow together, turning Saxony into a little economic miracle. His success was based among others on his 'lighthouse strategy' with the concept of focusing business development activities on a few future-oriented branches."

Together with the conurbation areas of Leipzig-Halle and Chemnitz-Zwickau, Dresden soon started to exert this desired radiance. Saxony's largest city became a motor that had suddenly picked up speed. Those living in more remote areas out in the country benefited less from the concentrated funding and complained of the preferential treatment being given to the state capital. At the same time, it was gradually understood that non-city states such as East Saxony cannot be equally competitive in all places all the time. Meanwhile the regions have established their own business profile in the Dresden chamber district, with many companies closely related to the greater Dresden area.

Value creation in a swarm

Clusters have meanwhile replaced the lighthouses. Clusters are also defined as bundles, bunches or swarms. In economic terms, clusters refer to regional networks of producers, suppliers, research facilities, service providers, skilled craftsmen and institutions. A shared supply chain pools the interests of all stakeholders, who become favourable location factors and innovation drivers for each other.

The Saxons are forming such consortiums right through to clusters of excellence for key technologies. They ensure that research results are implemented quickly and successfully on the market place, safeguarding constant growth and employment for the area. Future initiatives of this kind are backed by the creativity of the players involved, and also by the political will of the state. The Free State of Saxony has created an innovative climate. In the funding period through to 2013, it is concentrating nearly 43 percent of the EU's EFRE (European Regional Development Fund) on science, research, education and innovation, twelve percent more than between 2000 and 2006.

Since 1991, the WFS (Business Development Saxony) has been supporting German and foreign investors in Dresden. The

Continued on page 36

Information

Gründungsjahr: 1927

Mitarbeiter: Kunze gesamt ca. 500, in Dresden rund 150

Leistungsspektrum:
· nationale und internationale Landverkehre
· Projekt-, Kontrakt- und Distributionslogistik
· Mehrwertdienstleistungen entlang der logistischen Prozesskette

Year founded: 1927

Employees: Kunze altogether approx. 500, around 150 in Dresden

Range of services:
· national and international land transport services
· project, contract and distribution logistics
· value-added services along the logistics process chain

Spedition Kunze GmbH & Co. KG
Dresden

Spedition Kunze GmbH & Co. KG

Spedition Kunze GmbH & Co. KG belongs to the Kunze Group with other sites in Karlsdorf (near Bruchsal), Bielefeld and Karlsruhe.

The Kunze Group is a growth-oriented SME transport and logistics company currently run by the third generation of proprietors.

Together with Spedition Kunze GmbH & Co. KG, the Group also includes Walter Kunze Spedition GmbH & Co. KG and S+L Spedition GmbH (with own office in Dresden).

The range of services offered by Kunze in Dresden is supplemented by more than 30 regular truck services warranting nationwide coverage for general cargo and part loads.

The company operates its own fleet with its own swap bodies to organise its transportation services.

Der eigene Fuhrpark ist für die Kunden von Kunze europaweit unterwegs.

Kunze's own fleet is out and about on Europe's roads on behalf of the company's customers.

Warehousing and logistics services, including all conceivable value added services along the logistics chain, are provided on approx. 12,000 square metres premises.

Years of experience in enterprise resource planning, the deployment of innovative technology geared to the needs of customers and the team spirit of the workforce provides the foundations for further growth – both in the home region of Saxony and on an international scale.

Spedition Kunze GmbH & Co. KG

Die Spedition Kunze GmbH & Co. KG gehört zur Unternehmensgruppe Kunze mit weiteren Standorten in Karlsdorf (bei Bruchsal), Bielefeld und Karlsruhe.

Die Unternehmensfamilie Kunze ist ein in dritter Generation inhabergeführtes, mittelständisches und wachstumsorientiertes Speditions- und Logistikunternehmen.

Zur Unternehmensfamilie gehören neben der Spedition auch die Walter Kunze Spedition GmbH & Co. KG und die S+L Spedition GmbH (mit eigenem Büro in Dresden).

Die Leistungspalette von Kunze in Dresden wird ergänzt durch mehr als 30 Lkw-Linienverkehre, die täglich eine bundesweite Flächendeckung für Stückgut und Teilpartien gewährleisten.

Für die Transportorganisation steht ein eigener Fuhrpark mit eigenen Wechselbrücken zur Verfügung.

Lager- und Logistikdienstleistungen werden auf ca. 12 000 Quadratmetern Hallenfläche erbracht, alle denkbaren Mehrwertdienstleistungen entlang der logistischen Prozesskette werden angeboten.

Jahrelange Erfahrungen in der Warenwirtschaft, der Einsatz innovativer und an den Bedürfnissen der Kunden ausgerichteter Technik und der Teamgeist der Mitarbeiter sind das Fundament für weiteres Wachstum – sowohl in der Heimatregion Sachsen als auch im internationalen Maßstab.

Im Güterverkehrszentrum (GVZ) Dresden betreibt Kunze eine Speditions- und Logistikanlage: Blick ins Hochregallager der 5000 Quadratmeter großen Logistikhalle

Kunze operates a transport and logistics facility in Dresden cargo transport centre (GVZ): view of the high-bay stores in the logistics building measuring 5,000 square meters

Forschung im Kammerbezirk Dresden bringt jedoch Bewegung in die abgegrenzten Gefilde. Über die reine Fertigung hinaus delegieren die Großen vermehrt auch die Forschung an die Elbe.

Von der Holperpiste zu sechs Spuren

Freie Fahrt für freie Bürger. Nach diesem alten ADAC-Spruch konnte in Sachsen zur Wende niemand fahren. Das Straßennetz war katastrophal. Wer damals auf der A 4 von Chemnitz nach Dresden unterwegs war, musste vor der ramponierten Elbbrücke sein Auto auf Tempo 30 abbremsen. Selbst wenn heute noch nicht jede Holperpiste, rückständige Verkehrsführung oder überlastete Ortsdurchfahrt überwunden ist – es fährt sich gut und zügig. Mit Milliardeninvestitionen hat der Freistaat dem sprunghaft gestiegenen Verkehrsaufkommen nach der Wiedervereinigung entsprochen. Die Straßendichte liegt mit 760 Metern überörtliche Straße pro Quadratkilometer über dem Bundesdurchschnitt. Im Kammerbezirk Dresden hat sich neben der Qualität der Verkehrswege auch deren Ausdehnung erhöht um gut 130 Kilometer allein seit 2000.

Sachsens Straßen sind Teil eines leistungsfähigen internationalen Straßennetzes. Bei Dresden begegnen sich die Europastraßen E 40 von Frankreich nach Kasachstan und E 55 zwischen Schweden und Griechenland. Für den Kammerbezirk Dresden beste Voraussetzungen für Beschaffung und Absatz, für den Transfer der Touristen in Europa. Ein Aushängeschild ist die Bundesautobahn A 4 als West-Ost-Achse zwischen der niederländischen und der polnischen Grenze.

Mit diesem Verkehrsprojekt Deutsche Einheit Nr. 15 wurde die Strecke zwischen Chemnitz und Dresden sechsspurig ausgebaut. Vier neue Spuren erhielt der Abschnitt vom Dreieck Dresden-Nord, wo die A 13 nach Berlin abzweigt, bis Weißenberg. Damit verschwand eine Kuriosität: eine öffentlich gesperrte, 16 Kilometer lange Strecke zwischen Bautzen-Ost und Weißenberg mit 66 Getreidelagerhallen als DDR-Staatsreserve. Komplett neu wurde die A 4 zwischen Weißenberg und Görlitz Richtung Wrocław (Breslau) gebaut. Auf diesen 24 Kilometern durchquert die A 4 die Königshainer Berge im zweitlängsten Zwei-Röhren-Straßentunnel Deutschlands.

Kaffeetrinken in der goldenen Stadt

„Zum Frühstück nach Prag" – so lautete der Slogan für den Neubau der A 17. Mit Fertigstellung des tschechischen Autobahnabschnittes D 8 wird sie 2015 durchgängig in die „goldene Stadt" führen. Eine schnelle Verbindung zu den östlichen Nachbarn war mit der EU-Erweiterung unumgänglich geworden. Von 1998 bis 2006 flossen 646 Mio. Euro in den Bau: 45 Kilometer lang, fünf Tunnel, acht Anschlussstellen und zehn Großbrücken. Die A 17 entlastet Dresden, das obere Elbtal und das Osterzgebirge vom Transitverkehr.

Durch die südliche Oberlausitz rollt der Fernverkehr nicht so

Sächsische Aufbaubank (Saxon Reconstruction Bank) helps to shoulder the financial aspects of business projects. During the start-up and consolidation phase, new companies can use an on-line funding database run by the Free State and the "Saxon Business Atlas" of the three CCIs in Saxony and their partners.

Mixed feelings

When western corporations bought up eastern companies, generally they integrated them as "extended workbenches" in their own empire. This metaphor refers to production plants without a full supply chain. Most companies with more than 500 employees in the Dresden chamber district have this status, with local production activities restricted to certain components. This particular division of labour is typical for globalisation and offers advantages for both sides: the parent company invests in an established setting. The respective region starts to flourish. Industry is maintained, jobs are saved or new ones created.

On the other hand, there are also certain drawbacks: the crucial corporate functions remain with the parent company. The branch set-up has no decision-making powers where investment is concerned and has no individual development of its own. However, the density of education and research in the Dresden chamber district is starting to have an impact on the strictly demarcated structure, with research activities also being increasingly delegated to the area in addition to pure production.

From bumpy track to six-lane motorway

Clear roads for free citizens: after reunification, the claim made by the main motoring organisation missed the mark completely in Saxony. The road network was in a disastrous state. Those travelling on the A 4 motorway from Chemnitz to Dresden had to reduce speed to 30 kilometres per hour before trying to cross the battered bridge over the river Elbe. By contrast, today motorists can travel safely and swiftly in the Free State, even though not every last bumpy track, obsolete road layout or outdated village thoroughfare has been dealt with. Billions have been invested to cope with the dramatic increase in traffic volume since reunification. The density of the road network with 760 metres of cross-country roads per square kilometre is above the federal average. In the Dresden chamber district, every effort has been made to enhance not only the quality of the traffic infrastructure but also its expanse, by a good 130 kilometres since 2000 alone.

Saxony's roads are part of an efficient international road network. Dresden is close to the crossroads between the European route E 40 from France to Kazakhstan and the E 55 from Sweden to Greece. This offers the Dresden chamber district ideal conditions for procurement and sales and for the transfer of

Die neue A 17 vor dem Dölzschener Tunnel

The new A 17 in front of the Dölzschener tunnel

flüssig. Am Horizont zeigt sich aber Licht: Für die B 178 wird eine neue Trasse gebaut. Sie führt von der A 4 nach Zittau und wird die deutschen Autobahnen mit den Straßennetzen der böhmischen Kreise Liberec und Ústí nad Labem sowie der polnischen Woiwodschaft Niederschlesien verbinden. Von 42 Kilometern sind 16 bereits befahrbar. Die Oberlausitzer sehnen die Fertigstellung herbei, können doch dann auch Touristen ihre schöne, grenzübergreifende Natur- und Kulturlandschaft schneller und bequemer erreichen.

Größte Schienennetzdichte

Sachsen auf Gleisen: Beim Fernverkehr kämpft der Freistaat um eine bessere Anbindung und Vertaktung mit den großen Wirtschafts- und Kulturzentren in Deutschland und Europa. Zu den Prioritäten gehört der Ausbau von Dresden nach Berlin. Zwar fahren Züge – darunter der ICE – in kurzen Abständen in

tourists in Europe. One figurehead is the German motorway A 4 as West-East axis between the Dutch and Polish frontier.

The traffic project German Unity No. 15 upgraded the section between Chemnitz and Dresden to six lanes. Four new lanes were added to the section from Dresden North Interchange, where the A 13 turns off for Berlin, to Weißenberg. This finally did away with one oddity: a 16 kilometre long section between Bautzen-Ost and Weißenberg, barred from public use, with 66 grain warehouses as GDR state reserves. A completely new section of the A 4 motorway was built between Weißenberg and Görlitz towards Wrocław. On this 24 kilometre long section, the A 4 passes through the Königshain hills in Germany's second longest two-tube road tunnel.

Breakfast in the Golden City

This was the slogan for building the new A 17 motorway to Prague. On completion of the final section of the Czech D 8 motorway in 2015, this new road will go straight to the "Golden City". A fast link to the neighbours in the east had become vital with the expansion of the EU. 646 million Euro were invested in the construction work between 1998 and 2006, with five tunnels, eight motorway junctions and ten major bridges along

die Bundeshauptstadt, streckenweise aber schleichen sie eher, als dass sie brausen. Die Tempo reduzierenden Baustellen sind jedoch zugleich Hoffnungsschimmer für kürzere Fahrzeiten. Direkten internationalen Anschluss hat der Kammerbezirk Dresden über die Strecke Dresden–Prag mit den Grenzbahnhöfen Bad Schandau und Děčín.

Im Land selbst verfügt Sachsen mit einem Eisenbahnnetz von 2600 Kilometern über die höchste Schienennetzdichte aller Bundesländer. Im Kammerbezirk Dresden koordinieren die Verkehrsverbünde Oberelbe (VVO) und Oberlausitz-Niederschlesien (ZVON) die Verkehrsunternehmen und bieten flächendeckend Bahn- und Busleistungen an. Beliebte Raritäten sind drei Schmalspurbahnen aus dem 19. Jahrhundert: Die Weißeritztalbahn verbindet das Elbtal mit dem Osterzgebirge, die Zittauer Schmalspurbahn dampft ins Zittauer Gebirge, der „Lößnitzdackel" fährt von Radebeul nach Radeburg.

Last und Lust der Elbeschifffahrt

„Auf der Elbe bin ich gefahren / in dem wunderschönen Monat Mai..." Dieses Schifferlied spricht für die Poesie, die den Strom umgibt. Verwaltungsrechtlich gesagt ist die Elbe eine Bundeswasserstraße. Der umweltfreundliche Verkehrsweg verbindet den Kammerbezirk Dresden mittels Häfen in Dresden und Riesa mit dem internationalen Seehandel. Die Sächsische Binnenhäfen Oberelbe GmbH betreibt hochmoderne Umschlagplätze für Massen-, Stück- und Schwergüter sowie Container. Das Unternehmen mit Tochterfirmen in Tschechien und Sachsen-Anhalt kombiniert Wasser, Bahn und Straße für ihre Kunden. In ihren insgesamt sechs Häfen sind rund 70 Firmen mit 510 Mitarbeitern tätig. 2011 betrug das Umschlagvolumen 2,7 Millionen Tonnen.

Der 42 Hektar große Alberthafen in Dresden stammt von 1891, benannt nach Sachsenkönig Albert. Der Nordkai ist 730 Meter lang, der Südkai 1000 Meter. Seine Kräne tragen bis zu 90 Tonnen Last. Er gehört zum gut vernetzten Güterverkehrszentrum Dresden-Friedrichstadt. Stromabwärts bei Elbe-Kilometer 107,39 liegt der Riesaer Hafen, mit 50 Hektar Sachsens größter Binnenhafen. Der Bereich „Alter Hafen" – seit 120 Jahren in Betrieb – erhält derzeit eine neue, 540 Meter lange Kaimauer. Investitionsvolumen: 4,8 Mio. Euro. Zweistellige Zuwachsraten beim Güterumschlag hatten eine Kapazitätserweiterung herausgefordert.

Als Blickfang auf der Elbe laufen allerdings die neun historischen Raddampfer den Lastkähnen den Rang ab. Sie sind bis zu 133 Jahre alt. Das Dresdner Terrassenufer ist der Liegeplatz der ältesten und größten Raddampferflotte der Welt, zu der auch die Salonschiffe „August der Starke" und „Gräfin Cosel" gehören. Die Sächsische Dampfschifffahrt macht jährlich 700 000 Touristen mit den Schönheiten zwischen Bad Schandau und Seußlitz bekannt.

Fortsetzung Seite 40

---

the 45 kilometre long section of road. The A 17 relieves the pressure of transit traffic on Dresden, the upper Elbe valley and the eastern Erzgebirge.

Traffic through the southern Oberlausitz doesn't roll quite as smoothly, but there is light on the horizon, with a new route being built for the federal road B 178. It takes traffic from the A 4 motorway to Zittau and will link the German motorways with the road networks in the Bohemian districts of Liberec and Ústí nad Labem together with the Polish voivodeship (province) of Lower Silesia. Traffic is already running on 16 of the 42 kilometres. The population of Oberlausitz is longing for completion, which will give tourists faster, more convenient access to their lovely, cross-border natural and cultivated landscape.

Greatest rail network density

Saxony on the rails: where long-distance rail traffic is concerned, the Free State of Saxony is fighting for better links and more frequent services to the major business and cultural centres of Germany and Europe. One of the key priorities is to upgrade the line from Dresden to Berlin. Although there is a regular service of trains to the German capital at short intervals, also including the high-speed ICE trains, in parts they have to crawl rather than speed ahead. However, the construction sites that are causing the speed restrictions are at the same time a ray of hope for shorter journey times. The railway line between Dresden and Prague with the frontier stations of Bad Schandau and Děčín gives the Dresden chamber district a direct international connection.

Saxony itself has the greatest rail network density of all federal states with 2,600 kilometres of track. Transport undertakings in the Dresden chamber district are coordinated by the VVO and ZVON transport associations, offering widespread train and bus services. Three narrow gauge railways from the 19th century are popular rarities: the Weißeritztalbahn connects the Elbe valley with the eastern Erzgebirge mountains, the Zittauer narrow gauge railway steams into the Zittauer mountains and the "Lößnitzdackel" runs from Radebeul to Radeburg.

Freight and pleasure on the river Elbe

The river Elbe in Saxony is famed for its beauty and its commerce. In administrative terms, the river Elbe is a federal waterway. This environmentally friendly means of transport connects the Dresden chamber district with ports in Dresden and Riesa to international ocean-going trade. The Sächsische Binnenhäfen Oberelbe GmbH is the firm responsible for the inland ports where it operates state-of-the-art transhipment facilities for bulk goods, general cargo, heavy goods and containers. The company with subsidiaries in the Czech Republic and Saxony-Anhalt offers its customers intermodal services combining water, rail and road transport. Around 70 companies with 510

Continued on page 40

Information

Gründungsjahr: 1821
Mitarbeiter: rund 2000
Ranking:
· größte ostdeutsche Sparkasse
· unter den Top Ten der bundesdeutschen Sparkassen
Geschäftsgebiet: Landeshauptstadt Dresden, Landkreis Sächsische Schweiz-Osterzgebirge, Region Kamenz und Hoyerswerda
Vorstandsvorsitzender: Joachim Hoof
Bilanzsumme 2011: 11,6 Mrd. Euro
Filialen: 101

Year founded: 1821
Employees: around 2,000
Ranking:
· largest savings bank in Eastern Germany
· one of the top ten savings banks in Germany
Business area: State Capital Dresden, Rural District Sächsische Schweiz-Osterzgebirge, Kamenz and Hoyerswerda Region
Chairman of the Board: Joachim Hoof
Balance sheet total 2011: 11.6 billion Euro
Branches: 101

Ostsächsische Sparkasse Dresden

Ostsächsische Sparkasse Dresden

Seit über 190 Jahren ist sie in Sachsen zu Hause: die Ostsächsische Sparkasse Dresden. Mit einer Bilanzsumme von mehr als 11 Mrd. Euro ist sie die größte Sparkasse Ostdeutschlands und gehört damit zu den Top Ten der bundesdeutschen Sparkassen. Als wirtschaftlich stabiles und ertragsstarkes Haus bietet die Sparkasse ihren Privat- und Firmenkunden mit 101 Filialen ein dichtes Standortnetz und eine breite Palette an Finanzprodukten.

Wesentlicher Bestandteil der Geschäftspolitik ist dabei stets die persönliche Kundenbetreuung vor Ort – auf der Basis einer vertrauensvollen Zusammenarbeit in allen Finanzangelegenheiten: Mit mehr als 600 000 Kunden ist die Ostsächsische Sparkasse Dresden Marktführer in ihrem Geschäftsgebiet und etablierter Partner des regionalen Mittelstandes.

Die Ostsächsische Sparkasse ist Wirtschaftsmotor in der Region, um Investitionen der mittelständischen Wirtschaft zu finanzieren. Das zeigt ein Blick auf das Kreditgeschäft. So sagte die Sparkasse allein 2011 an mittelständische Firmen, Privatkunden und öffentliche Haushalte neue Kredite in Höhe von 959 Mio. Euro zu. Damit hat die Sparkasse nicht nur bewiesen, dass sie der Kreditgeber für die Firmen vor Ort ist, sie hat zudem auch ein positives Signal gesetzt: Der regionale Mittelstand kann sich auf die Ostsächsische Sparkasse Dresden verlassen.

Verantwortung übernimmt der Finanzdienstleister auch für seine fast 2000 Mitarbeiter. Besonderen Wert legt das Institut dabei auf eine qualifizierte und fundierte Ausbildung. Aktuell lernen mehr als 100 Jugendliche ihren künftigen Beruf bei der Sparkasse. Und schließlich dokumentiert die Sparkasse ihre Verbundenheit mit Land und Menschen durch die Förderung von Kunst, Kultur, Sport sowie Jugend und Soziales. Mehr als 3 Mio. Euro werden jährlich in Form von Spenden und Sponsoring sowie über Ausschüttungen der fünf sparkasseneigenen Stiftungen eingesetzt.

Ostsächsische Sparkasse Dresden

Ostsächsische Sparkasse Dresden has been at home in Saxony for more than 190 years. With a balance sheet total exceeding 11 billion Euro, this is the largest savings bank in Eastern Germany and also one of the top ten savings banks in Germany. As a financially stable, profitable bank, Ostsächsische Sparkasse Dresden offers its private and corporate customers a close-knit network of sites with 101 branches, together with a broad range of financial products.

The key element of the bank's business policy always focuses on personal, local customer service and support, based on trusting cooperation in all financial matters. With more than 600,000 customers, Ostsächsische Sparkasse Dresden leads this particular part of the market and is the established partner for the local SME sector.

Ostsächsische Sparkasse is the motor driving the region's economy, funding investment in and by the SME sector. This is illustrated by taking a look at the credit business. In 2011 alone, Ostsächsische Sparkasse granted new loans amounting to 959 million Euro to SME companies, private customers and the public sector, thus demonstrating its role as the key lender for local businesses. Moreover, these figures also set a positive signal, showing that the regional SME sector can rely on Ostsächsische Sparkasse Dresden.

The financial services provider also takes responsibility for its workforce of nearly 2,000 employees, devoting particular attention to sound, qualified training. At the moment, more than 100 youngsters are currently receiving vocational training with Ostsächsische Sparkasse Dresden. Furthermore, Ostsächsische Sparkasse Dresden demonstrates its close bonds with the region and the people living there by sponsoring art, culture and sport together with activities for the young generation, as well as shouldering its share of social tasks. More than 3 million Euro are dedicated to donations and sponsoring commitments every year, together with funds distributed by the bank's own foundations.

Neunmal mehr Fluggäste

Dynamische Wirtschafts- und Wissenschaftsregionen, beliebte Städteziele, Kulturmetropole Dresden... Wer mit diesen Pfunden wuchern will, der braucht internationale Luftstraßen. Sachsen verfügt – neben dem Airport Leipzig/Halle – über einen wettbewerbsfähigen Flughafen in der Landeshauptstadt. Am Standort im nördlichen Stadtteil Klotzsche erhob sich 1935 das erste Verkehrsflugzeug. 1957 wurde der DDR-Inlandsflugverkehr aufgenommen, 1967 die erste internationale Linie eröffnet. Das Areal hat sich inzwischen gründlich verändert. Das 2001 eröffnete Terminal gilt als eines der schönsten in Deutschland. Mit der S-Bahn kann man es direkt von der City aus erreichen. Seit 2005 betreibt die Flugsicherung einen neuen Tower. 2007 startete erstmals ein Jumbojet von der sanierten Piste, die um 350 Meter auf 2850 Meter erweitert worden war.

Der Airport – mit Millioneninvestitionen ins 21. Jahrhundert geholt und Arbeitsplatz für 3000 Menschen – trägt zu Recht den Namen „Dresden International". Zum einen haben sich im Umfeld weltweit agierende Firmen angesiedelt. Zum anderen ist er ein Tor zur Welt. Täglich starten Geschäftsreisende und Touristen in sechs deutsche und fünf europäische Metropolen. Wöchentlich werden rund 150-mal über 40 Ziele in Ost- und Südeuropa, am Mittelmeer, in Nordafrika und auf den Kanaren angesteuert. Seit 1990 hat sich die Zahl der Fluggäste auf 1,9 Millionen jährlich verneunfacht.

Flächen für Wachstum

Von der modernen Infrastruktur profitieren über 500 sächsische Gewerbegebiete, die seit 1990 auf der „grünen Wiese" oder auf altindustriellen Flächen entstanden sind. Davon befinden sich rund 200 im Kammerbezirk Dresden. Beste Vorausset-

employees work in the firm's total of six ports, with a transhipment volume of 2.7 million tons in 2011.

The 42 hectare Alberthafen port in Dresden dates from 1891 and is named after King Albert of Saxony. The north quay is 730 metres long, the south quay 1,000 metres. The cranes can lift loads of up to 90 tons. The port belongs to Dresden-Friedrichstadt cargo transport centre with its excellent infrastructure. Riesa port lies down river at Elbe kilometre 107.39. This is Saxony's largest inland port with 50 hectares. The "Alter Hafen" (old port) section has been in operation for 120 years and is currently being fitted with a new quay wall 540 metres in length. Investment volume: 4.8 million Euro. This had become necessary in order to expand the port's capacity so that it could keep pace with the double-figure growth rates in the transhipment of goods.

But when it comes to eye-catchers on the river, the nine historical paddle steamers leave the cargo barges far behind. They are up to 133 years old. Dresden is home to the world's oldest and largest fleet of paddle steamers, including the salon ships "August der Starke" and "Gräfin Cosel". Saxony's river boats introduce 700,000 tourists every year to the beautiful countryside between Bad Schandau and Seußlitz.

Nine times more air passengers

Dynamic business and science regions, popular city destinations, Dresden as cultural metropolis – to make the most of all these assets, international air transport has to be facilitated. Together with the Airport Leipzig/Halle, Saxony also has a competitive airport in the state capital. It was in 1935 that the first passenger airplane took off from the airport in the northern suburb of Klotzsche. In 1957, the GDR started operating domestic flights with the first international service starting in 1967.

Der Flughafen Dresden International ist für die Region ein wichtiger Standort- und Wirtschaftsfaktor.

The Dresden International Airport is an important location and economic driving force in the region.

zungen also für weitere auswärtige Investoren, hiesige Existenzgründer und expandierende Firmen. Der Technopark Nord in der Landeshauptstadt liegt nahe dem Flughafen und der A 4. Er hat sich zum Mikroelektronik-Standort entwickelt. Die verbindende Straße heißt nach dem berühmten Dresdner Technikpionier Manfred-von-Ardenne-Ring.

Am südlichen Stadtrand sind rund 50 Unternehmen im Gewerbegebiet Coschütz/Gittersee heimisch geworden. Dieses Gelände hatte die DDR vom Uranbergbau kontaminiert zurückgelassen. Die Stadt Dresden befreite es von den Altlasten. Richtung Meißen hat sich das Gewerbegebiet Klipphausen mit rund 90 Betrieben etabliert. Elbabwärts offeriert der Zeithainer Industriepark – mit Gleisanschluss zum Hafen Riesa – 124 Hektar

Meanwhile, the whole premises have been radically changed. The terminal opened in 2001 is said to be one of the most attractive in Germany and offers a direct rapid transit train link into the city. The air traffic control has been operating from a new tower since 2005, while 2007 saw the first jumbo jet taking off from the upgraded runway which had been lengthened by 350 metres to 2,850 metres.

Offering jobs for 3,000 people and upgraded to the 21st century at the costs of millions, the airport is rightly called "Dresden International". On the one hand, global players have settled in the surroundings. On the other hand, the airport is the city's gateway to the world. Every day, business travellers and tourists take off to fly to six German and five European metro-

Der Containerhafen Riesa bietet für Logistikunternehmen optimale Standortbedingungen.

The container port of Riesa provides logistic companies with an optimal business location.

Eines von zahlreichen Gewerbegebieten in Ostsachsen, auf dem sich stetig neue Unternehmen ansiedeln, ist in Heidenau, Landkreis Sächsische Schweiz-Osterzgebirge.

One of numerous industrial areas in East Saxony in which new companies are continually setting up business is in Heidenau, the administrative district of Saxon Switzerland's Osterzgebirge region.

Ansiedlungsfläche. In Richtung Bautzen liegt direkt an der A 4 das Gewerbegebiet Salzenforst, bei Görlitz der Industriestandort Kodersdorf. Dort steht eines der weltweit modernsten Säge- und Hobelwerke. Die Klausner Holz Sachsen hatte diesen Ort gewählt, um den ungenutzten Nadelholzvorräten im östlichen Sachsen und bei den Nachbarn Polen und Tschechien nahe zu sein.

Gute Leute und findige Köpfe

„It's all about the people." Diesen Satz hörte Richard Hornik vom „Time Magazin" 1998 von AMD-Managern. Der amerikanische Journalist wollte damals wissen, warum sich der Konzern ausgerechnet in Dresden niedergelassen hatte. Er erfuhr: Es geht um die Menschen. Wer in Zukunftstechnologien investiert, der braucht hoch qualifiziertes und motiviertes Fachpersonal. Das war wohl ohnehin ein entscheidender Grund für die Ansiedlungen auswärtiger Investoren in Sachsen.

politan destinations. Every week, around 150 flights set off for more than 40 destinations in East and South East Europe, on the Mediterranean, in North Africa and on the Canary Islands. Since 1990, the number of air passengers has increased nine fold to reach 1.9 million each year.

Space for growth

The modern infrastructure benefits more than 500 commercial estates in Saxony which have grown up on both green field and brown field sites since 1990. These include around 200 in the Dresden chamber district, offering ideal prerequisites for more foreign investors, local start-ups and expanding firms. Technopark Nord in the state capital is close to the airport and the A 4 motorway. It has become a microelectronics site. The estate road has been named Manfred-von-Ardenne-Ring after the city's famous technology pioneer.

On the southern outskirts, around 50 companies have found a home in Coschütz/Gittersee commercial estate. This land had been left in contaminated state by the GDR on account of uranium mining. The City of Dresden cleared up all the inherited pollution. The road to Meißen passes Klipphausen commercial estate with around 90 companies. Down river, Zeithain industrial park offers 124 hectares of space for companies to

Nirgendwo sonst in Deutschland ist die Quote der beruflichen Ausbildung so hoch wie in Sachsen.

Nowhere else in Germany is the share of persons with a vocational education as high as in Saxony.

Findige Fachleute hatten in DDR-Betrieben die Räder in Schwung gehalten. Die verfehlte Wirtschaftspolitik brachte eine eigene Spezies hervor: die Rationalisierungsmittelbauer. Sie tüftelten und werkelten bravourös, wenn Westimporte nicht möglich waren oder „abgelöst" werden mussten. Tugenden wie Fleiß, Gründlichkeit und Ordnungssinn verbanden sich nicht allein bei ihnen mit Flexibilität, Improvisationsvermögen, Pragmatismus und Einsatzbereitschaft. „Chaosqualifikationen" hat Soziologe Wolfgang Engler diese ostdeutsche Besonderheit genannt. Das Gespür der „fischelanten" Sachsen für die Wege zum Erfolg unter schwierigen Bedingungen – das wurde beim Neubeginn zum Wettbewerbsvorteil.

Das beste Bildungssystem

90 Prozent der sächsischen Erwerbstätigen verfügen über einen beruflichen Bildungsabschluss. Das ist ein innerdeutscher Spitzenwert. Jeder fünfte Absolvent der sächsischen Hoch- und Fachschulen beendet das Studium mit einem ingenieurwissenschaftlichen Abschluss. Diese Kaderschmieden haben seit 2000 sogar 27 000 Jungakademiker mehr hervorgebracht als zu erwarten waren. Die Wachstumskräfte werden schon früh geweckt. Der INSM-Bildungsmonitor 2011 stellte fest: Sachsen hat das beste und leistungsfähigste Bildungssystem aller Bundesländer. Bewertet wurden 13 Handlungsfelder und mehr als 100 Indikatoren.

Friede, Freude, Eierkuchen? Nein, seit der Wende wandern junge, gut qualifizierte Fachleute aus Sachsen ab. Bessere Chancen, mehr Geld. Vor allem wenig industrialisierte Regionen in der Oberlausitz oder im dünn besiedelten Norden des Kammerbezirkes Dresden sind betroffen. Sachsen wird immer älter. Die Einwohnerzahl soll bis 2020 von 4,8 Millionen im Jahr 1990 auf 3,9 Millionen sinken. Der Durchschnittssachse ist dann 49 Jahre alt, nicht 39 wie im Einheitsjahr.

Sachsens Ministerpräsident Stanislaw Tillich sagte dazu 2011 in der Dresdner Kammerzeitschrift „ihk.wirtschaft": „Zur Gefahr für die wirtschaftliche Entwicklung und den gesellschaftlichen Zusammenhalt wird der demografische Wandel erst dann, wenn wir nichts tun." Die Betriebe im Kammerbezirk Dresden verantworten 17 500 Ausbildungsplätze. Sie sind gefordert, dem Nachwuchs vor Ort eine Chance zu geben.

settle, with services including a railway siding to Riesa port. In turn, the A 4 motorway to Bautzen passes straight through Salzenforst commercial estate, while Kodersdorf industrial site is to be found near Görlitz. This is home to the world's most advanced sawmills and planing plants. Klausner Holz Sachsen chose this site for its close proximity to the unexploited conifer resources in eastern Saxony and in the neighbouring countries of Poland and the Czech Republic.

Good people and clever minds

"It's all about the people." Time Magazine journalist Richard Hornik heard these words in 1998 from AMD managers. He was trying to find out what had made the company settle in Dresden. He found out that it's all about the people. Anyone investing in future technology needs a highly qualified, motivated workforce. This would appear to have been one of the crucial reasons why foreign investors decided to settle in Saxony.

Resourceful experts had kept the wheels in motion in GDR companies. The failed economic policy had generated its very own species: rationed resources engineers. When imports from the west were not possible or had to be "done away with", they were simply brilliant at doing their very best in puzzling and tinkering with the resources available to them. They weren't the only ones to reveal unique combinations of virtues such as industriousness, thoroughness and a sense of order with flexibility, the ability to improvise, a pragmatic approach and dedicated commitment. "Chaos qualifications" is how sociologist Wolfgang Engler describes these East German characteristics.

Das Friedrich-Schiller-Gymnasium in Pirna ist das einzige deutsch-tschechische Gymnasium Deutschlands.

Friedrich Schiller grammar school in Pirna is Germany's first German/Czech grammar school.

Europas Mitte und weite Welt

Am Dreiländerpunkt bei Zittau in der Oberlausitz wehen vier Fahnen: die deutsche, tschechische und polnische Staatsflagge und die blaue Europaflagge. Mit seinen östlichen Nachbarn hat Sachsen eine 570 Kilometer lange Grenze, die etwa zur Hälfte den Kammerbezirk Dresden tangiert. Sie ist keine Trennlinie mehr zwischen „sozialistischen Bruderstaaten", sondern durchlässig für Zusammenarbeit und Tourismus. Dort beginnen die Wachstumsmärkte im Osten, zu denen sich der Kammerbezirk Dresden als Wegbereiter versteht. So hat die IHK Dresden in Görlitz und Zittau Kontaktzentren für die Sächsisch-Polnische und Sächsisch-Tschechische Wirtschaftskooperation eingerichtet.

Die Neisse University vernetzt die TU Liberec, die TU Wrocław und die Hochschule Zittau-Görlitz mit gemeinsamen Studiengängen. Das Friedrich-Schiller-Gymnasium in Pirna ist das einzige deutsch-tschechische Gymnasium Deutschlands. Das Augustum-Annen-Gymnasium in Görlitz bietet – ebenfalls einmalig – einen deutsch-polnischen Bildungsgang an. „Grenzenlos bilden – gemeinsam lernen" heißt das Motto der „Schkola". An fünf Oberlausitzer Standorten stellt diese Schule in freier Trägerschaft Nachbarsprache und interkulturelle Kompetenz in den Mittelpunkt.

The knack of the "fischelant" (vigilant) Saxons to find their way to success even under the most adverse conditions became a competition advantage when the economy restarted.

The best education system

90 percent of the gainfully employed in Saxony have vocational or professional qualifications, putting the state at the head of the field in Germany. One in five graduates from Saxony's universities comes away with an engineering degree. Since 2000, these talent pools have even produced 27,000 more young academics than expected. The growth forces are triggered early on. In 2011, the INSM education monitor ascertained that Saxony has the best, most efficient education system of all German states, based on 13 areas of action and more than 100 indicators.

So it's all peace and joy then? No, not really: since reunification, lots of young, well qualified skilled workers have left Saxony for better chances and more money elsewhere. The less industrialised regions of Oberlausitz and the sparsely populated north of Dresden chamber district are particularly affected. Saxony's population is getting older: by 2020, it will shrink to 3.9 compared to 4.8 million in 1990. By then, the average Saxon will be 49 years old, instead of 39 in the year of reunification.

Stanislaw Tillich, Minister-President of Saxony, commented on this in a 2011 interview with the Dresden chamber magazine "ihk.wirtschaft": "Demographic change will only endanger economic development and social cohesion if we do nothing about it." The companies in the Dresden chamber district are responsible for 17,500 traineeships. It's up to them to give local youngsters a chance.

The heart of Europe and the big wide world

There are four flags flying at the point where three countries meet near Zittau in the Oberlausitz: the German, Czech and Polish national flags, and the blue European flag. Saxony shares a 570 kilometre frontier with its eastern neighbours, with about half affecting the Dresden chamber district. It is no longer the border between "socialist brother states" but is open for cooperation and tourism. This is where the growth markets in the east begin, where the Dresden chamber district sees itself in the role of pioneer, setting up contact centres in Görlitz and Zittau for business cooperation between Saxony and Poland and between Saxony and the Czech Republic.

Neisse University networks with TU Liberec, TU Wrocław and Zittau-Görlitz University of Applied Sciences to offer joint courses. Friedrich Schiller grammar school in Pirna is Germany's first German/Czech grammar school. Augustum-Annen grammar school in Görlitz offers a unique German-Polish education. "Learning together in education without frontiers" is the

Sachsen hat das beste und leistungsfähigste Bildungssystem aller Bundesländer.

Saxony has the best and best-performing educational system of all of the federal states.

Die zentrale Lage begünstigt die Internationalität Sachsens. Seine Unternehmen setzen auch aus eigener Kraft globale Zeichen: Sie beeindrucken mit Spitzenleistungen und handeln mit aller Welt. Die Exportsumme stieg von 2000 bis 2011 von 10 auf 29 Mrd. Euro. Sachsens wichtigste Partner sind neben den EU-Staaten China und die USA. An Bedeutung gewinnen Indien und die Golfregion. Die IHK Dresden hilft ihren Mitgliedern, den Weg ins Ausland zu bahnen. Jährlich stellt sie rund 6000 Außenhandelsdokumente aus. Individuelle Beratungen, Unternehmerdelegationen, IHK-Exporttage, Messebeteiligungen und Kooperationsbörsen gehören zum weiteren Instrumentarium.

Land des geglückten Neuanfangs

Das moderne Sachsen, 22 Jahre alt, verglichen mit den drei DDR-Bezirken Dresden, Leipzig und Karl-Marx-Stadt – dazwischen liegen Welten. Der Aufbauwille der Ostdeutschen und die Solidarität der Westdeutschen scheinen Wunder vollbracht zu haben, versteht man Wunder als einen erstaunlichen, beeindruckenden, aufsehenerregenden Wandel in historisch kurzer Zeit. Der Sachse Gotthold Ephraim Lessing sagt: „Der Wunder höchstes ist, dass uns die wahren, echten Wunder so alltäglich werden können, werden sollen." Im normalen Leben liegen also die Wunder.

Diesem Leben spürt seit 2009 die Wochenzeitung „Die Zeit" auf den Seiten „Zeit für Sachsen" nach, inzwischen zu „Zeit im Osten" erweitert. Sie waren als Hommage an das Geburtsland der Friedlichen Revolution und Spiegel aktueller Veränderungen entstanden. „Sachsen, das Land der Revolution, das Land des geglückten Neuanfangs." So hieß es kurz und bündig in einem Beitrag am 15. Dezember 2011.

Solide Finanzen des Freistaates, intensive Ansiedlungspolitik, attraktive Förderprogramme, intakte Infrastruktur, historischer und kultureller Background, sympathische Einwohner, gute Fachleute, engagierte Global Player, kreative Mittelständler, effektive Netzwerke... Das alles sind Vorzüge „typisch Sachsen". Wie in einem Brennglas zeigen sie sich im Kammerbezirk Dresden.

motto of the "Schkola". This independent school works at five sites in Oberlausitz, with a focus on the neighbouring language and intercultural competence.

Saxony's central location fosters its international approach. Its companies are setting global signs under their own steam, with impressive first-rate achievements and trading with the whole world. Total annual exports increased between 2000 and 2011 from 10 billion to 29 billion Euro. In addition to the EU countries, Saxony's main partners are China and the USA, while India and the Gulf region are becoming increasingly important. Dresden CCI helps its members to do business abroad, issuing around 6,000 foreign trade documents every year, as well as offering individual advice and organising business delegations, CCI export days, trade fair participation and cooperation exchanges.

Successful restart

Compare modern Saxony, just 22 years old, with the three former GDR districts of Dresden, Leipzig and Karl-Marx-Stadt. They're simply worlds apart. The determination of the East Germans to forge ahead with recovery and the solidarity of the West Germans appear to have performed miracles, if a miracle is the right word for an amazing, impressive, sensational transformation process in a historically short period of time. Saxony's famous philosopher Gotthold Ephraim Lessing said: "The most amazing thing about miracles is that the real, genuine miracles can and should become commonplace." And so the real miracles are to be found in normal life.

Since 2009, the weekly newspaper "Die Zeit" has been on the trail of just that – normal life, in its "Time for Saxony" pages, meanwhile extended to "Time in the East". They pay homage to the birthplace of the peaceful revolution and reflect current changes. "Saxony, home to revolution and to a successful restart" was the brief conclusion reached in an article on 15 December 2011.

Sound financial policy in the Free State, intensive strategies to encourage businesses to settle here, attractive funding programmes, intact infrastructure, historical and cultural background, congenial citizens, good skilled workers, committed global players, a creative SME sector, efficient networks – all these and more are "typical Saxon" attributes, and can be found, as under a magnifying glass, throughout the Dresden chamber district.

Sechs Richtige im globalen Wettbewerb
Schwergewichte und Innovationstreiber

Sechs Richtige – das steht im Volksmund für den großen Gewinn. Im Lotto 6 aus 49 sind die Chancen gering. Sie stehen bei 1 zu 13 983 816. Sechs Richtige ganz anderer Art brachten dem Franzosen Louis Braille Erfinderglück. Er kombinierte sechs erhabene Punkte miteinander und schuf 1825 die Tastschrift für blinde Menschen. Sechs Richtige hat auch der Kammerbezirk Dresden. Und das in einem weiteren Sinn: Es sind die Branchen, die – umsatzstark, innovativ und wettbewerbsfähig – sein Wirtschaftsprofil charakterisieren.

Bei dieser Eingrenzung besteht die Qual der Wahl. Den Standort zeichnet Vielfalt aus, verbunden mit zahlreichen Zwischenstufen und Vermischungen, die in alle Bereiche hineinreichen. Sein Profil charakterisieren innovative Produkte und Technologien, weniger die Großserien. Das hilft, wirtschaftliche Schwankungen auszugleichen und ist ein Plus in Krisenzeiten. Landläufig assoziiert man den Kammerbezirk Dresden vor allem mit der Chipproduktion. Wer hätte gedacht, dass es in Wahrheit die Nahrungs- und Genussmittel sind, die hier das Zepter führen?

Was also sind die „Sechs Richtigen"? Statistiken, Markttrends und Zukunftsaussichten sprechen für diese Bereiche: Ernährungswirtschaft, Maschinen- und Anlagenbau, Mikroelektronik und Informationstechnologie, Metallerzeugung und -verarbeitung, Energie- und Umwelttechnologie sowie Bio- und Nanotechnologie.

Six winners in global competition
Heavyweights and innovation drivers

Six winning numbers are what it takes to win the lottery. The chances are pretty slight: only 1 to 13,983,816. Six winners of a completely different kind brought French inventor Louis Braille great success: in 1825 he combined six raised points to create the Braille alphabet for the blind. In yet another sense, the Dresden chamber district can also be said to have six winners, referring to the branches that characterise its economic profile: top-selling, innovative and competitive.

We're spoilt for choice when it comes to further differentiation. The location stands out on account of its diversity, paired with numerous intermediate stages and commingling effects extending into all areas. The profile is characterised by innovative products and technologies, rather than mass production. This helps to compensate for economic fluctuations and is a real benefit in times of crisis. The Dresden chamber district is generally associated with microchip production. Who would have thought that in fact it is the food and beverage industry that takes the lead?

Der Sachse liebt seinen Gerstensaft: Allein im Kammerbezirk Dresden gibt es 20 Bierbrauereien.

Saxons love drinking beer: Merely in the local region of Dresden, there are 20 beer breweries.

Genau richtig: Ernährungswirtschaft

Liebe geht durch den Magen, sagt das Sprichwort. Gute Chancen auf hohe Sympathiewerte für den Kammerbezirk Dresden: Über 300 IHK-Unternehmen (ab 50 Mitarbeiter) mit insgesamt mehr als 5000 Beschäftigten stellen Nahrungs- und Genussmittel sowie Getränke her. Ihr Jahresumsatz betrug 2011 rund 3,8 Mrd. Euro. Mit 18 Prozent am gesamten Industrieumsatz ist die Lebensmittelbranche mit Abstand die umsatzstärkste.

Der tägliche Verbrauch schafft immer wieder neuen Bedarf. Die Hersteller entsprechen ihm mit regionalen Erzeugnissen, verbunden mit bekannten Marken, speziellen Rezepten und sächsischer Esskultur. Vorbei ist die Zeit nach der Wende, als die Ostdeutschen fast ausschließlich nach Westprodukten griffen. Vorbei aber auch die Zeit der Ostalgie. Das Leipziger Marktforschungsinstitut belegte 2010: Die Ostherkunft von Produkten verliert vor allem für jüngere Konsumenten an Bedeutung. Sächsische Erzeugnisse haben gute Chancen, wenn sich nachvollziehbarer regionaler Charme, hohe Qualität, ein Vertrauensbonus und zeitgemäßes Marketing miteinander verbinden.

Doktoren des Genusses

Über drei Generationen führte der Weg der Unternehmerfamilie Doerr in Dresden. Dr. Herbert Doerr hatte vor fast 80 Jahren den heutigen Feinkostbetrieb gegründet, Sohn Dr. Udo Doerr dessen Zwangsverstaatlichung 1972 miterlebt und 1990 den Neustart gewagt. Inzwischen setzt der Enkel des Gründers, Christian Doerr, die Tradition mit 70 Mitarbeitern fort. Fast alle Dresdner kennen die Marke „Dr. Doerr". 2011 eröffnete der Betrieb ein neues Fertigwarenkühllager, eine 1,2-Mio.-Investition. Ministerpräsident Stanislaw Tillich sagte zur Einweihung: „Erfolgreiche Mittelständler wie die Dr. Doerr Feinkost GmbH bilden das Rückgrat der sächsischen Wirtschaft. Durch seinen hohen Anspruch, seine Marktkenntnis und seine Investitionsbereitschaft ist es dem Unternehmen gelungen, sich als regionaler Marktführer zu etablieren und den Kundenbedürfnissen optimal gerecht zu werden."

Eine weitere Marke verbindet sich mit dem Doktortitel: Dr. Quendt. Die Geschichte der Dresdner Spezialitätenbäckerei reicht bis 1876 zurück. Das „Russisch Brot" und andere Köstlichkeiten wurden dort erfunden. 1991 nahm Lebensmitteltechnologe Dr. Hartmut Quendt unter seinem Namen die Tradition auf. Inzwischen führt sie Sohn Matthias weiter. Seit 2000 produzieren über 100 Mitarbeiter in einem neuen Werk in Dresden-Coschütz, das 2008 um ein Besucherzentrum erweitert wurde. Klassiker und Neuheiten gehören gleichermaßen zum Sortiment, darunter „Echter Dresdner Christstollen" und „Original Dinkelchen".

Eine andere Gegend, eine weitere Erfolgsgeschichte: Im Gläsernen Nudelcenter in Riesa verfolgen täglich bis zu 250 Gäste den Werdegang von Hörnchen, Penne, Spaghetti… Die

So what are the six winners? According to statistics, market trends and future prognoses, we're talking about the following: the food industry, machine and plant construction, microelectronics and information technology, metal production and processing, energy and environment technology, and bio- and nanotechnology.

Big winner: Food industry

The way to the heart is through the stomach, or so the saying goes. So the Dresden chamber district stands a good chance of being popular: more than 300 CCI companies (from 50 employees) with a total workforce of more than 5,000 manufacture food and beverage products. In 2011, their annual turnover came to around 3.8 billion Euro. In terms of sales and turnover, the food branch is the strongest, accounting for 18 percent of total industrial turnover.

Daily consumption is constantly creating new demand. This is met by manufacturers with regional products, paired with well-known brands, special recipes and Saxon food culture. After reunification, the East Germans tended to choose west products. That's now over. But the nostalgic phase is also a thing of the past. In 2010, the Leipzig Market Research Institute found out that the eastern origin of products is increasingly losing significance, particularly for younger consumers. Saxon products have a good chance if they combine appropriate regional charm, high quality, an added confidence bonus and contemporary marketing.

Doctors of pleasure

Three generations of the Doerr family have been doing business in Dresden. Dr. Herbert Doerr founded today's delicatessen business here nearly 80 years ago; his son Dr. Udo Doerr witnessed forced nationalisation in 1972 and ventured to make a new start in 1990. Meanwhile, Christian Doerr, grandson of the company founder, continues the tradition with 70 employees. Almost everyone in Dresden knows the Dr. Doerr brand. In 2011, the company opened a new refrigerated warehouse for finished goods, having invested 1.2 million Euro in the project. At the inauguration, Minister President Stanislaw Tillich said: "Successful SME firms such as Dr. Doerr Feinkost GmbH form the backbone of Saxony's economy. High standards, market know-how and the willingness to invest have helped the company to become established as the regional market leader, always meeting customer demands in the best way possible."

Another brand associated with doctors is Dr. Quendt. The history of this Dresden speciality bakery goes back to 1876, and is where they invented "Russian Bread" biscuits and other tasty delights. In 1991, food technologist Dr. Hartmut Quendt took up the tradition under his name. Meanwhile his son Matthias holds the reins. Since 2000, more than 100 employees have been

Teigwaren GmbH verknüpft seit 2003 ihre Produktion von rund 100 Nudelsorten mit dem touristischen Erlebnis. Sie macht die gentechnikfreie Herstellung transparent und erinnert im hauseigenen 1. Deutschen Nudelmuseum an die Firmengeschichte. Diese begann 1914 in einem roten Backsteinbau, der bis in die Gegenwart zum Areal gehört. Mit 240 000 Tonnen Teigwaren und einem Anteil von knapp einem Drittel sind die Riesaer heute ostdeutsche Marktführer. Die 150 Beschäftigten freuen sich, dass die Deutschen immer mehr Nudeln essen und einen jährlichen Pro-Kopf-Verbrauch von acht Kilogramm ansteuern.

Hightech-Milch und Käse-Patent

Eine weißes „müller" auf rotem Grund an einer silbergrauen Fassade, Gruppen schlanker Türme, quaderförmige Gebäude, Milchlastzüge. Wer auf der A 4 die Abfahrt Pulsnitz Richtung Bautzen passiert, sieht rechter Hand Europas größte und modernste Molkerei. Die Sachsenmilch AG ist der Gigant der Lebensmittelproduzenten im Kammerbezirk Dresden. Sie verarbeitet jährlich 1,7 Milliarden Kilogramm Milch. Von 1994 an investierte die Theo-Müller-Gruppe rund 700 Mio. Euro. Mit 2000 Beschäftigten gehört die Sachsenmilch Leppersdorf AG zu den größten Arbeitgebern in Ostsachsen. Sie produziert Handelswaren und führt die eigenen Linien „Sachsenmilch" und „Käsemeister". „Sachsenmilch" mit mehr als 40 Produkten zählt zu den bekanntesten Marken im Freistaat.

Milch wird auch im nahen Radeberg verarbeitet. Über 60 Landwirtschaftsbetriebe aus Ostsachsen und Südbrandenburg liefern sie in den Ortsteil Heinrichsthal für jährlich 22 000 Tonnen Schnittkäse. 40 Prozent des „Heinrichsthalers" werden exportiert. Agathe Zeis heißt die Stammmutter der 200 Mitarbeiter in der Heinrichsthaler Milchwerke GmbH. Sie hatte 1884 als Erste in Deutschland das französische Patent für Camembert und Brie erworben. 1893 wurde die Meierei „Königlich Sächsischer Hoflieferant", was die heutige Vermarktung als „Königliche Käsespezialitäten" erklärt, unter ihnen Camembert.

Zweimal Radeberger

Radeberg. Den Namen haben gleich zwei Firmen aufgegriffen. Die eine heißt Radeberger Fleisch- und Wurstwaren Korch GmbH. Gründer Georg Korch und jetzt Sohn Michael haben der langen Fleischereitradition auf dem Firmengelände eine Zukunft gegeben. Gläserne Produktion auch dort: Beim Rundgang können die Feinschmecker beobachten, wie sich Qualitätsfleisch in Schinken- und Würstchenspezialitäten verwandelt. Die Marke „Original Radeberger" ist in vielen Teilen Deutschlands erhältlich. 2011 vergab die DLG (Deutsche Landwirtschafts-Gesellschaft) den 180 Mitarbeitern zum 14. Mal in Folge den „Preis der Besten", den wiederum zum fünften Mal nacheinander in Gold.

Radeberger? Kann man das nicht trinken? Stimmt, die zweite Firma mit Stadtbezug ist die Radeberger Exportbierbrauerei. TV-

Die Lebensmittelbranche ist die umsatzstärkste Industrie in Sachsen.

The food and beverage industry has the highest turnover in Saxony.

making the company's products in a new facility in Dresden-Coschütz, to which a visitor's centre was added in 2008. The product range includes both classic items and new products, such as "Echter Dresdner Christstollen" (genuine stollen) and "Original Dinkelchen" (spelt biscuits).

Another area, another success story: the glass pasta centre in Riesa shows up to 250 visitors every day how elbow pasta, penne and spaghetti are made... Since 2003, Teigwaren GmbH has turned the production of its approx. 100 types of pasta into a tourist event. It makes GMO-free production transparent, while its very own first pasta museum in Germany recalls the company history. This began in 1914 in a red brick building which is still on the company premises today. Meanwhile the company from Riesa leads the market in eastern Germany with 240,000 tons of pasta and a share of just about one third. The 150 employees are glad that Germans are eating ever increasing quantities of pasta, heading for an annual per capita consumption of eight kilograms.

Spots haben sie weithin bekannt gemacht und – so sagt man – manch Auswärtigen staunen lassen, aus welch prunkvollem Brauhaus das Bier kommt. Sie wirbt mit der Dresdner Semperoper. Sachsens Brautradition ist jahrhundertealt. Die Nähe zum böhmischen Plzeň belebte sie zusätzlich. 1872 brauten die Radeberger als Erste in Deutschland Gerstensaft nach Pilsner Art. Heute ist die Brauerei – im Besitz der Dr. August Oetker KG – eine der modernsten in Europa.

Flüssiges für jeden Geschmack

Sachsen trinken jährlich pro Kopf 145 Liter Bier, fast 38 Liter mehr als die Durchschnittsdeutschen. Sicher auch, weil das Einheimische mit 310 Sorten gut schmeckt. Diese Biere produzieren 58 industrielle Brauereien und Gasthausbrauereien, davon 20 im Kammerbezirk Dresden. Einige Namen: „Schwerter" in Meißen – mit 550 Jahren Sachsens älteste Privatbrauerei –, „Landskron" in Görlitz und „Bergquell" in Löbau. Neben den Großen wie „Feldschlößchen" in Dresden behaupten sich die Kleineren. Spezialität der Privatbrauerei Eibau ist das Schwarzbier. Sie stellt auch das Klosterbräu für die Zisterzienserinnenabtei St. Marienstern her, das älteste Kloster des Ordens in Deutschland.

Hochprozentiges und Spritziges gleich in der Nachbarschaft. Die „Wilthener Goldkrone" aus der Weinbrennerei Wilthen – mit Tradition seit 1842 und seit 1992 eine Niederlassung der norddeutschen Hardenberg-Wilthen AG – zählt zu den meistgekauften Spirituosen in Deutschland. Die Oppacher Mineralquellen GmbH & Co. KG wiederum gewinnt natürliches Mineralwasser aus elf Brunnen, die bis zu 300 Meter tief sind. Die Anfänge der Firma liegen im Jahr 1886. Heute erquickt sie mit 24 Produkten Durstige in ganz Mitteldeutschland.

Wohlschmeckend und touristisch attraktiv ist der gute Tropfen aus dem Elbtal zwischen Pirna und Diesbar-Seußlitz. Die 55 Kilometer lange „Sächsische Weinstraße" führt ins zweitkleinste Weinbaugebiet Deutschlands. Sachsens Winzer – darunter das Staatsweingut Schloss Wackerbarth in Radebeul – werben mit dem Slogan „Eine Rarität. Weine aus Sachsen". Da nur 0,2 Prozent der deutschen Weine aus diesem Gebiet kommen, ist der hiesige Rebensaft – oft abgefüllt in der „Sachsenkeule" – selbst für Kenner etwas Besonderes.

Lecker, scharf und vielfältig

Wein mundet zu Fisch. Während der Oberlausitzer Fischwochen im Herbst verbünden sich acht Teichwirtschaften mit Gastronomen und Touristikern der Region. Die Veranstaltungsfolge reicht vom Schaufischen bis zum Zubereiten von Fischdelikatessen. Qualität aus der Region dominiert auch das sommerliche Oberlausitzer Genussfestival. Restaurants servieren Speisen nach heimatlichen Rezepten, aus heimischen Zutaten und im Ambiente des Landstrichs.

High-tech milk and patented cheese

White "müller" on a red background against a silver grey facade, groups of slender towers, cuboid buildings, milk trucks. Whoever drives past the Pulsnitz exit on the A 4 motorway travelling towards Bautzen will see Europe's largest and most modern dairy on the right-hand side. Sachsenmilch AG is the giant of all food producers in the Dresden chamber district, processing 1.7 billion kilograms of milk every year. From 1994 on, the Theo Müller Group invested around 700 million Euro here. 2,000 employees make Sachsenmilch Leppersdorf AG one of the largest employers in East Saxony. The company produces trade goods together with its own brands "Sachsenmilch" and "Käsemeister". "Sachsenmilch" with more than 40 products is one of the best known brands in the Free State.

Milk is also processed in nearby Radeberg, supplied to the suburb of Heinrichsthal by more than 60 farms in East Saxony and South Brandenburg for the production of 22,000 tons of cheese every year. 40 percent of the products are exported. The original ancestress of the 200 employees at Heinrichsthaler Milchwerke GmbH was called Agathe Zeis: back in 1884, she was the first German to acquire the French patent for making Camembert and Brie. In 1893, the dairy became "Royal Purveyor to the Court of Saxony", which explains today's advertising claim that the products, including Camembert, are "royal cheese specialities".

Radeberg twice over

Radeberg. Two companies use the name. One is Radeberger Fleisch- und Wurstwaren Korch GmbH. Founder Georg Korch and now his son Michael have given a future to the long butcher's tradition on the company premises. Glass production here too: during a tour of the company, gourmets can see how quality meat is turned into ham and sausage specialities. The "Original Radeberger" brand is available in many parts of Germany. In 2011, the DLG (German Agricultural Society) awarded the "Prize of the Best" to the company's 180 employees for the 14th time in succession and also for the fifth time in succession in gold.

Radeberger? Isn't that a drink? That's right, the second company using the town's name is Radeberger Exportbierbrauerei. TV spots have made it well known, and strangers are said to be amazed at the ornate building involved: the company advertises with Dresden's Semperoper. Saxony has a centuries old brewing tradition, which was further enlivened by the close proximity to Plzeň in Bohemia (famous for the original Pilsner beer): in 1872, Radeberger was the first brewery in Germany to produce Pilsner beer. Today, the brewery is owned by Dr. August Oetker KG and is one of the most modern in Europe.

Die 55 Kilometer lange „Sächsische Weinstraße" führt ins zweitkleinste Weinbaugebiet Deutschlands.

The Saxon wine route is 55 kilometres long taking visitors through Germany's second smallest wine-growing area.

Wer's zu Tisch scharf mag, wird zum „Bautz'ner" greifen. Der Senf ist eine sächsische Legende und eine der bekanntesten Ostmarken. Viele halten die Sorte „Bautz'ner Senf mittelscharf" für unübertroffen. Die Senf-Jahresproduktion könnte eine Bockwurst garnieren, die sich viermal um den Erdball windet. Unter dem Markendach produzierte die Bautz'ner Senf & Feinkost GmbH – seit 1992 zum bayerischen Unternehmen Develey gehörend – inzwischen über 30 weitere Produkte.

Was alles müsste man noch probieren! Eierschecke natürlich, den Dresdner Christstollen, „Werners Kloßmehl" aus einer Freitaler Familienfirma, Fruchtsäfte aus Sohland, Ebersbach und Heidenau, Altenberger Kräuterlikör, Leinöl aus Hoyerswerda, Obst aus Dohna und Schleinitz, Zwieback aus Neukirch, „Sonja" aus dem Dresdner Margarinewerk des europäischen Konzerns Vandermoortele... Der Kammerbezirk Dresden ist eine Region des guten Geschmacks. Die Warnung „Rauchen kann tödlich sein" vorausgeschickt, gehört selbst das Aroma der „f 6" dazu. Die erste DDR-Filterzigarette hat überlebt und wird in der denkmalgeschützten Zigarettenfabrik Jasmatzi von 1900 im Dresdner Stadtteil Striesen hergestellt. Seit 1990 gehört die „f 6" zum Philip-Morris-Konzern und liegt in der gesamtdeutschen Rauchergunst auf Platz acht.

Beverages for every taste

Saxony has a per capita beer consumption of 145 litres per year, nearly 38 litres more than the German average. This is sure to be because the local beer with 310 different varieties tastes so good. The beer is produced by 58 industrial breweries and microbreweries, including 20 in the Dresden chamber district. Names include Schwerter in Meißen – 550 years old and Saxony's oldest private brewery –, Landskron in Görlitz and Bergquell in Löbau. Alongside the big names such as Feldschlößchen, smaller breweries also manage to survive in Dresden. The speciality produced by the Eibau private brewery is dark beer. It also makes the cloister beer for the Cistercian convent of St. Marienstern, which is the oldest of the order's convents in Germany.

High-proof and sparkling refreshment just around the corner: one of Germany's best selling spirits is Wilthener Goldkrone from the Wilthen distillery, with a tradition going back to 1842. Since 1992, the firm belongs to the North German company Hardenberg-Wilthen AG. On the other hand, Oppacher Mineralquellen GmbH & Co. KG produces natural mineral water from eleven springs that go down to 300 metres in depth. The company's roots go back to 1886. Today it offers a range of 24 thirst-quenching products for the whole of Central Germany.

The Elbe valley between Pirna and Diesbar-Seußlitz produces good wines that have become an added tourist attraction. The Saxon wine route is 55 kilometres long, taking visitors through Germany's second smallest wine-growing area. Saxony's winegrowers, including the state vineyard Schloss Wackerbarth in Radebeul, advertise with the slogan "A rarity: Saxon wine".

Genau richtig: Maschinen- und Anlagenbau

Eine klassische Ingenieurdisziplin ist zweitstärkste Branche im Kammerbezirk Dresden: der Maschinen- und Anlagenbau. Sein Jahresumsatz beträgt fast 3 Mrd. Euro. Diesen erwirtschaften 340 Betriebe (ab 50 Mitarbeiter) mit mehr als 13 000 Beschäftigten. Sachsen ist die Wiege des deutschen Maschinenbaus: 1826 begann Carl Friedrich Haubold in Chemnitz mit der Maschinenfabrikation, 1839 fertigte Johann Andreas Schubert in Dresden die erste deutsche Dampflok, nach 1850 erobern sächsische Maschinen den Weltmarkt.

Sprung ins Jahr 1990: Die Ostmärkte brachen weg, die DDR-Maschinenbaukombinate zerbröselten, mittelständische Unternehmen entstanden und orientierten sich von nun an am Weltmarkt. Der Neuansatz gelang. Investitionen von mehr als 2,7 Mrd. Euro haben die alte sächsische Tradition neu belebt. Seit 2000 verdoppelten die Maschinen- und Anlagenbauer ihren Umsatz und führen vor den anderen neuen Bundesländern. Sie erwirtschaften fast die Hälfte des ostdeutschen Branchenumsatzes. 52 Prozent ihrer Erzeugnisse gehen ins Ausland.

Lob des Ingenieurs

Ohne Maschinenbau geht im produzierenden Gewerbe nichts. Die Ingenieure gelten als Alleskönner, Tüftler und Visionäre. 1871 pries Schriftsteller und Maschinenbauingenieur Heinrich Seidel diesen Typus: „Dem Ingenieur ist nichts zu schwere, / Er lacht und spricht: ‚Wenn dieses nicht, so geht doch das!'" Auch den Maschinenbau im Kammerbezirk Dresden hat dieser Typus neu erblühen lassen. Sein Nachwuchs wächst unter anderem an der TU Dresden, der Hochschule für Technik und Wirtschaft Dresden, der Hochschule Zittau/Görlitz und der Berufsakademie Sachsen mit den Standorten Dresden, Bautzen und Riesa heran.

Die aktuellen Zeichen stehen auf Verflechtung: Maschinenbauer, Dienstleister und Forscher bündeln ihre Kräfte. Dafür stehen Netzwerke wie die „Verbundinitiative Maschinenbau Sachsen" (VEMAS), der Verein „ELEWER – Der Elektronenstrahl als Werkzeug e.V." in Dresden und „Team 22 – Maschinenbau- und Metallbearbeitung in Ostsachsen". VEMAS beispielsweise fördert Firmenkooperationen und den Technologietransfer aus der Forschung. Sie hilft, neue Märkte zu erschließen und Fachpersonal heranzubilden.

Hochburg Oberlausitz

Im „Team 22" haben sich über 20 ostsächsische Firmen des Maschinenbaus und der Metallverarbeitung verbündet. Sie beherrschen hoch entwickelte Fertigungsverfahren und bieten Systemlösungen aus einer Hand an. Die Kooperationsbörse nutzt ihren Standort im Dreiländereck, um die Geschäftsbeziehungen nach Osteuropa zu intensivieren. Mitgliedsbetriebe sind beispielsweise die SSL Maschinenbau GmbH in Eibau mit einem

Fortsetzung Seite 54

Accounting for only 0.2 percent of German wine, the local products, frequently found in the specially shaped Sachsenkeule bottle, are often something special even for experts.

Tasty, hot and varied

Wine goes well with fish. During the Oberlausitz fish weeks in the autumn, eight pond farms join forces with the region's restaurant owners and tourism managers to offer a whole series of events including a fishing show and how to prepare fish delicacies. Quality products from the region also dominate Oberlausitz's summer food-and-drink festival. Restaurants serve dishes made according to local recipes from local ingredients, set in a regional ambience.

Those who like their food hot will enjoy Bautz'ner mustard. This is a Saxon legend and one of the best known eastern brands. For many, Bautz'ner mustard medium hot is unsurpassed. The annual mustard production could garnish a sausage stretching four times around the globe. Part of the Bavarian company Develey since 1992, Bautz'ner Senf & Feinkost GmbH meanwhile makes another 30 products under the company brand.

What else is there to try? Eierschecke cake, Dresden stollen, dumpling flour by Werner, a family company in Freital, fruit juice from Sohland, Ebersbach and Heidenau, Altenberg herbal liqueur, linseed oil from Hoyerswerda, fruit from Dohna and Schleinitz, rusks from Neukirch, "Sonja" from the Dresden margarine factory of the European Vandermoortele Group... The Dresden chamber district is certainly a region of good taste. As long as people note the warning "Smoking can kill", this claim even extends to the aroma of the "f 6". The GDR's first filter cigarette has survived and is still made in the listed cigarette factory Jasmatzi that dates back to 1900 in the Dresden suburb of Striesen. Since 1990, "f 6" has been part of the Philip Morris Group and is the eighth most popular cigarette in Germany.

Big winner: Machine and plant construction

A classic engineering discipline is the second strongest branch in the Dresden chamber district: machine and plant construction, with an annual turnover of nearly 3 billion Euro. This is generated by 340 companies (from 50 employees) with a total workforce of more than 13,000. Saxony is the birthplace of German machine construction. It was here in Chemnitz back in 1826 that Carl Friedrich Haubold started to make machines; in Dresden in 1839, Johann Andreas Schubert produced Germany's first steam locomotive, and after 1850, machines from Saxony conquered the world market.

Leap forward to 1990: the eastern markets collapsed and the GDR machine construction collectives started to fall apart; SME companies emerged and geared their activities to the global market. The new start was a success, with capital expenditure

Continued on page 54

VEM Sachsenwerk GmbH

Information

Gründungsjahr: 1886

Mitarbeiter: 605

Leistungsspektrum:
Entwicklung, Produktion und Vertrieb von Mittel- und Großmaschinen in Drehstromausführung im Leistungsbereich 500 kW bis 35 MW

Fertigungsfläche:
30 195 m²

Lagerfläche: 8975 m²

Zertifizierungen:
DIN EN ISO 9001:2008
DIN EN ISO 14001:2009
IRIS Certification

Year founded: 1886

Employees: 605

Range of services:
development, production and sale of medium and large rotating electrical machines power range 500 kW up to 35 MW

Production area:
30,195 m²

Stacking ground:
8,975 m²

Certification:
DIN EN ISO 9001:2008
DIN EN ISO 14001:2009
IRIS Certification

VEM Sachsenwerk GmbH, Dresden

VEM Sachsenwerk GmbH: Kompetenz für höchste Ansprüche von Großmaschinen

Als Spezialist für die Fertigung von Mittel- und Hochspannungsmaschinen konzentriert sich VEM Sachsenwerk gezielt auf ausgewählte Marktsegmente aller Industriebranchen, in denen komplexe Anforderungen gestellt werden. Die hohe Ausnutzung durch elektromagnetische Optimierung bei geringem Einbauvolumen kennzeichnen die Groß- und Spezialmaschinen von VEM. Das Unternehmen fertigt Asynchron- und Synchronmaschinen vom Niederspannungsbereich bis zu 13,8 kV mit einer Leistung bis zu 35 000 kW für individuelle Applikationen.

Die Produktpalette reicht von Kompressor- und Walzwerksantrieben über Wind- und Wasserkraftgeneratoren bis hin zu POD-Antrieben für Schiffe und Traktionsmotoren für die Verkehrstechnik. Die Maschinen entstehen überwiegend als Einzelanfertigungen in einer Kombination aus qualifizierter Handarbeit und modernster Technik. Nicht alltägliche Aufträge wie Twin Drives für Walzwerksapplikationen oder Kompressorantriebe, die im zweistelligen Megawatt-Bereich liegen, führen die Referenzliste an.

VEM Sachsenwerk GmbH: Competence for the highest demands on large machines

As a specialist in the manufacture of medium and high-voltage machines, VEM Sachsenwerk intentionally focuses on selected market segments of all industrial sectors in which complex demands are made. The high level of utilization through electromagnetic optimization with a minimal installation volume characterize the large and special machines of VEM. The company manufactures asynchronous and synchronous machines from the low voltage range up to 13.8 kV with an output of up to 35,000 kW for individual applications.

The product range spans from the compressor and rolling mill drives via wind and hydroelectric generators to POD drives for ships and traction motors for transport engineering. The machines are created primarily as individual production in a combination of quality craftsmanship and cutting-edge technology. Unusual commissions, such as twin drives for rolling mill applications or compressor drives in the double-digit megawatt range, top our list of references.

Spezialisiert auf Unikate: Das VEM Sachsenwerk, der Dresdner Standort der VEM-Gruppe, zählt mit seiner über 125-jährigen Geschichte zu den traditionsreichsten Elektromaschinenbauern in Deutschland.

Specializing in unique innovations: VEM Sachsenwerk, the Dresden location of the VEM Group, is among the electrical machinery manufacturers with the richest history in Germany with its history spanning over 125 years.

robotergeführten Bandschleifsystem als Spezialität und die 120-jährige FWH Federnfabrik Wilhelm Hesse GmbH mit Qualitätsfedern für viele Industriezweige.

Die Oberlausitz ist eine Hochburg des sächsischen Maschinenbaus. Die TruLaser 7040 NEU gilt als produktivste Laserschneidanlage der Welt. Ihr Schöpfer, die TRUMPF Sachsen GmbH in Neukirch, ging aus dem Rationalisierungsmittelbaubetrieb des DDR-Landmaschinenkombinates Fortschritt hervor. Die Siemens AG hat ihren Geschäftsbereich für Industriedampfturbinen in Görlitz angesiedelt, wo schon ab 1847 Turbinen gebaut wurden.

Für Ford, BMW, Volvo und Rolls-Royce ist Neugersdorf ein Begriff. Die MBN Maschinenbaubetriebe Neugersdorf GmbH hat den Ortsnamen mit Fahrzeugmontageanlagen in die Welt getragen. Die Endmontagelinie für den Phaeton in der VW-Manufaktur in Dresden stammt aus dem Betrieb. 1991 gelang der neue Aufbruch: Unternehmer Ernst Lieb – aus der Nähe von Wolfsburg stammend – gründete die Firma aus Hinterlassenschaften des DDR-Textilmaschinenbaukombinates. „Es gab hier gut ausgebildete Facharbeiter. Darauf konnten wir aufbauen", erinnert er sich. Qualität und Qualifizierung gehören für ihn zusammen. Unter seinen 230 Mitarbeitern sind 45 Auszubildende.

Karl May und von Ardenne

Die Gruppe König & Bauer – weltweit zweitgrößter Druckmaschinenhersteller – signalisiert auf ihrer Webseite einen Superlativ: „Die neue Rapida 105 – Die modernste Maschine ihrer Klasse." Die seit Jahren marktbestimmende Mittelformat-Bogenoffset-Druckmaschine habe einen konstruktiven Schub erhalten, so mit neuem Greifersystem. Diese Neuheit wird in Radebeul bei Dresden hergestellt. 1600 Mitarbeiter produzieren dort die Bogenoffsetmaschinen der erfolgreichen Rapida-Serie. Erste Druckmaschinen entstanden schon 1898, als noch Karl May in der Elbestadt wohnte und schrieb. Vorgänger des jetzigen Werkes war Planeta Radebeul, der größte DDR-Druckmaschinenhersteller.

Der Name „von Ardenne" steht für sächsischen Forschergeist. Manfred von Ardenne erwarb im 20. Jahrhundert rund 600 Patente, viele davon in seiner Dresdner Zeit ab 1955. Sein privates Forschungsinstitut war das größte seiner Art im Ostblock. 1991 schlug die Geburtsstunde der VON ARDENNE Anlagentechnik GmbH: 67 Entschlossene gründeten sie aus dem Ardenne-Institut aus. Seither hat sich die Belegschaft fast verzehnfacht. Sie führt den berühmten Namen weiter und das Wertesystem fort, das sich mit ihm verbindet: wissenschaftliche Neugier, ständige Suche nach innovativen Lösungen, Qualitätsbewusstsein, nachhaltiges Handeln und Zuverlässigkeit.

2011 veröffentlichte „Die Welt" eine Studie mit einem Ranking der 100 besten von 1600 deutschen Mittelständlern. Ihnen wurden „dauerhafte Spitzenleistung, unternehmerische Weitsicht und Durchhaltevermögen" bescheinigt. Platz zwölf belegten die

Fortsetzung Seite 58

---

of more than 2.7 billion Euro reviving the old Saxon tradition. Since 2000, the machine and plant construction sector has doubled its turnover and now takes the lead ahead of the other new German states, generating nearly half of the branch's turnover in eastern Germany. 52 percent of their products go abroad.

An engineer's praise

Manufacturing simply doesn't work without machine construction. The engineers are deemed to be all-rounders, boffins and visionaries. In 1871, author and mechanical engineer Heinrich Seidel praised the whole fraternity: "Nothing is too hard for the engineer, / He laughs and says: 'if this won't work, then that will!'" This is a fraternity that was instrumental to resurrecting mechanical engineering in the Dresden chamber district. Young engineers are meanwhile learning all they need to know at the Technical University of Dresden, Dresden University of Applied Sciences, Zittau/Görlitz University of Applied Sciences and the Saxon Vocational College with its sites in Dresden, Bautzen and Riesa.

At the moment, networking is all the rage, with mechanical engineers, service providers and researchers pooling their forces. This results in networks such as the joint initiative VEMAS (Mechanical Engineering in Saxony), ELEWER (Electron Beam as a Tool) in Dresden and Team 22 (Mechanical Engineering and Metal Processing in East Saxony). VEMAS for example funds cooperation between companies and the transfer of technology from research. It helps to cultivate new markets and train new skilled staff.

Engineering stronghold Oberlausitz

"Team 22" groups together more than 20 mechanical engineering and metal processing firms in East Saxony, offering highly developed production methods and providing system solutions from a single source. The cooperation exchange uses its location at the three-nation triangle to intensify business relations with Eastern Europe. Member companies include for example the specialist company SSL Maschinenbau GmbH in Eibau with its robot-guided belt grinder, and FWH Federnfabrik Wilhelm Hesse GmbH with a 120-year tradition of supplying quality springs for many branches of industry.

The Oberlausitz is a stronghold for engineering in Saxony. The TruLaser 7040 NEU is deemed to be the most productive laser cutting system in the world. It was created by TRUMPF Sachsen GmbH in Neukirch, which grew out of the rationalisation toolmaking division of the GDR agricultural machinery collective "Fortschritt". Siemens AG chose Görlitz for its industrial steam turbine division, settling in a town where turbines were already being made back in 1847.

Continued on page 58

Information

Gründungsjahr: 1991

Gesellschafter:
zu 100 Prozent die Familien von Ardenne

Mitarbeiter:
ca. 600 in Sachsen

Produkt- und Leistungsspektrum:
Anlagenlösungen für die Vakuumbeschichtung von Glas, Metallband oder Folie

Tochtergesellschaften:
in China, Malaysia, Taiwan und in den USA

Vertriebsnetzwerk weltweit:
in China, Indien, Japan, Korea, Taiwan, den USA, Kanada, Mexiko, den Vereinigten Arabischen Emiraten, Saudi-Arabien u. a.

Year founded: 1991

Shareholders: wholly owned by the von Ardenne families

Employees: approx. 600 in Saxony

Range of products and services: equipment solutions for vacuum coating of glass, metal strip or plastic foil

Subsidiaries: in China, Malaysia, Taiwan and in the USA

Global sales network: in China, India, Japan, Korea, Taiwan, the USA, Canada, Mexico, the United Arab Emirates, Saudi Arabia, etc.

VON ARDENNE Anlagentechnik GmbH Dresden

VON ARDENNE Anlagentechnik GmbH

VON ARDENNE gehört zu den weltweit führenden Herstellern von Anlagen für industrielle mikro- bis nanometerdünne Beschichtungen von Glas, Metallband oder Folie. Kunden des Dresdner Unternehmens stellen beispielsweise Produkte wie Wärmeschutzglas, Solarabsorber oder Reflektoren her, die einen besonderen Nutzen aufweisen: Sie vermeiden Wärmeverlust oder Überhitzung, unterstützen ökologisches Heizen und Kühlen oder erhöhen die Lichtausbeute von Leuchten.

Bei VON ARDENNE wird ständig an innovativen Lösungen für Technologien und Komponenten geforscht. Dabei wird Wert auf eine Zusammenarbeit mit verschiedenen Forschungseinrichtungen und Universitäten gelegt.

Das Unternehmen fühlt sich eng mit der Region und ihren Einwohnern verbunden. So vergibt VON ARDENNE unter anderem seit 2009 die Physikpreise für besondere Lernleistungen an den Nachwuchs und finanziert in der „KITA am Hochwald" das spielerische Erlernen von Englisch.

VON ARDENNE Anlagentechnik GmbH

VON ARDENNE is a leading global manufacturer of equipment for industrial micro- to nanometre-thin coating of glass, metal strip or plastic foil. Customers served by the Dresden company manufacture products such as heat protection glass, solar absorbers or reflectors, offering a special benefit: they prevent heat loss or overheating, support ecological heating and cooling, or increase the light yield of lamps.

VON ARDENNE constantly works at research into innovative solutions for technologies and components, attaching importance to cooperating with various research institutions and universities.

The company feels closely related to the region and its inhabitants. Since 2009, among others VON ARDENNE has awarded the Physics Prize to youngsters for special learning achievements, while also providing the necessary funds for kindergarten children at the "KITA am Hochwald" to learn English in play.

slr-Elsterheide GmbH

Information

Gründungsjahr: 2008

Mitarbeiter: 350

Produkte:
· Baumaschinenteile
· Achsen
· Roboterarme

Year founded: 2008

Employees: 350

Products:
· construction parts
· axes
· robotic arms

slr-Elsterheide GmbH
Elsterheide

slr-Elsterheide GmbH

Right at the heart of the Lausitz lake district is the world's most advanced foundry: slr-Elsterheide GmbH.

The headquarters of the slr-Group are in St. Leon-Rot. Castings are developed in Eging am See. The Group has a machining facility in Hungary, together with cooperation partners in Austria and in the Czech Republic. At slr-Elsterheide, 60,000 tonnes of spheroidal graphite iron are cast, blasted and checked. The young company enjoys constant growth, while increasing order quantities mean that the number of furnaces is being doubled from two to four by 2013. The products consist of top quality castings for drive systems, construction machinery, commer-

cial vehicles, railways and many other branches of industry.

The Chairman of the slr-Group, Rudi Seiz, attaches great importance not just to product quality but also to efficient, well-functioning environmental management. The Elsterheide foundry is equipped with state-of-the-art filter systems to clean the exhaust air.

Characteristic features of the foundry include the modern core shooting machines in operation since the start of production, together with the automatic moulding installation. The moulding boxes are used to produce castings with a weight from 15 to 800 kilograms. Every batch undergoes quality inspection using a spectrometer to check compliance with the quality parameters, and corresponding records are kept. These entire processes form the quality basis which is further expanded and assured by the 350 highly motivated employees.

Spheroidal graphite iron is a very tough, high-strength material with similar stability to cast steel. The motto of "The heart of quality is the blank" applies to the entire production process.

slr-Elsterheide GmbH

Mitten im Herzen des Lausitzer Seenlandes befindet sich die modernste Gießerei der Welt – die slr-Elsterheide GmbH.

Der Stammsitz der slr-Gruppe befindet sich in St. Leon-Rot. Die Entwicklung der Gussteile findet in Eging am See statt. Ein Bearbeitungswerk ist in Ungarn. Kooperationspartner der slr befinden sich in Österreich und Tschechien. Bei der slr-Elsterheide werden jährlich 60 000 Tonnen Sphäroguss gegossen, gestrahlt und anschließend kontrolliert. Das junge Unternehmen befindet sich im stetigen Wachstum, und dank steigender Auftragszahlen wird bis 2013 die Anzahl der Schmelzöfen von zwei auf vier Öfen erhöht. Verkauft werden hochwertige Gussstücke für Antriebstechniksysteme, Baumaschinen, Nutzfahrzeuge, Eisenbahnen und für viele andere Industriezweige.

Der Geschäftsführer der slr-Gruppe, Rudi Seiz, legt nicht nur großen Wert auf die Qualität der Produkte, sondern auch auf ein gutes und funktionierendes Umweltmanagement. Im Werk in Elsterheide sind modernste Filteranlagen, um die Abluft zu reinigen.

Charakteristisch für das Werk sind die zu Produktionsbeginn verwendeten modernen Kernschießmaschinen und die automatische Formanlage. In den Formkästen werden Gussteile mit einem Gewicht von 15 bis 800 Kilogramm produziert. Anschließend wird jede Charge mit Hilfe eines Spektrometers auf ihre Qualitätsparameter geprüft und dokumentiert. Diese ganzen Prozesse legen die Qualitätsgrundlage, die durch die 350 hoch motivierten Mitarbeiter ausgebaut und gesichert wird.

Sphäroguss ist als Werkstoff sehr zäh und hochfest und hat eine Stabilität ähnlich dem Stahlguss. Darum zieht sich das Motto „Die Keimzelle der Qualität liegt im Rohteil" durch die gesamte Produktion.

Dresdner Wach- und Sicherungs-Institut GmbH

Information

Gründungsjahr: 1990
Mitarbeiter: ca. 1000
Dienstleistungen:
· Objekt- und Werkschutz
· Mobile Sicherheit & Intervention
· Veranstaltungsservice
· Rezeptions- und Empfangsdienst
· Museale Sicherheit & Service
· Geld- und Werttransport, Geldbearbeitung
· Kaufhausdetektive & Shopguards
· Alarmanlagenaufschaltungen
· Personenschutz
· Aus- und Fortbildung in BDSW-zertifizierter Sicherheitsfachschule

Standorte:
Dresden (Hauptsitz), Riesa-Großenhain, Kamenz, Marienberg, Löbau, Neustadt (Sachsen), Leipzig, Berlin

Year founded: 1990
Employees: approx. 1,000
Services:
· property and factory security
· mobile security & intervention
· event service
· reception service
· museum security & service
· transport of cash and valuables, cash handling
· store detectives & shop guards
· activating alarm systems
· personal security
· initial and advanced training in security college certified by BDSW (Federal Security Association)

Locations:
Dresden (headquarters), Riesa-Großenhain, Kamenz, Marienberg, Löbau, Neustadt (Saxony), Leipzig, Berlin

Dresdner Wach- und Sicherungs-Institut GmbH
Dresden

Dresdner Wach- und Sicherungs-Institut GmbH – Mit Sicherheit flexibel, menschlich, nah!

Mit seinem breiten Dienstleistungsspektrum ist die Dresdner Wach- und Sicherungs-Institut GmbH eines der größten Sicherheitsunternehmen im Freistaat Sachsen. Rund um die Uhr betreuen die operativen Einsatzkräfte des DWSI ca. 5000 Objekte von über 2700 Kunden.

Entsprechend deren Anforderungsprofil werden neben Dienstleistungen, die der präventiven Sicherheit von Mensch und Eigentum dienen, zahlreiche angrenzende Serviceleistungen wie beispielsweise das Besucher- und Ausweismanagement im Rahmen des Werkschutzes angeboten.

Mit den meisten seiner Kunden arbeitet das DWSI bereits seit vielen Jahren in enger Kooperation zusammen. Sicherheitsdienstleistungen sind oftmals nicht skalierbar und basieren deshalb auf Vertrauen, welches das Unternehmen durch individuelle Sicherheitskonzepte, eine hohe Serviceorientierung und durch das große Engagement der Mitarbeiterinnen und Mitarbeiter, besonders bei sich plötzlich verändernden Rahmenbedingungen, gewinnt.

Dresdner Wach- und Sicherungs-Institut GmbH - Flexible, human and local security services close at hand!

The Dresdner Wach- und Sicherungs-Institut GmbH (DWSI) with its wide range of services is one of the largest security companies in Saxony. Day and night the employees take care of approx. 5,000 properties belonging to more than 2,700 customers.

On the one hand the DWSI offers typical security services for the protection of people and properties. On the other hand it offers numerous related services such as visitor management and identification management depending on the specific requirements of each client.

DWSI has been working together with most of its clients already for many years in a very close cooperation. Security services are often not scalable and are therefore based on trust, which the company wins by individual customized security concepts, great focus on service quality and the extensive commitment shown by its staff, particularly in the context of suddenly changing framework conditions.

Die zentrale Organisation von Aufgaben wie Ausweiskontrollen, Schlüsselausgabe oder die Lieferabfertigung sollten besonders unter Sicherheitsaspekten nicht dem Zufall überlassen werden.

The central organisation of tasks such as checking identification, issuing badges or dealing with deliveries should not be left to chance, particularly where security aspects are concerned.

www.dwsi.de

Dresdner. Das Unternehmen brilliert weltweit mit Plasma- und Elektronenstrahltechnologien. Vakuum-Beschichtungsanlagen für die Fotovoltaik – Umwandlung von Licht- in Elektroenergie – ermöglichen es, die Sonnenstrahlung neuartig zu nutzen. Andere Anlagen, die dünne Schichten auf Architekturglas aufbringen, helfen, in verglasten Gebäuden Wärme besser zu dämmen und Energie zu sparen.

Automatisch, schnell, präzise

Mut zum Risiko und Vertrauen in die eigenen Fähigkeiten hatten 1990 auch elf Unentwegte im VEB Robotron-Messelektronik Dresden. Sie formten den Rationalisierungsmittelbau in ein eigenes Unternehmen um. Inzwischen ist die XENON Automatisierungstechnik GmbH ein Spezialist von internationalem Ruf. Über 130 Mitarbeiter projektieren, entwickeln und produzieren Maschinen und Anlagen, die beim Kunden Fertigungsprozesse maßgeschneidert automatisieren. 2011 erhielt XENON Sachsens Innovationspreis für die vielseitig adaptierbare 3-D-Montagelinie für Motorradschalter.

Süße Sachen sind Sache der Theegarten-Pactec GmbH & Co. KG in Dresden. So schnell wie ihre Anlagen wickelt sonst niemand Bonbons ein. Das Familienunternehmen mit 300 Mitarbeitern zählt zu den führenden Herstellern von Verpackungsmaschinen. Im Namen vereint es jahrzehntelange Traditionslinien aus West und Ost. Die eine ist Kölner, die andere Dresdner Ursprungs. Seit 1997 wird nur noch in Dresden produziert. Auf Messen unterstreicht der Betrieb immer wieder seine Spitzenposition bei Anlagen für kleinstückige Süßwaren, darunter mit dem neuen Modell MCH, das pro Minute bis zu 1000 Gelee-Artikel verpackt.

Die Maxime der Mikromat GmbH in Dresden lautet: „Wir setzen auf das produktive µ." Der zwölfte Buchstabe im griechischen Alphabet steht für Mikro, das Millionstel. Mikromat denkt, konstruiert und produziert in diesem Maßbereich. Die Produkte befähigen die Kunden, im gesamten Arbeitsraum einer Maschine Werkstücke hochgenau herzustellen. Zu den Abnehmern gehören Automobilbau und Luftfahrtindustrie. Die Leipziger Messe vergab ihren „intec-Preis 2011" für ein Bravourstück: die Präzisionsportal-Bohr-Fräsmaschine 40V. „Ihre Innovation besteht darin, dass wir unseren Hochgenauigkeitsanspruch übertragen konnten in den Bereich der großen Werkzeugmaschinen, die bis zu 17 Meter lange Teile bearbeiten können", sagt Geschäftsführer Dr.-Ing. Horst Hermsdorf.

Ein weiteres Beispiel für sächsische Innovationskraft: Ende 2011 nahm der Schlachthof in Zürich eine „thermeco2" in Betrieb. Diese CO_2-Wärmepumpenanlage stammt aus der thermea. Energiesysteme GmbH in Freital. Sie hat diese weltweit neue Generation von Wärmepumpen, die den Arbeitsstoff CO_2 verwendet, gemeinsam mit dem Dresdner Institut für Luft- und Kältetechnik erfunden.

Neugersdorf means something to Ford, BMW, Volvo and Rolls-Royce as the home to MBN Maschinenbaubetriebe Neugersdorf GmbH. The firm exports vehicle assembly plants all over the world. The finishing line for the VW Phaeton in the Dresden factory comes from here. The big breakthrough came in 1991. Ernst Lieb, a businessman from near Wolfsburg, founded the company from the legacy of the GDR textile machine collective. "There were plenty of well trained, skilled workers around, giving us the foundation we needed", he remembers. Quality and qualification go hand in hand for Ernst Lieb, who has 45 trainees and apprentices among his 230 employees.

Karl May and von Ardenne

The König & Bauer Group – second largest printing press manufacturer in the world – anounces a superlative on its website: "The new Rapida 105 – the most advanced machine of its class." The medium format sheet offset printing press has dominated the market for years and has now been given a design remake, including a new gripper system. This new feature is made in Radebeul near Dresden, where 1,600 employees produce the sheet offset presses in the successful Rapida series. The first printing presses were being made here already back in 1898, when German author Karl May still lived and wrote in Dresden. The current factory is the successor to Planeta Radebeul, the largest printing press manufacturer in the GDR.

The name "von Ardenne" stands for Saxony's inventive spirit. Manfred von Ardenne acquired around 600 patents during the 20th century, many during his period in Dresden since 1955. His private research institute was the largest of its kind in the Eastern Bloc. 1991 then saw the birth of VON ARDENNE Anlagentechnik GmbH as a spin-off from the Ardenne Institute, thanks to the determined motivation of 67 employees. Since then, the workforce has increased nearly tenfold. The firm keeps the famous name and upholds the values associated with it: scientific curiosity, constant search for innovative solutions, quality awareness, sustainable approach and reliability.

In 2011, the German newspaper "Die Welt" published a study putting the 100 best of 1,600 German SME businesses in order of preference. The ranking was based on "constant top performance, corporate perspicacity and staying power". The firm from Dresden came in twelfth. It stands out on a global scale with its plasma and electron beam technologies. Vacuum coating equipment for photovoltaic applications that convert light into electricity permits new uses of sunlight. Other systems apply thin layers to architectural glass in order to improve the heat insulation of glazed buildings, thus saving energy.

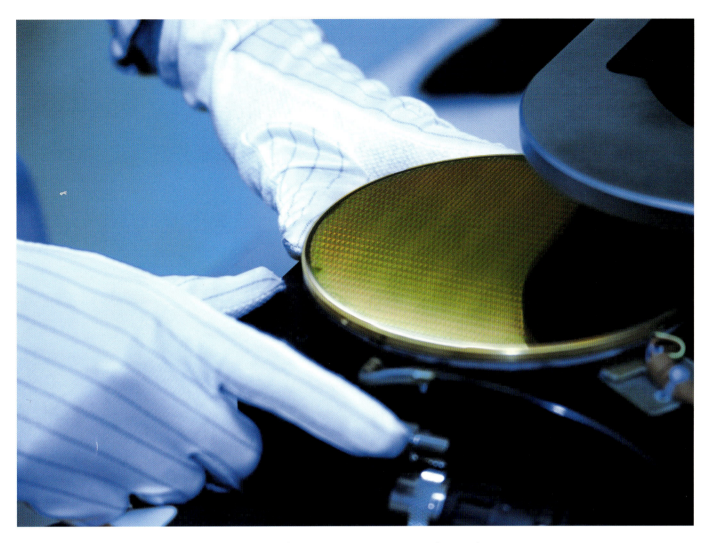

Sachsen ist das Zentrum der europäischen Chip-Herstellung. Das Bild zeigt einen sogenannten Wafer. Die polykristallinen (Halbleiter)-Rohlinge sind die Basis für Mikrochips.

Saxony is the centre of European chip-manufacturing. This image shows a so-called wafer. The polycrystalline (semi-conductor)-blanks form the basis for microchips.

Genau richtig: Mikroelektronik und Informationstechnologie

„AMD zieht sich aus Dresdner Chip-Werk zurück." Unter dieser Überschrift berichtete die „Sächsische Zeitung" am 6. März 2012 über den Abschied des US-Herstellers von seiner hiesigen Fertigungstochter. AMD gebe seinen noch verbliebenen 8,6-Prozent-Anteil an GLOBALFOUNDRIES ab, alleiniger Eigentümer sei damit Advanced Technology Investment Company (ATIC) aus Abu Dhabi aus den Vereinigten Arabischen Emiraten. „Das schafft mehr Flexibilität für beide Unternehmen", zitierte die Zeitung den AMD-Vorstandschef Thomas Seifert. Der Kontakt bleibe jedoch erhalten: „AMD plant in diesem Jahr, für rund 1,1 Mrd. Euro Wafer bei GLOBALFOUNDRIES zu kaufen, die in Dresden hergestellt werden."

Automatic, fast and precise

Confidence in their own capabilities and a willingness to take risks – that's what it took in 1990 when eleven stalwarts from the state-owned Robotron-Messelektronik Dresden set up their own company from the collective's rationalisation toolmaking division. XENON Automatisierungstechnik GmbH is meanwhile a specialist of international renown. More than 130 employees plan, develop and produce machinery and equipment for tailor-made automation of customer manufacturing processes. In 2011, XENON received Saxony's Innovation Prize for the highly adaptable 3-D assembly line for motorbike switches.

Sweets are what it's all about at Theegarten-Pactec GmbH & Co. KG in Dresden. No-one else can wrap sweets as quickly as their machines. The family company with 300 employees is one of the leading manufacturers of packing machines. The name combines decades of tradition from west and east, one from Cologne, the other from Dresden. Since 1997, the firm has been concentrating all its production activities in Dresden. At shows and trade fairs, they like to demonstrate their leading position when it comes to machines for small-sized sweets, including the new MCH model that packs up to 1,000 jelly items per minute.

In der Mikroelektronik ist viel in Bewegung. Und sie bewegt viel. Ihr Einsatzgebiet scheint grenzenlos, ihr Markt unersättlich. Die miniaturisierten elektronischen Schaltungen, die auf Halbleitern – vorrangig Silicium – basieren, sind in alle Lebensbereiche eingezogen. Auf einer Siliciumscheibe können Millionen von Transistoren untergebracht werden. Sie vervollständigen sich zu einem integrierten Schaltkreis, dem Chip.

Jeder zweite Chip, der in Europa gefertigt wird, kommt aus Sachsen. Anders gesagt: Sachsen ist die Chipwerkstatt Europas. Unterstützt von Politik und öffentlicher Hand sind leistungsfähige Ansiedlungen gelungen. Der Kammerbezirk Dresden ist ein Kerngebiet des Know-hows. Rund 290 Unternehmen – davon etwa die Hälfte in Dresden – vertreten diese Schlüsseltechnologie. 30 von ihnen haben 50 und mehr Mitarbeiter, insgesamt über 10 000. Allein diese Gruppe setzt jährlich 2,8 Mrd. Euro um, gut 60 Prozent des gesamten Zweiges in Sachsen.

Von Silicon Valley zu Silicon Saxony

Silicium – englisch Silicon – mit der Ordnungszahl 14 im Periodensystem der Elemente hat Karriere gemacht. Als Halbleiterwerkstoff und Namenspatron. Dem Gebiet südlich der San Francisco-Bucht gab 1971 ein Journalist den Namen „Silicon Valley", wimmelte es doch dort vor Halbleiter-Forschern und -Firmen. Der Begriff wurde zum Synonym für die US-Elektronik- und Computerindustrie. Zum Silicium-Tal gesellte sich um 2000 das Silicium-Sachsen. Selbstbewusst gab sich ein Verein den Namen Silicon Saxony e. V. Ihm gehören 300 Hersteller, Zulieferer, Dienstleister, Hochschulen, Forschungsinstitute und öffentliche Einrichtungen an. Der Verein teilt das positive Schicksal seines Vorbilds: Sein Name kombiniert Weltoffenheit, Modernität und Regionalbezug und kennzeichnet treffend Sachsens geballte Hightechkompetenz überhaupt.

„Silicon Saxony" ist Europas größter Cluster der Mikro- und Nanoelektronik-, Software-, Fotovoltaik- und Mikrosystemindustrien. Weltweit gehört er zu den Top Five. Die Konkurrenz ist in Kalifornien, Nordamerika und Südostasien zu Hause. Auf allen Stufen der Wertschöpfungskette sind in der sächsischen Informations- und Kommunikationstechnologie 1500 Unternehmen mit mehr als 43 000 Mitarbeitern tätig. Kerngebiet ist die Landeshauptstadt mit hoher Firmenkonzentration und einschlägiger Tradition.

Große Männer und ein Kürzel

Zu den Stammvätern der Elektronik zählt der Physiker Heinrich Barkhausen. Er hatte ab 1911 an der TU Dresden das Institut für Schwachstromtechnik aufgebaut, das erste in Deutschland. Er forschte und lehrte zu den Grundlagen der Telefonie und Telegrafie, später verfasste er grundlegende Arbeiten zu Elektronenröhren. Heute vergibt die Fakultät für Elektrotechnik und Informationstechnik der TU Dresden alljährlich den Heinrich-Barkhausen-Preis.

Fortsetzung Seite 64

Mikromat GmbH in Dresden swears by the "productive µ". The twelfth letter in the Greek alphabet stands for micro, which is one millionth. This is the scale in which Mikromat thinks, designs and produces. The products enable customers to produce items with the greatest of precision in the complete working area of a machine. The customer base includes the automotive sector and the aviation industry. In 2011 it received the "intec Prize" from Leipzig Trade Fair for a pièce de resistance: its precision portal drilling/milling machine 40V. "The special thing about this machine is that we have been able to transfer our high-precision quality standard to the large-scale machine tool sector for processing parts measuring up to 17 metres in length", says Managing Director Dr.-Ing. Horst Hermsdorf.

Yet another example for Saxony's innovation powers: at the end of 2011, Zurich abattoir started operations with a "thermeco2". This CO_2 heat pump system came from thermea. Energiesysteme GmbH in Freital. The firm worked together with the Dresden Institute of Air Handling and Refrigeration to develop this new generation of heat pumps working with carbon dioxide.

Big winner: Microelectronics and information technology

"AMD pulls out of Dresden chip factory." This heading in the Sächsische Zeitung on 6 March 2012 told the city that the US manufacturer was taking leave of its local manufacturing subsidiary. AMD renounced its remaining 8.6 percent share in GLOBALFOUNDRIES, leaving Advanced Technology Investment Company (ATIC) from Abu Dhabi in the United Arab Emirates as the sole proprietor. "This gives greater flexibility to both companies" is how the newspaper quoted AMD Chairman Thomas Seifert. However, a certain contact would remain: "This year, AMD plans to buy wafers for around 1.1 billion Euro from GLOBALFOUNDRIES, which will be made in Dresden."

The microelectronic sector is constantly on the move. It gets things moving too. There are practically no limits to its possible applications and its market seems insatiable. The miniaturised electronic circuits based on semiconductors, mainly silicon, have become an integral part of all ways of life. Millions of transistors fit on a silicon wafer to form an integrated circuit or chip.

Every second chip made in Europe comes from Saxony. In other words, Saxony is Europe's chip workshop. Efficient sites have become established, with support from the political sector and public bodies. The Dresden chamber district has become a key area for chip know-how, with around 290 companies (about half of them in Dresden) involved in this key technology. 30 of them have 50 and more employees with a total workforce of more than 10,000. This group alone generates annual turnover of 2.8 billion Euro, a good 60 percent of the total branch in Saxony.

Continued on page 64

SMT & HYBRID GmbH

Information

Gründungsjahr: 1990

Mitarbeiter: ca. 130

Umsatz 2011:
rund 21,5 Mio. Euro

Leistungsspektrum:
Entwicklung und Fertigung elektronischer Baugruppen für verschiedenste Anwendungen aus den Branchen Industrie, Verkehr, Medizin und Automotive

Zertifizierungen:
Qualitätssicherung nach
· ISO 9001:2008
· ISO/TS 16949:2009
· ISO 14001:2004

Year founded: 1990

Employees: approx. 130

Turnover 2011: around 21.5 million Euro

Range of services: development and production of electronic components for many different applications in industry, traffic, medicine and automotive engineering

Certification:
quality assurance certified to
· ISO 9001:2008
· ISO/TS 16949:2009
· ISO 14001:2004

SMT & HYBRID GmbH, Dresden

SMT & HYBRID GmbH

Der inhabergeführte EMS-Dienstleister (Auftragsfertiger und Auftragsentwickler für kundenspezifische elektronische Produkte) SMT & HYBRID wurde 1990 gegründet und ist einer der Mitbegründer von Dresdens Ruf als Zentrum der deutschen Elektronik- und Halbleiterindustrie. Das Kundenspektrum umfasst die Bereiche Industrie, Verkehr, Medizin und Automotive. Am Standort Dresden ist das Unternehmen sehr eng vernetzt in der Forschung. Ein hoch qualifiziertes Expertenteam arbeitet Hand in Hand mit Universitäten und Hochschulen und hebt die Entwicklung in der Elektroniktechnologie stets auf den neuesten Stand von Wissenschaft und Technik.

SMT & HYBRID GmbH produziert ausschließlich mit modernster technologischer Ausrüstung auf höchstem Qualitäts- und Fertigungsniveau. Ziel ist dabei stets, dem Kunden bei maximaler Flexibilität eine individuelle Produktion jenseits starrer Großserien zu garantieren, um langfristige und partnerschaftliche Geschäftsbeziehungen aufzubauen. Bestückt werden SMD- und THD-Bauelemente in verschiedenen Bauformen auf FR4, Flex-, Starr-Flex-, Keramik- und Metallkernleiterplatten.

SMT & HYBRID GmbH

The proprietor-run EMS service provider SMT & HYBRID (contract manufacturer and contract developer for customised electronic products) was founded in 1990 and is one of the co-founders of Dresden's reputation as Germany's electronic and semiconductor centre. The client base extends from industry, traffic and medicine to automotive engineering. Here in Dresden, the company is closely involved in the technology research network. A highly qualified team of experts works hand-in-hand with university research institutions, keeping developments in electronic technology in line with state-of-the-art science and technology.

Baugruppen im Produktionsprozess

Components in the production process

SMT & HYBRID GmbH produces only with ultra-modern technology equipment to the very highest quality and production standards. The aim is always to guarantee maximum flexibility for the customer together with individual production beyond rigid bulk series, in the interests of long-term business relations working together as partners. SMD and THD components are mounted in various designs on FR4, flexible, flex-rigid, ceramic and metal-core circuit boards.

ADZ NAGANO GmbH
Gesellschaft für Sensortechnik

Dresden, die sächsische Metropole am östlichen Ende der Autobahn 4 bezeichnet sich als das größte Halbleiterzentrum in Europa und fünfwichtigster Standort auf der Welt. Hier gründeten die beiden ehemaligen Mitarbeiter des Forschungszentrums Mikroelektronik Dresden (ZMD) Dietmar Arndt und Wolfgang Dürfeld 1998 zusammen mit zwei Geschäftsfreunden die ADZ Sensortechnik.

Erste Produkte waren Drucktransmitter für industrielle Anwendungen. Die verwendete Technologie führte zu qualitativ hochwertigen Produkten, die sich schnell am Markt einen Namen machten. Die sogenannte SML Baureihe wird mit verschiedenen Ausgangssignalen geliefert.

Die von ADZ NAGANO produzierte, technisch ausgereifte und robuste Sensorik wird weltweit in verschiedensten industriellen Anwendungen eingesetzt. Sensoren sind die Sinne automatisierter Anlagen und Maschinen. Sie spielen eine wesentliche Rolle, wenn es darum geht, qualitativ hochwertige Produkte herzustellen oder Maschinen zuverlässig und sicher zu betreiben. Das junge, mittelständische Unternehmen entwickelt schwerpunktmäßig kundenspezifische Lösungen aus dem Bereich Druckmesstechnik. Heute beschäftigt die ADZ NAGANO GmbH am Firmenstandort Ottendorf-Okrilla nördlich von Dresden fast 100 Mitarbeiter. Davon sind allein zwölf in der Entwicklung tätig. Hier werden mit viel Kreativität und Ideenreichtum nicht nur individuelle Kundenlösungen realisiert, sondern auch neue Standardprodukte auf dem aktuellen Stand der Technik zur Fertigungsreife gebracht.

Kunden aus der Prozesstechnik, der Automobilindustrie und allen Bereichen, in denen pneumatische und hydraulische Anlagen eingesetzt werden, vertrauen auf Lösungen von ADZ NAGANO. Auch die technisch anspruchsvolle Luftfahrtindustrie setzt auf Produkte des sächsischen Sensorik-Spezialisten.

Jährlich verlassen mehrere Hunderttausend Drucktransmitter in 3000 verschiedenen Varianten die Produktion zu Kunden in aller Welt. Von Asien über Europa bis nach Amerika sind immer mehr Anwender von den Produkten von ADZ NAGANO überzeugt.

ADZ NAGANO GmbH
Gesellschaft für Sensortechnik

Dresden, Saxony's metropolis at the eastern end of the A 4 motorway, is said to be Europe's largest semiconductor centre and the world's fifth key semiconductor location. This is where ADZ Sensortechnik was founded in 1998 by Dietmar Arndt and Wolfgang Dürfeld, two former employees of Dresden's microelectronic research centre ZMD (Zentrum Mikroelektronik Dresden), together with two business friends.

The first products consisted of pressure transmitters for industrial applications. The technology that was used led to top quality products which soon made a name for themselves on the market. The so-called SML series is supplied with various output signals.

The technically mature, robust sensors produced by ADZ NAGANO are used all over the world in many different industrial applications. Sensors are the sensory organs of automated plants and machinery. They play a crucial role when it comes to making top quality products or ensuring reliable, safe operation of machines. Development work in the young SME company focuses primarily on customised solutions for pressure measuring technology. Today, ADZ NAGANO GmbH has a workforce of nearly 100 employees at the company site in Ottendorf-Okrilla to the north of Dresden, including a development team of twelve. This is where not only individual customised solutions are produced, but where new standard products are also designed in accordance with state-of-the-art technology.

Customers in process engineering, the automotive industry and all sectors using pneumatic and hydraulic systems have come to place their trust in solutions by ADZ NAGANO. The technologically challenging aerospace industry also advocates products by Saxony's sensory specialists.

Every year, several hundred thousand pressure transmitters in 3,000 different variants are supplied to customers all over the world. From Asia via Europe to America, increasing numbers of users are convinced by the ADZ NAGANO products.

Dresden ist eines der weltweit bedeutendsten Zentren der Halbleiterbranche.

Dresden is one of the world's main centres for the semiconductor branch.

Information

Gründungsjahr: 1998

Mitarbeiter: etwa 100

Produktspektrum:
· Drucktransmitter
· Druckschalter
· Durchflussmesser
· kundenspezifische Entwicklungen

Einsatzgebiete:
· Mobilhydraulik
· Industrietechnik
· Fahrzeugtechnik
· Luft- und Raumfahrttechnik
· Klima- und Kältetechnik
· Umwelttechnik
u. a.

Year founded: 1998

Employees: about 100

Product range:
· pressure transmitters
· pressure switches
· flowmeters
· customised developments

Applications:
· mobile hydraulics
· industrial technology
· vehicle engineering
· aerospace engineering
· air-conditioning and refrigeration technology
· environmental technology
and much more besides

ADZ NAGANO GmbH
Gesellschaft für Sensortechnik
Ottendorf-Okrilla

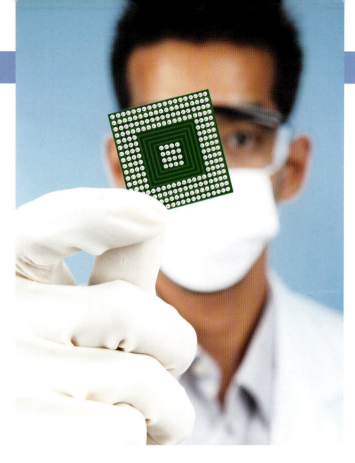

Die Forschung und Entwicklung in der Mikroelektronik hat in Sachsen eine lange Tradition und ist ein Baustein dafür, dass die Region heute in der Branche unter dem Namen Silicon Saxony bekannt ist.

Research and development in the field of microelectronics has a long tradition in Saxony, and it is one of the building blocks that has contributed to the region becoming known in the branch as Silicon Saxony.

Ein weiterer Wegbereiter: 1961 gründete Physiker Werner Hartmann im Regierungsauftrag die Arbeitsstelle für Molekularelektronik (AME). Er gilt als Vater der DDR-Mikroelektronik. Über Zwischenstufen wuchs die AME zum Forschungszentrum Mikroelektronik Dresden (ZMD) mit 3000 Beschäftigten heran. 1988 präsentierte es den „U61000". So hieß der erste 1-Megabit-Speicherchip der DDR. Das erste funktionsfähige Muster verwahrt heute das Deutsche Museum Bonn.

Mit dem Kürzel ZMD verbindet sich inzwischen marktwirtschaftlicher Langzeiterfolg. Die Forscher und Praktiker brachten ihre Fähigkeit zu kreativen Lösungen in das neue Wirtschaftssystem ein. Die Staatsregierung förderte den Überlebenswillen. Heute gehört die Zentrum Mikroelektronik Dresden AG (ZMDI) zu den Schwergewichten in Silicon Saxony. Übrigens, auch weitere Ausgründungen des Ursprungsinstituts haben es in die Mikroelektronik-Elite Sachsens geschafft.

Weltweite Gießereien?

Das Wort Gießerei weist nicht auf einen Mikroelektronik-Riesen hin, seine englische Entsprechung „foundry" schon eher. Sie wird für Halbleiterwerke verwendet, die im Auftrag mikroelektronische Bauelemente herstellen. Die GLOBALFOUNDRIES Inc. in Dresden ist mit rund 3700 Mitarbeitern solch ein Auftragsfertiger. Und ein Wachstumsunternehmen, wie eine Pressemitteilung der EU-Kommission von 2011 belegt: „Die Kommission hat ein Regionalbeihilfepaket in Höhe von 219 Mio. Euro für ein mit rund 2 Mrd. Euro ausgestattetes Investitionsvorhaben von GLOBALFOUNDRIES genehmigt. Mit der Investition im sächsischen Dresden sollen die bestehenden Anlagen des Unternehmens, mit denen bislang nur Computer-Mikroprozessoren für AMD (Advanced Micro Devices) hergestellt werden konnten, auf die Produktion aller Arten von Halbleiterwafern

From Silicon Valley to Silicon Saxony

The element silicon with atomic number 14 in the periodic table has made a name for itself, and not just as a semiconductor material. In 1971, a journalist coined the name "Silicon Valley" for the area south of San Francisco Bay on account of the many semiconductor activities and firms based there. The expression became synonymous with the electronic and computer industry in the USA. By around 2000, Silicon Valley was joined by Silicon Saxony: an association confidently gave itself the name Silicon Saxony e. V. It includes 300 manufacturers, suppliers, universities, research institutes and public institutions. The association shares the positive fate of its role model: its name combines a cosmopolitan, modern approach with regional links, appropriately conjuring up all of Saxony's high-tech expertise.

Silicon Saxony is Europe's largest cluster for the micro- and nanoelectronic industries together with the software, photovoltaic and microsystem sectors. It is one of the Top Five in the world, facing competition in California, North America and Southeast Asia. Right across the supply chain, the information and communication technology industry in Saxony has 1,500 companies with more than 43,000 employees, focused on the state capital with a high concentration of companies offering a wealth of relevant tradition.

Great men and an abbreviation

Physicist Heinrich Barkhausen is one of the fathers of electronics. In 1911, he set up the Institute for Weak Current Engineering at TU Dresden, the first of its kind in Germany. His remit included teaching and research into the principles of telephony and telegraphy; later he wrote fundamental papers on electron tubes. Today, the Faculty for Electrical and Computer Engineering at TU Dresden awards the Heinrich Barkhausen Prize every year.

Another pioneer: in 1961, physicist Werner Hartmann was instructed by the government to set up the Arbeitsstelle für Molekularelektronik (AME – Department for Molecular Electronics). He is known as the father of microelectronics in the GDR. The AME went through various stages of development to become the Research Centre Microelectronics Dresden (ZMD) with 3,000 employees. In 1988 it presented the "U61000". That was the first 1-megabit memory chip in the GDR. The first functional specimen is kept today by Deutsches Museum Bonn.

umgestellt werden." Kurz gesagt: Bis 2013 entsteht in Dresden Europas größtes Halbleiterwerk.

Die Fab 1 (Fabrication Plant) – innerhalb eines Netzwerkes mit Chip-Fabriken in Singapur und den USA – zählt schon jetzt zu den erfolgreichsten Werken für innovative Halbleitertechnologien. Sie produziert 200- und 300-Millimeter-Wafer. Diese Silicium-„Waffeln" tragen die integrierten Schaltkreise. Je größer der Wafer, desto mehr Platz für elektronische Bauteile.

Die Dresdner Fab wird um einen 10 000-Quadratmeter-Reinraum erweitert. Damit steigt es zur ersten Gigafab Europas auf. Sie ermöglicht monatlich bis zu 80 000 Waferstarts bei den 300-Millimeter-Scheiben („Pizza-Wafer"). In den Standort am Flughafen sind bereits Milliarden geflossen. Den Grundstein legte der kalifornische Hersteller AMD 1999 mit dem ersten und 2005 mit dem zweiten Werk. 2009 übernahm GLOBALFOUNDRIES die Fertigungsstätten.

Start, Rückschlag, Weltspitze

Nachbar ist ein weiterer Riese: Infineon Technologies Dresden. Der Halbleiterhersteller mit 1900 Mitarbeitern gehört zur weltweit tätigen bayerischen Infineon Technologies AG. Der Name verbindet das englische „infinity" für Grenzenlosigkeit mit dem griechischen „aeon" für Leben und Ewigkeit. Die Wurzeln der Ansiedlung reichen bis 1994 zurück, als die Siemens AG die Stadt Dresden als Zukunftsstandort erkannte. Aus ihrer Halbleitersparte ging 1999 Infineon hervor. Schon kurz darauf trumpfte der Namensneuling als weltweit Erster mit der 300-Millimeter-Technologie und einem entsprechenden Werk auf. 2006 wurde die Speicherchipsparte ausgegliedert und als Qimonda-Konzern mit Qimonda Dresden weitergeführt. Mit dessen Insolvenz 2009 durch rasanten Preisverfall auf dem Weltmarkt ging zugleich der größte private Arbeitgeber im Raum Dresden zu Boden.

Infineon Dresden stellt heute auf Basis von 220-Millimeter-Siliciumscheiben hochwertige und innovative Logikchips her. Diese Schaltkreise speichern und verarbeiten Informationen. Mit Strukturen von 0,25 Mikrometer bis 90 Nanometer deckt das Werk ein großes Technologie- und Produktspektrum mit kundenspezifischen Lösungen ab. Es ist der weltweit zweitgrößte Chiphersteller für die Automobilelektronik und führt bei den Sicherheitsanwendungen wie für Kredit- und Zugangskarten.

Ein quirliges Taubennest

Alt-Ministerpräsidenten Kurt Biedenkopf wird der Satz zugesprochen: „Wo Tauben sind, fliegen Tauben hin." Tatsächlich hat sich Dresden auf diese Weise zum Wachstumskern entwickelt. Ingenieurpotenzial, Lage und Liebreiz zogen – neben milliardenschweren Förderpaketen – die Großen an. Ihr Aufstieg ließ andere wachsen. „Die Geschäftsfelder der ansässigen Firmen umfassen die vollständige Wertschöpfungskette von der Chipherstellung bis hin zu Produkten der Anwenderindustrie. Darüber hinaus begünstigt dieses breite Spektrum von Unter-

The abbreviation ZMD is meanwhile associated with long-term market economy success. The researchers and practitioners contributed their skills to producing creative solutions in the new economic system. The state government fostered their will to survive. Today, ZMDI (Zentrum Mikroelektronik Dresden AG) is one of the heavyweights in Silicon Saxony. By the way, other spin-offs from the original institute have also joined Saxony's microelectronic elite.

Global foundries?

The word foundry does not necessarily make you think of microelectronics. But in this day and age, foundry also refers to semiconductor factories for contract production of microelectronic components. GLOBALFOUNDRIES Inc. in Dresden with 3,700 employees is one such contract manufacturer – and a growth company as well, as confirmed by a press release issued by the EU Commission in 2011: "The Commission has approved of a regional aid package amounting to 219 million Euro for an investment project worth around 2 billion Euro by GLOBALFOUNDRIES. The investment in Dresden, Saxony, is intended to change the company's production facilities, hitherto capable only of producing computer microprocessors for AMD (Advanced Micro Devices), so that they can be used to produce all kinds of semiconductor wafers." In other words: by 2013, Dresden will be hope to Europe's largest semiconductor factory.

Fab 1 (Fabrication Plant) – part of a network with chip factories in Singapore and the USA – is already one of the most successful facilities for innovative semiconductor technologies. It produces 200 and 300 millimetre wafers. These silicon wafers carry the integrated circuits. The larger the wafers, the more space for electronic components.

A 10,000 square metre clean room is being added to Dresden's Fab, making it the first Gigafab in Europe. Every month it will be used for up to 80,000 wafer starts for the 300 millimetre "pizza" wafers. Billions have already been ploughed into the site near the airport. The corner stone for the first fab was laid in 1999 by the Californian manufacturer AMD, followed by the second fab in 2005. The production sites were taken over by GLOBALFOUNDRIES in 2009.

Start, setback, best in the world

There's another giant just next door: Infineon Technologies Dresden. The semiconductor manufacturer with 1,900 employees belongs to the Bavarian global player Infineon Technologies AG. The name combines infinity with the Greek word "aeon" for life and eternity. The roots go back to 1994, when Siemens AG saw Dresden's potential as a future site. Its semiconductor division became Infineon in 1999. Only just afterwards, the new name was the first company in the world to use the 300 millimetre technology together with a corresponding factory. In 2006, the memory chip division was hived off and continued at

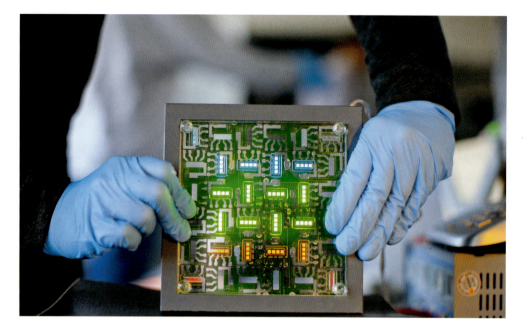

Grüne Technologie für ultraflache Bildschirme und transparente Leuchten – hocheffiziente OLEDs mit Novaled-Material und Know-how

Green technology for ultra-flatscreen monitors and transparent luminaires – highly-efficient OLEDs with Novaled material and know-how

nehmen ganz unterschiedlicher Größe den Austausch von Know-how sowie die Vernetzung der Service- und Lieferbeziehungen", heißt es in der städtischen Broschüre „Vernetztes Denken".

Heute schon mobil telefoniert? An innovativen Mobilfunklösungen der Zukunft forscht der Weltkonzern Intel in Dresden. Die Niederlassung an der neuen Waldschlößchenbrücke – bundesweit bekanntes Streitobjekt und ingenieurtechnische Meisterleistung gleichermaßen – ging aus einem kleinen Start-up-Unternehmen hervor. Dessen Kompetenz für die neue Datenfunktechnik LTE (Long Term Evolution) fließt jetzt bei erhöhter Mitarbeiterzahl in die neue Generation der Mobilfunktechnik des weltgrößten Halbleiterherstellers ein.

Heute schon mit dem Auto gefahren? Der Mittelständler SAW Components Dresden GmbH mit 25 Mitarbeitern gehört zur Spitzengruppe bei mikromechanischen SAW-Bauelementen (Surface Acoustic Wave). Wöchentlich verlassen drei Millionen dieser Chips das Werk. Als Filter und Resonatoren werden sie in drahtlosen Geräten angewendet, beispielsweise in Autoschlüsseln und Funkuhren.

Heute schon Fernsehen geschaut? Bildschirme, Displays, Lichtquellen – bei diesen Produkten ist die organische Leuchtdiode, kurz OLED, auf dem Vormarsch. Die organischen halbleitenden Materialien auf hauchdünnem Trägermaterial wie Glas oder Folie ermöglichen zukünftig den biegsamen Bildschirm oder die transparente Lichtquelle. Die Novaled AG in Dresden ist ein führendes Unternehmen im OLED-Bereich. Mit ihren Erfindungen – über 500 Patente sind bewilligt oder beantragt – treibt die junge Firma die Organische Elektronik weltweit voran. 2011 erhielten die Novaled Gründer den Deutschen Zukunftspreis. Novaled's Technologien und Materialien machen OLEDs langlebiger und effizienter im Energieverbrauch.

Fortsetzung Seite 69

the Dresden site with Qimonda Dresden as the Qimonda Group. When Qimonda went bankrupt in 2009 on account of the rapid price decline on the world market, the largest private employer in the Dresden region had gone to pieces.

Today, Infineon Dresden produces top quality, innovative logic chips based on 220 millimetre silicon wafers. These circuits save and process information. The company offers structures from 0.25 micrometres to 90 nanometres, covering a broad range of technology and products with specific customised solutions. This is the world's second largest chip manufacturer for automotive electronics and also plays a leading role in security applications and for credit and access cards.

Lively nest of pigeons

Former Minister-President Kurt Biedenkopf is supposed to have said "Pigeons will gather where pigeons have settled." Actually, this is the approach with which Dresden has become a growth centre. Together with weighty funding packages worth billions, engineering potential, location and charm attracted the big names. Their success let others grow. "The areas of business offered by local firms cover the entire supply chain from chip production through to products for the user industry. Furthermore, this wide range of companies of all different sizes encourages the sharing of know-how and the networking of service and supplier relations", as described in the city brochure "Networked Thinking".

Used your mobile yet today? Global player Intel in Dresden is researching into innovative mobile communications solutions for tomorrow. The company's branch next to the new Waldschlößchenbrücke – object of national dispute and engineering masterpiece at the same time – emerged from a small start-up company. The firm's expertise in the new LTE (Long Term

Continued on page 69

Infineon Technologies Dresden GmbH

Information

Gründungsjahr: 1994

Mitarbeiter:
über 2000

Produkte:
innovative Halbleiter- und Systemlösungen, die drei zentrale Herausforderungen der modernen Gesellschaft bedienen:
· Energieeffizienz
· Mobilität
· Sicherheit

Investitionen:
über 3 Mrd. Euro seit der Gründung

Year founded: 1994

Employees:
more than 2,000

Products:
innovative semiconductor and system solutions addressing the three central challenges of modern society:
· energy efficiency
· mobility
· security

Investment:
more than 3 billion Euro since the company was founded

Infineon Technologies Dresden GmbH
Dresden

Seit der Gründung im Jahr 1994 wurden in Dresden über 3 Mrd. Euro investiert.

More than 3 billion Euro have been invested in Dresden since the company was founded in 1994.

Infineon Technologies Dresden GmbH

Die Infineon Technologies Dresden GmbH ist einer der größten Fertigungsstandorte der Infineon Technologies AG – Deutschlands größtes Halbleiterunternehmen mit Hauptsitz in München und weltweit rund 25 000 Mitarbeitern.

In Dresden werden über 200 verschiedene Produkte für innovative Automobilelektronik-, Sicherheits- und Chipkarten- sowie für Power Management- und Multimarketanwendungen hergestellt. Jede Woche durchlaufen Tausende von Siliziumscheiben (Wafer) die hochkomplexe Fertigung in den Reinsträumen.

Bei der Entwicklung und Produktion sind die über 2000 Mitarbeiter wichtigstes Kapital und zugleich wesentliche Voraussetzung für den nachhaltigen Unternehmenserfolg. Schon heute ist Infineon Dresden ein Leuchtturm der Wirtschaftsregion Sachsen, künftig wird das Werk der weltweit erste Standort für die Hochvolumenproduktion von Leistungshalbleitern auf Basis von 300-mm-Wafern sein. Damit beginnt ein neues Kapitel mit großem Zukunftspotenzial für den Standort Dresden.

Auf jeder Scheibe hochreinen Siliziums werden in den Reinsträumen gleichzeitig Tausende von Chips hergestellt.

Thousands of chips are manufactured simultaneously on every silicon wafer in the clean rooms.

Infineon Technologies Dresden GmbH

Infineon Technologies Dresden GmbH is one of the largest production sites of Infineon Technologies AG – Germany's largest semiconductor company with headquarters in Munich and around 25,000 employees worldwide.

The Dresden site manufactures more than 200 different products for innovative automotive electronics, security and chip cards, power management and multi-market applications. Every week, thousands of wafers pass through the highly complex manufacturing process in the clean rooms.

The human resources consisting of more than 2,000 employees are the key capital in development and production and the prime prerequisite for sustainable corporate success. Today already, Infineon Dresden is a lighthouse in the Economic Region Saxony; in future, the factory will be the world's first site for high-volume production of power semiconductors based on 300 mm wafers, thus opening a new chapter with great future potential for the Dresden site.

www.infineon.com

PRETTL Electronics AG

Information

Gründungsjahr: 2000

Mitarbeiter: insgesamt 750

Leistungsspektrum: Entwicklung und Fertigung von elektronischen Baugruppen und Komplettsystemen für die Bereiche Medizin, industrielle Anwendungen bis hin zu Applikationen für Automotive und Telekommunikation

Year founded: 2000

Employees: altogether 750

Range of services: development and production of electronic components and complete systems for medical technology and industrial applications through to automotive and telecommunications engineering

PRETTL Electronics AG Radeberg

SMD-Bestückung

SMD mounting

PRETTL Electronics AG

Vom Konzept bis zur Serienreife entwickelt und produziert PRETTL kundenspezifische elektronische Baugruppen und Geräte und blickt dabei auf eine über 10-jährige Vergangenheit als Elektronikfertiger zurück.

Die PRETTL Electronics AG (vormals PRETTL Elektronik Radeberg GmbH) wurde in ihrer heutigen Form im Jahr 2000 gegründet. Ihre Kernkompetenzen sind insbesondere im Hightechbereich die Entwicklung und Fertigung von Baugruppen, Geräten und Systemen der Telekommunikationstechnik, Automobiltechnik, Industrieelektronik, Medizintechnik sowie ein leistungsstarker Reparatur- und Servicebereich. Die lesswire AG als Tochter steht für die Entwicklung von (drahtloser) Kommunikationstechnik.

Außer am Hauptsitz in Radeberg ist PRETTL Electronics mit weiteren fünf Standorten in Lübeck und Berlin sowie in Ungarn, Mexiko und den USA präsent.

Mikroskoplöten

Microscopic soldering

PRETTL Electronics AG

From the initial concept through to the start of production, PRETTL develops and manufactures electronic components and devices, looking back on more than 10 years of company history as an electronic producer.

PRETTL Electronics AG (formerly PRETTL Elektronik Radeberg GmbH) in its current form was founded in 2000. In the high-tech sector, its core expertise consists particularly in the development and production of components, devices and systems for telecommunications, automotive engineering, industrial electronics and medical technology, together with a highly efficient repair and service division. The subsidiary lesswire AG stands for the development of (wireless) communications technology.

Together with company headquarters in Radeberg, PRETTL Electronics has another five sites in Lübeck and Berlin, Hungary, Mexico and the USA.

www.prettl-electronics.com

Jünger des Computererfinders

Konrad Zuse, der 1941 den ersten funktionstüchtigen Computer der Welt baute, streifte in seinem Leben auch die Oberlausitz. In Hoyerswerda legte er 1927 sein Abitur ab. Ein gutes Omen für die Informationstechnologie in diesem Landstrich. Die einheimische Marketinggesellschaft spricht von mehr als 450 ansässigen IT-Unternehmen von Softwareentwicklern, Ingenieurbüros und Webgestaltern über Systemhäuser bis zu weltweit agierenden Serviceunternehmen. Die Oberlausitz führt insbesondere ihre SAP-Kompetenz ins Feld. Das Kürzel bedeutet „Systeme, Anwendungen und Produkte in der Datenverarbeitung".

Firmen in Bautzen und Görlitz besitzen Zertifizierungen der SAP AG in Walldorf, dem drittgrößten unabhängigen Softwareanbieter der Welt. Die Oberlausitzer betreuen SAP-Anwender weltweit. Sie helfen mit ihren Lösungen, rentabel zu wirtschaften und nachhaltig zu wachsen. Bautzen ist Standort der Itelligence AG Bielefeld, die seit gut 20 Jahren Betrieben ganzheitliche Lösungen maßschneidert. Das Bautzener Unternehmen BIT betreut seit 2004 SAP-Kunden. Für die Cideon AG in Bautzen – deutsche Niederlassung des weltweiten Spezialisten für Engineering – sind kluge Köpfe sowohl in der einstigen Hauptstadt der Oberlausitz selbst als auch im nahen Görlitz tätig.

In Görlitz ist ebenso die eigentümergeführte Deutsche Software Engineering & Research GmbH zu Hause. Sie zählt zu den führenden europäischen Softwareanbietern für Finanzdienstleister. Dazu kooperiert sie mit der Hochschule Zittau/Görlitz. In Dresden und weit darüber hinaus ist „Robotron" ein Begriff. 1969 als zentrales ostdeutsches IT-Unternehmen gegründet und 1990 durch mutige Privatisierung mit 26 Mitarbeitern erhalten, ist die Robotron Datenbank-Software GmbH heute mit 230 Beschäftigten und fünf Tochterunternehmen in Europa ein strahlender Stern am IT-Himmel. Der Neuaufstieg verbindet sich eng mit Dr. Rolf Heinemann, zupackender und erfindungsreicher Chef vor und nach der Wende. Für sein Lebenswerk als IT-Wegbereiter wurde er 2010 zum „Unternehmer des Jahres" in Sachsen geehrt.

Der Kammerbezirk Dresden ist nicht allein mit seinen Firmen, sondern auch als Messestandort zum Schaufenster für Mikroelektronik und IT geworden: Die 1976 gegründete „SEMICON Europa" ist nach Genf, Zürich, München und Stuttgart 2009 nach Silicon Saxony übergesiedelt. Im Oktober 2012 findet die bedeutendste und größte europäische Halbleitermesse zum vierten Mal in Dresden statt.

Genau richtig:
Metallerzeugung und -verarbeitung

Das moderne Leben ist aus Metall gemacht. Es wird sogar als Mutter aller Sachwerte bezeichnet. Kein produzierender Industriezweig kommt ohne diese Werkstoffe aus. Die weltweite Nachfrage nach ihnen ist unermesslich. Selbst ein Musikstil

Evolution) data radio technology is now being used by a much larger workforce in the new generation of mobile communications technology at the world's largest semiconductor manufacturer.

Used your car yet today? The SME business SAW Components Dresden GmbH with 25 employees belongs to the leading group involved in micromechanical SAW (Surface Acoustic Wave) parts. Three million of these chips leave the factory every week. They are used as filters and resonators in wireless devices such as car keys and radio clocks.

Used your television yet today? Screens, displays, light sources – the OLED (organic light-emitting diode) is on the advance with all these products. The organic semiconductor materials on a wafer-thin flexible carrier permit pliable screens. Novaled AG in Dresden leads the world OLED market. The SME company with its wealth of inventions – more than 500 patents have been granted or applied for – drives organic electronics on into the future. In 2011 it was awarded the German Future Prize to-gether with partners. OLED technologies dramatically reduce energy consumption in the products and prolong the service life.

Disciples of the man who invented the computer

The life of Konrad Zuse, who invented the world's first functional computer in 1941, also touched on the Oberlausitz: it was in Hoyerswerda that he obtained his university entrance qualifications in 1927 – a good omen for information technology in this region. The local marketing company speaks of more than 450 IT companies based here, from software developers, engineering firms and web designers via system houses through to global service companies. In particular, the Oberlausitz has SAP expertise on offer: the abbreviation means "Systems, Applications and Products in data processing".

Companies in Bautzen and Görlitz are certified by SAP AG in Walldorf, the world's third largest independent software provider. The Oberlausitz service companies offer support for SAP users worldwide. Their solutions help clients to do profitable business with sustainable growth. Bautzen is a site of Itelligence AG Bielefeld with more than 20 years of experience in offering clients holistic customised solutions. The BIT company in Bautzen has been providing support for SAP customers since 2004. And Cideon AG in Bautzen, the German branch of the global engineering specialists, has clever minds working on its behalf both in the former capital of the Oberlausitz and in nearby Görlitz.

Görlitz is also home to the proprietor-led Deutsche Software Engineering & Research GmbH, one of Europe's leading software providers for the financial services industry. To this end, the company cooperates with Zittau/Görlitz University of Applied Sciences. Robotron is well-known in Dresden and way beyond. Founded in 1969 as the central East German IT company and kept alive in 1990 through courageous privatisation

bezieht Härte und Wucht ausdrücklich auf den Begriff: Heavy Metal. Power auch im Kammerbezirk Dresden: Die ansässige Metallindustrie erbringt mit 1,2 Mrd. Euro 40 Prozent des jährlichen Branchenumsatzes in Sachsen. In 65 mittelständischen Betrieben (ab 50 Mitarbeiter) arbeiten 7300 Beschäftigte.

In der Finanz- und Wirtschaftskrise zwischen 2008 und 2009 hatten sie den stärksten Einbruch zu verkraften. Der Umsatz sank auf 56 Prozent. Ein breites Produktspektrum und hohe Flexibilität der Firmen verhinderten Schlimmeres. Die Erholung ist noch nicht auf dem Vorkrisenniveau angekommen. Der Dachverband „Sachsenmetall" ist vorsichtig optimistisch. In neue Produkte und moderne Anlagen investieren, mit Hochschulen und Instituten kooperieren – darin sieht er die Wege, um international wettbewerbsfähig zu bleiben und Marktanteile hinzuzugewinnen.

Die Italiener an der Elbe

„Stahl Riesa", so heißt ein Fußballverein. Kürzer kann man auch das jahrzehntelange Profil der Elbestadt nicht fassen. Stahlproduktion, Stahlarbeiterstadt und Fußball bildeten eine Einheit. 16-mal spielte die BSG (Betriebssportgemeinschaft) in der höchsten DDR-Spielklasse. 2003 wurde sie als TSV (Traditionssportverein) wiedergeboren. Riesa ist weiterhin mit dem Stahl verbunden, aber nicht mehr ausschließlich. Den DDR-Mammutbetrieb mit 13 000 Beschäftigten hat die ESF Elbe-Stahlwerke Feralpi GmbH abgelöst, zugleich das größte Werk im weltweit tätigen italienischen Konzern Feralpi Stahl. 430 Mitarbeiter produzieren hochwertige Erzeugnisse, darunter Stranggussknüppel, Betonbandstahl und Walzdraht.

Die Italiener sind zu viert an der Elbe: Auch die Elbe-Drahtwerke Feralpi GmbH, die Feralpi-Logistik GmbH und die Feralpi Stahlhandel GmbH gehören zur Ansiedlung. Die Drahtwerker stellen Betonstahllagermatten, Betonstahllistenmatten und Gitterträger her, die Logistiker schaffen sie zu den Kunden. Vielen deutschen Bauwerken gibt Riesaer Stahl inneren Halt, darunter der Centrum-Galerie in Dresden und der Airbus-Montagehalle in Hamburg.

1843 errichteten die Brüder Schönberg das erste Eisenhüttenwerk in Riesa. Die Elbe und gute Bahnverbindungen machten es für die deutsche Schwerindustrie interessant. Von 1949 bis 1989 galt es als sozialistischer Vorzeigebetrieb. Die Italiener brachten ein neues Stahlzeitalter mit nach Riesa: Auf historischem Grund floss 1994 der erste Stahl in einer neuen Produktionsstätte, 1995 ging das Walzwerk mit jährlich 500 000 Tonnen Betonstahl in Betrieb. Bis heute entstand eine der modernsten Anlagen Europas. Bis 2013 investiert Feralpi weitere 20 Mio. Euro in Umweltschutz- und Verfahrenstechnologien. Mit ihnen soll der Energieverbrauch um ein Viertel reduziert werden.

Fortsetzung Seite 72

with 26 employees, today Robotron Datenbank-Software GmbH is one of the bright stars in the IT sky with 230 employees and five subsidiaries in Europe. The company's new start is closely associated with Dr. Rolf Heinemann, the hands-on, resourceful boss before and after reunification. In 2010 he was awarded title of "Entrepreneur of the Year" in Saxony in honour of his life's work as IT pioneer.

The Dresden chamber district has become a shop window for microelectronics and IT, not just thanks to its companies but also as a trade-fair centre. Following Geneva, Zurich, Munich and Stuttgart, in 2009 the SEMICON Europa founded in 1976 moved to Silicon Saxony. October 2012 was the fourth time that Europe's largest and most important semiconductor trade-fair was held in Dresden.

Big winner: Metal production and processing

Modern life is made of metal. They even call it the mother of all assets. No branch of manufacturing can manage without metal. Global demand for metal is immeasurable. It is even used to express a style of music to refer explicitly to hardness and power: Heavy Metal. Metal also reflects power in the Dresden chamber district, where the local metal industry generates 1.2 billion Euro or 40 percent of the annual branch turnover in Saxony, with 7,300 employees working in 65 SME companies (from 50 employees).

This was the sector that suffered the most from the financial and economic crisis between 2008 and 2009. Turnover fell by 56 percent. A broad range of products and highly flexible companies prevented the situation from getting any worse. The general trend towards recovery has still not restored the pre-crisis level. The umbrella organisation "Sachsenmetall" is cautiously optimistic, seeing investment in new products and modern equipment alongside cooperation with universities and institutes as the way to remain competitive on the international scale and to win over new market shares.

Italian firms on the Elbe

"Stahl Riesa" is the name of a football club. For decades, this was also the shortest possible profile applying to the town on the Elbe. Steel production, steelworker town and football formed one unit. The BSG (company sport club) played 16 seasons in the GDR's highest division, and was reborn in 2003 as TSV (traditional sport club). Riesa is still associated with steel, but not exclusively. The GDR's giant company with 13,000 employees has been replaced by ESF Elbe-Stahlwerke Feralpi GmbH, which in turn is the largest plant belonging to the Italian global player Feralpi Stahl. 430 employees produce top

Continued on page 72

Information

Gründungsjahr: 1901

Mitarbeiter: ca. 100

Leistungsspektrum:
Kaltgewalzte Profile
· Spezial/Standard
· gelocht

Komponenten und Systeme
· Schweißen/Widerstandsschweißen
· Dornbiegen
· Konfektionierung

Branchen:
· Sanitär
· Solar
· Automobilindustrie
· Elektroindustrie
· Bauindustrie
· Verkehrstechnik

Year founded: 1901

Employees: approx. 100

Range of services:
cold-rolled sections
· special/standard
· punched

components and systems
· welding/resistance welding
· mandrel bending
· order picking

Branches:
· sanitary systems
· solar technology
· automotive industry
· electrical industry
· construction industry
· traffic engineering

Kirchhoff & Lehr GmbH, Arnsdorf

Kirchhoff & Lehr GmbH

Das traditionsreiche mittelständische Unternehmen Kirchhoff & Lehr aus dem sächsischen Arnsdorf ist ein europaweit bekannter Hersteller kaltgewalzter Profile. Das Produktspektrum reicht von einfachen Standardprofilen über Spezialprofile bis hin zu komplexen Systemen.

Die Herstellung der Profile erfolgt auf modernen Profilieranlagen durch geschultes Personal. Zur weiteren Anarbeitung der Profile setzt Kirchhoff & Lehr verschiedenste Technologien ein, u. a. Schweißen, Lochen, Perforieren, Biegen und Toxen. Im Anschluss werden die Oberflächen je nach Kundenwunsch pulverbeschichtet, lackiert, galvanisch veredelt oder verzinkt.

Profile, Baugruppen und Komponenten von Kirchhoff & Lehr begleiten nahezu jeden Mitteleuropäer tagtäglich. Ob im Badezimmer, im Auto, in der Regal- und der Lagertechnik: Produkte von Kirchhoff & Lehr bilden im Verborgenen oft die Grundlage des Gesamtteils.

Kirchhoff & Lehr GmbH

Kirchhoff & Lehr is a medium-sized company with a long tradition in Arnsdorf/Saxony, and is a renowned European manufacturer of cold-rolled sections. The production programme extends from standard and specialised sections through to complex systems.

The sections are produced by highly skilled staff on modern forming machinery. A wide range of different technologies are then used for subsequent processing of the sections, including welding, punching, perforating, bending and toxing. Surfaces can subsequently be powder-coated, lacquered, electro-galvanised and hot-dip galvanised to customer specifications.

Sections, assemblies and components by Kirchhoff & Lehr can be found in almost every aspect of the daily lives of the population in Central Europe. Whether in the bathroom or in the car, in shelving or warehousing systems, products by Kirchhoff & Lehr will often be involved behind the scenes in providing the fundamental basis for the overall whole.

Rohre warm und kalt

Eine andere Branchengröße forscht in Riesa: Vallourec & Mannesmann Tubes. Der Weltmarktführer bei nahtlos warmgefertigten Stahlrohren hat 2010 im Ortsteil Gröba ein Rohrforschungszentrum eingeweiht, ein weltweit einzigartiges Labor. In dem Miniaturwalzwerk testet er Produktinnovationen.

Rohrproduktion auch im fünf Kilometer entfernten Zeithain: Die Salzgitter Mannesmann Sachsen GmbH gehört zum führenden europäischen Hersteller kaltgezogener nahtloser und geschweißter Präzisionsstahlrohre sowie geschweißter maßgewalzter Präzisionsstahlrohre, Sitz in Mühlheim an der Ruhr. Eine Investition 2008 brachte dem sächsischen Werk den Durchbruch: Die Zeithainer kombinierten erstmals auf der Welt ein Drei-Walzen-Schrägwalzwerk mit einer Stoßbank. Das Verfahren ermöglicht eine Produktionssteigerung von jährlich 170 000 Tonnen auf 205 000 Tonnen.

Wiederbelebte Standorte

Ein Koloss im nahen Gröditz war das Stahl- und Walzwerk mit 5300 Beschäftigten. Der Standort mit Wurzeln bis 1779 ist erhalten geblieben, die Produktion hat sich seit 1990 aufgefächert. Die Elektrostahlwerke Gröditz erzeugen Rohblöcke unterschiedlicher Formate. Abnehmer sind die Schmiedewerke Gröditz GmbH, zu deren Kunden die Gröditzer Kurbelwelle Wildau GmbH zählt. Den Reigen in der Stadt vervollständigt die Stahlguss Gröditz GmbH. Sie liefert dem Schiffsbau, der Energiewirtschaft und dem Maschinenbau bis zu 50 Tonnen schwere handgeformte Gussteile.

Die Bierstadt Radeberg beheimatet die Gießerei Radeberg GmbH mit 80 Beschäftigten. Gegründet 1860, ist sie sogar älter als die Exportbierbrauerei. Die Wellenbewegungen ostdeutscher Geschichte kennzeichnen ihre Entwicklung: 1974 Verstaatlichung des Traditionsbetriebes, 1993 Reprivatisierung, Aufschwung als Unternehmen für filigrane Gussteile ebenso wie für schwere, kompakte Stücke. Im Glasformenbau gehört sie zur europäischen Spitzengruppe.

Unikate, Umstrukturierung, Umfeld

Zwei Edelstahlgießereien flankieren Dresden: die Edelstahlwerke Schmees GmbH in der Sächsischen Schweiz und die BGH Edelstahlwerke Freital GmbH am Fuße des Osterzgebirges. Der Familienbetrieb Schmees aus dem rheinischen Langenfeld hatte sich 1993 mit zweitem Standbein in Pirna etabliert und bald den Hauptsitz dorthin verlagert. Die 360 Mitarbeiter in beiden Werken haben sich internationalen Ruf erworben. „Wir bezeichnen uns als die Handwerker unter den Gießern", sagt Geschäftsführer Clemens Schmees. Mit jährlich rund 35 000 Abgüssen einer durchschnittlichen Losgröße von 3,5 tragen die Produkte Unikatcharakter.

Fortsetzung Seite 74

---

quality products, including billets, reinforcement flat steel and wire rods.

The Italians have four sites on the Elbe, with Elbe-Drahtwerke Feralpi GmbH, Feralpi-Logistik GmbH and Feralpi Stahlhandel GmbH. The Drahtwerke produce reinforcement steel support matting, meshes and lattice beams, while the logistics division brings them to the customers. Steel from Riesa gives the inner strength to many building structures in Germany, including the Centrum-Galerie in Dresden and the Airbus assembly plant in Hamburg.

In 1843, the Schönberg brothers constructed the ironworks in Riesa. The river Elbe and the good railway connections made it interesting for Germany's heavy industry. From 1949 to 1989, this was a role model company in the socialist regime. After reunification, the Italians brought a new steel age to Riesa: in 1994, the first steel flowed into a new production facility on the historic site, and in 1995 the rolling mill was commissioned with an annual output of 500,000 tons of reinforcement steel. Meanwhile this has become one of Europe's most advanced plants. Through to 2013, Feralpi will be investing a further 20 million Euro in environment protection and processing technologies, aiming to reduce energy consumption by a quarter.

Hot and cold tubes

Another branch giant does research in Riesa: Vallourec & Mannesmann Tubes. The world market leader for seamless hot-rolled steel tubes inaugurated a tube research centre in 2010 in the suburb of Gröba, with a unique laboratory like no other in the world. Product innovations are tested in the miniature rolling mill.

Tubes are also produced five kilometres down the road in Zeithain: Salzgitter Mannesmann Sachsen GmbH is one of Europe's leading manufacturers of cold-drawn seamless and welded precision steel tubes together with welded size-rolled precision steel tubing, based in Mühlheim an der Ruhr. An investment made in 2008 put the Saxon plant on the road to success: here in Zeithain they were the first in the world to combine a three-roller piercing mill with a push bench. The process has boosted annual production output from 170,000 tons to 205,000 tons.

Revitalised sites

One behemoth in nearby Gröditz was the steel and rolling mill with 5,300 employees. Dating back to 1779, the site has been retained to the present day with production diversifying since 1990. Elektrostahlwerke Gröditz produces ingots in differing formats, purchased by Schmiedewerke Gröditz GmbH, whose customers include Gröditzer Kurbelwelle Wildau GmbH. Stahlguss Gröditz GmbH is yet another steel firm in the town: it supplies hand formed castings weighing up to 50 tons to the

Continued on page 74

Schmiedewerke Gröditz GmbH

Information

Gründungsjahr: 1779

Mitarbeiter:
724 (Ende 2011)

Produkt- und Leistungsspektrum:
Die Schmiedewerke Gröditz GmbH fertigt Schmiedestücke und Ringwalzerzeugnisse aus unlegierten, legierten und hochlegierten Stählen in gewünschter chemischer Zusammensetzung nach nationalen und internationalen Qualitätsstandards:
· Edelbaustähle
· RSH-Stähle
· Werkzeugstähle
· Stähle für den Energiemaschinenbau
· Sonderstähle

Year founded: 1779

Employees:
724 (end of 2011)

Range of products and services:
Schmiedewerke Gröditz GmbH produces forgings and rolled rings from unalloyed, alloyed and high-alloyed steels in the desired chemical composition in accordance with national and international quality standards:
· high-grade construction steel
· stainless steel
· tool steel
· steel for power generation application
· special purpose steel

Schmiedewerke Gröditz GmbH
Gröditz

Chargieren des Wechselstrom-Lichtbogenofens im Elektrostahlwerk

Charging process of the AC electric arc furnace in the steel plant

Zukunft braucht Stahl

Die Schmiedewerke Gröditz GmbH stellt auf Basis eines eigenen Elektrostahlwerkes Freiformschmiedestücke und Ringwalzerzeugnisse her, die wärmebehandelt, auf Wunsch mechanisch vor- oder fertigbearbeitet und umfangreichen Qualitätsüberprüfungen unterzogen werden. Sie verfolgt damit ein Ziel: die Herstellung von Produkten, die den Erwartungen der Kunden voll entsprechen.

Für die Kunden ergeben sich daraus vielfältige individuelle Lösungen. Auch die Werkstoffpalette von rund 300 produzierten Stahlmarken in mehr als 1700 Analysemodifikationen spiegelt diese Vielfalt wider.

Aus Edelstählen, die sich durch spezielle Materialeigenschaften wie hohe Reinheitsgrade, gleichmäßiges Gefüge, Verschleiß- und Korrosionsbeständigkeit auszeichnen, entstehen Produkte für einen weltweiten Kundenkreis. Schwerpunkte sind der allgemeine Maschinen-, Schiffs- und Energiemaschinenbau, die chemische Industrie, die Offshore-Industrie und der Fahrzeugbau.

Das Unternehmen setzt auf durchgängige Qualität – von der Beschaffung über die Produktion bis hin zur Auslieferung.

Future needs steel

Schmiedewerke Gröditz GmbH turns steel supplied by its own steel plant into open-die forgings and rolled rings; after heat treatment, these can be mechanically rough or finish-machined on request, before undergoing extensive quality tests. In this way, the company pursues the objective of manufacturing products that comply fully with customer expectations. And in this way it pursues an important goal: the manufacture of products which completely fulfill the expectations of the customers.

As a result of this the company can offer its customers a wide range of individual solutions. The material range of around 300 produced steel grades in more than 1,700 analysis modifications reflects this variety.

Schmiedewerke Gröditz produces parts for customers throughout the world which are distinguished by special material properties such as high degrees of purity, even structure, resistance to wear and corrosion. Principal customers are the general mechanical engineering industry, shipbuilding, the power generation industry, the chemical industry, the offshore industry and vehicle construction.

The company implements a strict quality system throughout – from purchasing through production to delivery.

Schmiedestück auf dem Weg zur 60MN-Schmiedepresse

Forging on its way to the 60MN-press

www.stahl-groeditz.de

Der Freitaler Branchenvertreter gehört zur Boschgotthardshütte (BGH) in Siegen. Einst war das hiesige Edelstahlwerk mit 5000 Beschäftigten größter Edelstahllieferant der DDR. Der Standort ist – komplett erneuert – mit 600 Mitarbeitern erhalten geblieben. So zählt die Horizontalstranggussanlage weltweit zu den modernsten. Mit 70 Mitarbeitern ist die nahe gelegene Hainsberger Metallwerk GmbH deutlich kleiner. Sie fertigt Metall- und Kunststofferzeugnisse, darunter Verpackungsmaschinenteile und Möbelbeschläge.

Wiederum nicht weit entfernt weist der Name Schmiedeberg auf ein Hammerwerk von 1492 hin. Mit der Schmiedeberger Gießerei GmbH ist seine Geschichte lebendig geblieben. Im Dorf verzahnen sich – typisch für Sachsen – Wirtschaft und Kultur: Die barocke Kirche wurde nach Plänen von George Bähr, dem Baumeister der Frauenkirche, gebaut, und aus dem Ort stammte der Vater von Friedrich Gerstäcker, dem Autor des Abenteuerromans „Flusspiraten des Mississippi".

Genau richtig: Energie- und Umwelttechnologie

Weltweit einzigartig – dieses Begriffspaar hat Klang im globalen Wettbewerb. Im März 2012 vermeldete die Heliatek GmbH Dresden eine solche Neuheit. Sie weihte eine weltweit einzigartige Produktionslinie für flexible Solarfolien ein, die auf organischen Halbleitern basieren. Gegenüber bisherigen Verfahren besitzt die 14-Mio.-Investition Vorzüge wie höhere Effizienz und längere Lebensdauer. Ihre Erzeugnisse können vielseitiger eingesetzt werden als traditionelle Fotovoltaikprodukte. Das Unternehmen mit 75 Mitarbeitern – 2006 als Ausgründung der TU Dresden und Universität Ulm entstanden – zählt zu den Solar-Weltmarktführern.

Mit innovativen Produkten können Herausforderungen wie Energiewende, Rohstoffknappheit und Klimawandel gemeistert werden. Für eine sichere, bezahlbare und emissionsarme Energieversorgung hat Sachsen die Weichen für die Zukunft gestellt und der EU dazu einen 10-Punkte-Plan vorgelegt. So soll in knapp zehn Jahren mindestens ein Drittel des Bruttostrombedarfs im Freistaat mittels erneuerbarer Energien abgedeckt werden.

Braunkohle bleibt aber unverzichtbar. 80 Prozent des Stroms in Sachsen werden mit diesem fossilen Energieträger erzeugt. Mit der schwedischen Vattenfall AB hat sich ein europäischer Energiegigant im Kammerbezirk Dresden angesiedelt. Er betreibt in der nordöstlichen Oberlausitz das Braunkohlenkraftwerk Boxberg, das zweitgrößte des Konzerns in Deutschland.

Drei Blöcke mit modernster Umwelttechnik erbringen eine Leistung von 1900 Megawatt. Mit einem neuen Kraftwerksblock soll sie ab 2012 auf 2575 Megawatt steigen. Damit wird das Kraftwerk für die Gesamtleistung bis zu 30 Prozent weniger Kohle benötigen als Kraftwerke im weltweiten Durchschnitt. Die Braunkohle kommt aus den benachbarten Tagebauen Nochten und Reichwalde. In beiden werden jährlich 29 Millionen Tonnen gewonnen.

shipbuilding industry, energy sector and machine construction branch.

The beer town of Radeberg is home to Gießerei Radeberg GmbH, a foundry with 80 employees. It was founded in 1860, which makes it older even than the brewery. Its development is marked by the ups and downs of East German history: in 1974 the long-standing company was nationalised, followed by reprivatisation in 1993 when it enjoyed a revival as a specialist for filigree castings as well as heavy, compact pieces. Today it is one of Europe's leading firms for glass mould manufacturing.

Unique products, restructuring, surroundings

Not far from Dresden there are two stainless steel foundries: Edelstahlwerke Schmees GmbH in Saxon Switzerland and BGH Edelstahlwerke Freital GmbH at the foot of the East Erzgebirge mountains. Schmees is a family business from Langenfeld in the Rhineland which set up a second site in Pirna in 1993 and soon moved its headquarters over here too. The 360 employees in both plants have acquired an international reputation. "We call ourselves the skilled craftsmen of the steel branch", says Managing Director Clemens Schmees. The products are unique in character with an annual output of around 35,000 castings in average batch sizes of 3.5.

The branch representative in Freital belongs to Boschgotthardshütte (BGH) in Siegen. At one time, the local stainless steel works had a workforce of 5,000 employees and was the largest stainless steel supplier in the GDR. The completely revamped site now operates with 600 employees. The horizontal continuous casting plant is one of the most advanced in the world. Nearby Hainsberger Metallwerk GmbH is much smaller with 70 employees, making metal and plastic products including packing machine components and furniture fittings.

Again not far away, the name Schmiedeberg refers to a hammer mill back in 1492. Schmiedeberger Gießerei GmbH keeps the history alive. The village offers the typical Saxon combination of business and culture: the baroque church was built according to plans drawn up by George Bähr, the architect who built Dresden's Frauenkirche, while Schmiedeberg was also home to the father of German author Friedrich Gerstäcker who wrote the adventure story "River pirates of the Mississippi".

Big winner: Energy and environment technology

Globally unique – a popular claim in global competition. In March 2012, Heliatek GmbH Dresden announced an innovation living up to this claim. It inaugurated a globally unique production line for manufacturing flexible solar films based on organic semiconductors. Compared to previous methods, the 14 million Euro investment offered advantages such as higher efficiency and longer service life. The products can be put to far more flexible use than traditional photovoltaic products. The company with 75 employees which was founded in 2006 as a

Der Braunkohlentagebau erlebt in Ostsachsen gerade eine Renaissance.

Currently the brown coal open-pit mining is undergoing a renaissance in East Saxony.

Boxberg – drittgrößte Gemeinde in Sachsen – lebt in Eintracht mit dem Energieareal. Auf ihrer Internetseite wirbt Bürgermeister Roland Trunsch für die waldreiche Gegend und touristische Anziehungspunkte. „Die Rückkehr der Wölfe in die Lausitz offenbart den Gleichklang der Natur und dem Industriestandort Boxberg", schreibt er. Touristischer Trumpf ist der nahe Bärwalder See, mit 13 Quadratkilometern Sachsens größtes stilles Gewässer. Dieses Erholungsgebiet ist eine Bergbaufolgelandschaft. Von 1997 bis 2009 wurde das Tagebaurestloch geflutet. Heute ist das Gewässer Wassersportparadies und Brauchwasserspender für das Kraftwerk.

Vom Turmblick zur Industriekultur

Im Lausitzer Revier – mit Gebieten der Oberlausitz auf sächsischer und der Niederlausitz auf brandenburgischer Seite – lagern Milliarden Tonnen des Bodenschatzes Braunkohle. 1911 wurde in Hirschfelde bei Zittau das erste deutsche Braunkohlenkraftwerk in Betrieb genommen. In der DDR schadete der extensive Braunkohlenabbau Menschen und Umwelt. Ab 1990 wurde die sächsische Braunkohlenwirtschaft umgestaltet. Neue, effiziente Anlagen entstanden, Tagebaulandschaften wurden rekultiviert. Seither sind in Sachsen etwa zwei Drittel der Tagebaufläche wieder nutzbar gemacht.

spin-off from TU Dresden and Ulm University is now one of the world market leaders in the solar branch.

Innovative products are the best way to meet challenges such as the energy turnaround, raw material shortages and climate change. Saxony has set the points for a reliable, affordable and low-emissions energy supply in the future, based on a 10-point plan. The aim is for at least one third of the gross power demand in the Free State to be covered by renewable energy sources in just ten years.

Even so, lignite remains indispensable. 80 percent of Saxony's electricity is generated from this fossil fuel. Vattenfall AB, one of Europe's energy giants, has settled in the Dresden chamber district; it operates Boxberg lignite-fired power station in the north-eastern Oberlausitz, the company's second largest in Germany.

Three blocks with state-of-the-art environmental technology generate output of 1,900 megawatts. A new power station block should bring the output to 2,575 megawatt as from 2012. The

Das Revier wandelt sein industrielles Gesicht in ein touristisch attraktives Antlitz. Aus dem kargen Kohlengrubenland wird mit 14 000 Hektar Fläche die größte künstliche Gewässerlandschaft Europas. Ausblick und Rückblick: Vom 30 Meter hohen Turm auf dem Schweren Berg bei Weißwasser aus sieht man den Tagebau Nochten. Ein Infozentrum von Vattenfall im Turm macht mit historischer und neuer Abbautechnik bekannt.

Das südlich gelegene Kraftwerk Hirschfelde – zu DDR-Zeiten mit 5000 Beschäftigten und seit 1992 außer Betrieb – ist als Technisches Denkmal und Museum wiedererstanden. Seinen Brennstoff bezog es einst auch aus dem Olbersdorfer Tagebau. Als Erholungsgebiet mit Badestrand, Segeln, Camping und einem internationalen Crosstriathlon direkt am deutsch-polnisch-tschechischen Dreiländerpunkt ist er nicht wiederzuerkennen.

Die Erneuerbaren kommen

Heute arbeitet Sachsen dreimal energieeffizienter als 1990. Wie aber können Industrie, Gewerbe, Verkehr und Haushalte noch sparsamer und rationeller mit dem unentbehrlichen Stoff des modernen Lebens umgehen? Wie können erneuerbare Energien dem Klassiker Braunkohle immer mehr Arbeit abnehmen? Produzenten und Forscher im Kammerbezirk Dresden finden Antworten, die international aufhorchen lassen.

Der Sonne wendet sich in der Landeshauptstadt die SOLARWATT AG zu. Sie ist einer der führenden internationalen Hersteller kristalliner Solarmodule. Ihre 490 Mitarbeiter verfügen über eine der modernsten Fertigungslinien in Europa. Die FHR Anlagenbau GmbH im Gewerbepark Ottendorf-Okrilla ist Spezialist für Vakuumprozesstechnologien und deren maßgeschneiderte anlagentechnische Umsetzung. Eine Gruppe erfahrener und couragierter Ingenieure hatte sie 1991 gegründet. Seit 2008 gehören die 165 Mitarbeiter zur centrotherm photovoltaics AG Blaubeuren. Weltweite Fotovoltaik-Autorität ist die bereits vorgestellte VON ARDENNE Anlagentechnik GmbH.

Dünnschicht-Technologie und Organische Fotovoltaik repräsentieren schon die zweite und dritte Generation von Solarzellen. In und um Dresden wird der Vorsprung greifbar: Vier der zehn größten Fotovoltaik-Anlagenbauer weltweit sind hier beheimatet. Auch einschlägige Wissenschafts- und Forschungskompetenz von Weltklasse bündelt sich im Herzen des Kammerbezirks Dresden. So errichten drei der zwölf Dresdner Fraunhofer-Einrichtungen derzeit das Fraunhofer-RESET, ein Zentrum für ressourcenschonende Energietechnologie.

Energieträger mit innerem Geheimnis

Mit dem Auto emissionsfrei unterwegs? In Kamenz arbeitet die Li-Tec Battery GmbH am Antrieb von morgen. Das Unternehmen der Evonik Industries AG Essen und der Daimler AG Stuttgart stößt die Tür auf zur künftigen umweltverträglichen Mobilität. Hochleistungsfähige Lithium-Ionen-Batterien

power station will need up to 30 percent less lignite for its total output than power stations in the global average. The lignite comes from the neighbouring open-cast mines in Nochten and Reichwalde where 29 million tons are produced every year.

Boxberg – Saxony's third largest municipality – lives in harmony with the energy site. On the Boxberg website, mayor Roland Trunsch promotes the wooded countryside and tourist attractions. "The return of the wolves to the Lausitz reveals the balance achieved with nature and the industrial activities around Boxberg", he writes. Nearby Bärwalder See is the key tourist attraction, Saxony's largest lake covering 13 square kilometres. This recreation area is a renaturised former open-cast mine that was flooded between 1997 and 2009. Today it acts as a water sport paradise while at the same time providing a source of service water for the power station.

Industrial culture seen from the tower

The Lausitz coalfield covering parts of Oberlausitz in Saxony and Niederlausitz in Brandenburg contains billions of tons of lignite. Germany's first lignite-fired power station started up in 1911 in Hirschfelde near Zittau. In the GDR, extensive lignite mining harmed both man and the environment. As from 1990, Saxony's lignite industry was reorganised. New efficient systems were introduced and open-cast mining landscapes were renaturised. Since then, about two thirds of Saxony's open-cast mines have been restored to other use.

The coalfield is changing its industrial uniform into an attractive tourism dress. The barren mining countryside has become Europe's largest man-made water landscape. Outlook and retrospective: the 30 metre high tower at Schwerer Berg near Weißwasser offers a view of Nochten open-cast mine. Vattenfall has an information centre in the tower with plenty of details about past and present mining technology.

Hirschfelde power station to the south used to have 5,000 employees in GDR times; it was decommissioned in 1992 and now functions as a technical monument and museum. In the old days, its fuel came from Olbersdorf open-cast mine. Today, it is past recognition as a recreation area with beach, sailing, camping and an international cross triathlon directly on the German/Polish/Czech border.

The renewables are coming

Today Saxony is three times more efficient with its energy than in 1990. But how can industry, trade, traffic and private households be even more economical and rational in handling the indispensable component of modern life? How can renewable energies take on even more tasks from the classic fuel lignite? Producers and researchers in the Dresden chamber district are finding answers that make them sit up and listen on an international scale.

Vier der zehn größten Fotovoltaik-Anlagenbauer weltweit sind in der Region Dresden ansässig.

Four of the world's ten largest photovoltaic system manufacturers are at home in and around Dresden.

werden das Kernstück von Elektroautos sein. Die junge Batteriezellen-Fabrik will in Europa die Nummer eins unter den Herstellern dieser Power-Batterien werden.

Ihre weltweit einzigartige Speichertechnologie kombiniert Keramik-Materialien und hochmolekulare Ionenleiter. Die patentierte hauchdünne, hitzefeste, keramische Membran macht die großformatigen Zellen besonders effizient und sicher. Die Kamenzer stellen die Energiespeicher der Zukunft in einem der größten Trockenräume Europas her. Schlüsselkomponenten wie keramische Seperatoren und Elektroden liefert die ortsansässige Schwester Evonik Litarion GmbH.

Hohe Energiedichte zeichnet auch die Brennstoffzelle aus. Sie wandelt chemische Energie in Strom, wie beim Space Shuttle praktiziert. Die Riesaer Brennstoffzellentechnik GmbH beschreitet diesen Weg. 2005 entwickelte sie eine Fünf-Kilowatt-Anlage, die sie seither im Feldversuch testet. Ab 2013/14 soll der Strom- und Wärmespender für Gebäude zunächst in kleiner Serie gefertigt werden.

In the state capital, the sun is the main business of SOLARWATT AG. The company is a leading international manufacturer of crystalline solar modules. The 490 employees work on one of the most advanced production lines in Europe. FHR Anlagenbau GmbH in Ottendorf-Okrilla industrial estate is a specialist for vacuum process technology and its customised implementation in equipment and systems. The company was founded in 1991 by a group of experienced and courageous engineers. Since 2008, the 165 employees belong to centrotherm photovoltaics AG Blaubeuren. The already mentioned company VON ARDENNE Anlagentechnik GmbH is the global authority in the photovoltaic branch.

Thin-film technology and organic photovoltaics stand for what is already the second and third generation of solar cells. There are visible signs in and around Dresden of the area's technological lead: four of the world's ten largest photovoltaic system manufacturers are at home here. There's also a cluster of pertinent world-class science and research expertise at the heart

Frischer Wind in der Windkraft

Der Brockhaus erklärt Wind als „Luftströmung, hervorgerufen durch Luftdruckgegensätze und Temperaturunterschiede". Dieser Vorgang ist das Lebenselixier der Eickhoff Wind Power GmbH, zu Hause im Gewerbegebiet Klipphausen bei Meißen. Seit 2009 stellt sie Getriebe für Windkraftanlagen her. Die 50-Mio.-Investition der Bochumer Eickhoff-Gruppe hat den klassischen Maschinen- und Anlagenbau im Kammerbezirk Dresden ebenso gestärkt wie sein Profil bei erneuerbaren Energien. Eickhoff gehört zu den weltweit führenden Lieferanten von Windkraftgetrieben.

Ein echt Dresdner Gewächs ist die WSB Neue Energien GmbH. 1997 hatten Andreas Dorner und Vater Achim den Traum von der Windkraft als Zukunftsenergie. Das damalige kleine Planungsbüro ist zu einem der größten Windkraftunternehmen Deutschlands herangewachsen. Visionen, Mut und Innovationen haben ein Team von 180 Mitarbeitern formiert. 300 Windenergie- und Solaranlagen sind inzwischen errichtet. Mit ihnen können jährlich über 860 000 Tonnen CO_2, 470 Tonnen Stickoxide und fast 3700 Kilogramm radioaktive Abfälle vermieden werden.

Abprodukte und Zugewinn

Umwelttechnologie – wer den Begriff googelt, erhält über eine Million Treffer. Einst Sache weniger Enthusiasten, ist sie zum globalen Markt geworden. Vom Kammerbezirk Dresden aus agieren Anbieter mit intelligenten Lösungen in aller Welt. 500 Referenzanlagen in mehr als 40 Ländern belegen den Ruf der STRABAG Umweltanlagen GmbH. Das Dresdner Unternehmen entwickelt und baut Anlagen für die mechanisch-biologische Abfallbehandlung und die Biogaserzeugung. Die DAS Environmental Expert GmbH in Dresden kümmert sich um schädliche Abprodukte in der Halbleiter- und Solarindustrie. „Die großen Halbleiter-Fabs weltweit vertrauen seit mehr als zwei Jahrzehnten unserer Kompetenz für Abgasreinigung", sagt Dr. Guy Davis, der diesen Geschäftsbereich leitet.

Wie verbreitet sich Zukunftswissen? „Partnerschaft für Klimaschutz, Energieeffizienz und Innovation" heißt ein Projekt des Bundes und des Deutschen Industrie- und Handelskammertages (DIHK). In diesem Rahmen hilft die IHK Dresden Unternehmen, Einsparpotenzial aufzuspüren. 180 Firmen vertrauten bisher dem IHK-Energieberater. In der „Umweltallianz Sachsen" setzt der Freistaat seit 1998 auf Eigenverantwortung und Kooperation seiner Unternehmen und Einrichtungen bei nachhaltiger Wirtschaftsweise. Die Sächsische Energieagentur SAENA GmbH und die Verbundinitiative Industrielles Netzwerk Erneuerbare Energien Sachsen (EESA) – beide mit Sitz im Kammerbezirk Dresden – beraten und bilden zur Energieeffizienz.

of the Dresden chamber district. Three of Dresden's twelve Fraunhofer institutes are currently involved in building the Fraunhofer-RESET, a research centre for resource-friendly energy technologies.

Energy source with its own secret

Do you have an emission-free car? In Kamenz, Li-Tec Battery GmbH is working on drive systems for tomorrow. The company belonging to Evonik Industries AG Essen and Daimler AG Stuttgart is opening the door to future environmentally friendly mobility. In future, electric cars will run on high-powered lithium ion batteries. The young battery cell factory wants to be Europe's Number One manufacturer of these power batteries.

Their globally unique storage technology combines ceramic materials with high-molecular ionic conductors. The patented wafer-thin heat-resistant ceramic membrane makes the large-sized cells particularly efficient and safe. In Kamenz, they make the future energy storage batteries in one of Europe's largest drying rooms. Key components such as ceramic separators and electrodes are supplied by the local affiliate Evonik Litarion GmbH.

Fuel cells also stand out with high energy density. They convert chemical energy into electricity, as used in the Space Shuttle. This is the path being followed by Riesaer Brennstoffzellentechnik GmbH. In 2005, the firm developed a five kilowatt system which has been going through field trials ever since. The plan is to start small-series production of the power and heat source for buildings in 2013/2014.

Fresh breeze for wind power

Dictionaries define wind as "air current generated by opposite air pressure levels and differences in temperature". This is the life blood of Eickhoff Wind Power GmbH, based in Klipphausen industrial estate near Meißen. Since 2009 the company has been producing gears for wind turbines. The Eickhoff Group from Bochum has invested 50 million Euro here, enhancing the Dresden chamber district's machine construction sector as well as its renewables profile. Eickhoff is one of the world's leading suppliers of wind turbine gears.

WSB Neue Energien GmbH is a genuine Dresden development. In 1997, Andreas Dorner and his father Achim dreamt of wind power as a future energy. Their small planning firm has turned into one of German's leading wind power companies. Vision, courage and innovation have led to a team of 180 employees. Meanwhile, 300 wind turbines and solar systems have been installed, helping to avoid more than 860,000 tons of carbon, 470 tons of nitrogen oxide and nearly 3,700 kilograms of radioactive waste.

Genau richtig: Bio- und Nanotechnologie

Wie fertigte sich der Homo sapiens vor 40 000 Jahren ein Messer? Erfahrung ließ ihn einen geeigneten Stein auswählen. Auf den schlug er geschickt mit anderen Steinen. Das Wort Technologie war für diesen durchdachten Vorgang noch nicht erfunden. Die Steinbearbeitung ist aber eines der ältesten technologischen Verfahren der Menschheit, Bio- und Nanotechnologie gehören zu den jüngsten.

Die Sachsen sind besonders neugierig. Der Kammerbezirk Dresden gehört auf beiden Gebieten zu den fortschrittlichsten Forschungslandschaften der Welt. Die Landeshauptstadt als Metropole vereint Wissenschaftler, Forscher und Praktiker auf engstem Raum und mit unbegrenztem Blick. Im Biotechnischen Zentrum (BIOTECH) der TU Dresden beispielsweise widmen sich rund 230 Experten querbeet den Lebenswissenschaften (Life Sciences), darunter dem Molekularen Bioengineering, das keinerlei Barrieren zwischen den Disziplinen mehr kennt.

Der Übergang zwischen Bio und Nano ist fließend. Grundlagenforschung, angewandte Forschung und industrielle Anwendung sind eng verwoben. Dieses Miteinander verschiedener Spezialisten ist der Quell für Inspiration und Leistung, die vom sächsischen Standort ausgeht und ihn anziehend macht.

Waste products and profit

Environmental technology gets more than a million hits on Google. What used to be a niche sector for a few enthusiasts has meanwhile become a global market. Based in the Dresden chamber district, a whole number of providers offer intelligent solutions to customers all over the world. 500 reference installations in more than 40 countries verify the reputation of STRABAG Umweltanlagen GmbH. The Dresden company develops and builds systems for mechanical/biological waste treatment and biogas production. DAS Environmental Expert GmbH in Dresden looks after harmful waste from the semiconductor and solar industry. "For more than two decades, the major semiconductor fabs depend on our expertise for treating exhaust gas", says Dr. Guy Davis, who runs this division.

How does future know-how spread? "Partnership for climate protection, energy efficiency and innovation" is the name of a project by the Federal Government and the DIHK (Association of German Chambers of Commerce and Industry). Dresden CCI uses this framework to help companies to ascertain what potential savings they may be able to make. Up to now, 180 companies have turned to the CCI energy advisors. Since 1998, the "Environment Alliance Saxony" advocates direct responsibility and cooperation in the Free State's companies and institutions together with a sustainable business approach. Saxon Energy Agency SAENA GmbH and the EESA (Initiative Industrial Network Renewables in Saxony), both based in the Dresden chamber district, provide advice and training under the overall heading of energy efficiency.

Die Beratungsangebote der IHK Dresden helfen vielen Unternehmen, ihre Potenziale zu erkennen und noch besser auszunutzen.

The consultancy services of the Dresden CCI support numerous companies, helping them to recognise and fully utilize their full potential.

Der Kammerbezirk Dresden gehört in der Biotechnologie zu den fortschrittlichsten Forschungslandschaften der Welt.

In biotechnology the Dresden chamber district offers one of the most progressive research landscapes in the world.

Bio-Sachsen mit vielen Vorzügen

Silicon Saxony hat Konkurrenz bekommen namens biosaxony e. V. Der Verein engagiert sich für die Biotechnologie von der Materialwirtschaft über die Umwelt- und Energietechnik bis zur Medizin. Mit der Gründung 2009 gab er der seit 2000 prosperierenden Biotech-Region einen weiteren Schub. Rund 80 Biotechnologie- und Pharmaunternehmen sowie über 30 universitäre und außeruniversitäre Forschungseinrichtungen haben Sachsen in die Spitzengruppe der Bio-Regionen Europas gebracht.

Warum hat sich 2010 die RESprotect GmbH in Dresden verwurzelt? Professor Dr. Rudolf Fahrig, ihr Gründer, nennt Motive: die vernetzten Strukturen mit der Nähe zu Kliniken und Instituten, die Aufgeschlossenheit der Dresdner und die Stadt selbst als eine der schönsten Großstädte Deutschlands. „Kurz: Hier lässt sich einfach gut leben und arbeiten", sagt er. Seine Firma – eine Ausgründung der Fraunhofer-Gesellschaft – entwickelt als erste weltweit ein Medikament, das die Resistenz von Krebszellen gegenüber der Chemotherapie verhindert.

Mit der alkoholischen Gärung und der Hefe im Brot nutzen die Menschen Biotech seit Jahrtausenden. Mikrobiologie und Molekularbiologie ermöglichen einen immer tieferen Griff in die Werkzeugkiste der Natur. Unter dem Namen Biotechnologie sammeln sich mittlerweile unzählige Verfahren und Produkte. Farben helfen, ihre Spielarten zu unterscheiden. Die rote Biotechnologie bezieht sich auf die Medizin, die weiße auf die Industrie und die grüne auf die Landwirtschaft.

Big winner: Bio- and nanotechnology

How did homo sapiens make knives 40,000 years ago? Experience led him to choose a suitable stone, which he knocked into shape skilfully with another stone. The word technology for this well thought-out procedure had not yet been invented. But working stone is still one of the oldest technological procedures in the history of mankind. Bio- and nanotechnology are among the youngest.

Saxons are curious people. In both of these areas, the Dresden chamber district offers one of the most progressive research landscapes in the world. The state capital as metropolitan centre brings together scientists, researchers and practitioners in a relatively confined area with an unlimited view. The Biotechnical Centre (BIOTEC) at TU Dresden for example is the research home for around 230 scientists investigating the full range of life sciences including bioengineering, and has brought down all the interdisciplinary barriers.

The transition between bio and nano is a fuzzy one. Pure research, applied research and industrial application are closely entwined. Working together at the cutting edge of science, all these specialists act as a source for the inspiration and achievements that make Saxony such an attractive place.

BioSaxony with many advantages

Silicon Saxony now faces competition called biosaxony e. V. The association advocates biotechnology from materials science via environmental and energy technology through to medicine. Founded in 2009, it gave a further boost to the biotech region that has been prospering since 2000. Around 80 biotechnology and pharmaceutical companies together with 30 university and non-university research institutes have pushed Saxony into Europe's leading group of bio-regions.

Why did RESprotect GmbH settle in Dresden in 2010? Company founder Professor Dr. Rudolf Fahrig names the reasons: the networked structures with close proximity to hospitals and institutes, the open-minded local population and Dresden itself as one of the loveliest cities in Germany. "In brief: this is a good place to live and work", he says. His company, a spin-off from the Fraunhofer Society, is the first in the world to develop a drug to prevent cancer cells from resisting chemotherapy.

For thousands of years, people have been using biotech procedures such as the fermentation of alcohol and of yeast in bread. Microbiology and molecular biology permit an ever deeper insight into nature's toolbox. Biotechnology has meanwhile spawned countless processes and products. Colours help to distinguish the various types: red biotechnology refers to medicine, white biotechnology refers to industry and green biotechnology refers to agriculture.

Bio-Wissenschaft und Bio-Wirtschaft haben im Dresdner Stadtteil Johannstadt unter dem Namen „BioPolis" ein bedeutendes Zentrum gefunden.

In the Dresden district of Johannstadt, under the name of "BioPolis", bio-science and bio-economy have found a centre of significant importance.

Viel Wissen und Wirken unter einem Dach

„BioPolis" hat Dresden seinen Stadtteil Johannstadt getauft. Das altgriechische „polis" bedeutet Stadt oder Staat. Nahe der City und dem Universitätsklinikum Carl Gustav Carus konzentrieren sich Bio-Wissenschaft und Bio-Wirtschaft. Kurze Wege und unerschöpfliche Synergien beschleunigen in diesem Terrain den Transfer bis hin zur Produktionsreife. 21 Firmen und Einrichtungen vereint das 2004 gegründete BioInnovationsZentrum unter einem Dach, Start-ups ebenso wie Etablierte. Sie nutzen Büros, Labore, Reinräume, Service- und Gerätepools. BIOTECH der TU gehört zu den Mietern, daneben die Novaled AG, die wir bereits als OLED-Spezialisten kennen. Auch sechs Biotechnologie-Lehrstühle der TU Dresden fühlen sich dort wohl.

Die Brücke zur Medizin schlägt das Netzwerk BioMeT. Es ist ebenso in BioPolis zu Hause. Über 200 Partner aus Wissenschaft, Industrie, Verbänden, Kommunen und staatlichen Einrichtungen wirken zusammen. Mit dabei ist das Max-Planck-Institut für Molekulare Zellbiologie und Genetik Dresden. Gemeinsam mit der TU Dresden hat es die „Dresden International Graduate School for Biomedicine and Bioengineering" ins Leben gerufen.

Know-how and working under one roof

"BioPolis" is the name Dresden has given its suburb of Johannstadt. The Ancient Greek word "polis" means city. Bio-science and bioindustry is accumulated here near to the city centre and also near the Carl Gustav Carus University Hospital. Short distances and inexhaustible synergies on this campus accelerate the transfer processes involved in getting new ideas ready for production. 21 companies and institutions are housed in the BioInnovationCentre founded in 2004, including both start-ups and established firms. Here they find offices, laboratories, clean-rooms, service facilities and equipment pools. The tenants include the TU's BIOTECH as well as Novaled AG, already featured in the section on OLED. Six university chairs in biotechnology at TU Dresden are also at home here.

Das Projekt zielt auf eine neue Wissenschaftlergeneration: Bis zu 300 Doktoranden beschäftigen sich mit Molekularer Zell- und Entwicklungsbiologie, Regenerativer Medizin, Nanobiotechnologie, Biophysik und Bioengineering. Für Laien rätselhafte Disziplinen, deren Erkenntnisse und Ergebnisse aber zu grundlegend neuen Therapien vorstoßen.

Von neuen Knochen bis Aids-Test weltweit

Mit neuartigem Implantatmaterial beschäftigt sich das Dresdner Max-Bergmann-Zentrum für Biomaterialien. Zusammen mit der TU Dresden und dem Leibniz-Institut für Polymerforschung Dresden arbeitet es an Werkstoffen, die Knochen und Knorpel ersetzen können. Das Zentrum für Medizinische Strahlenforschung ZIK OncoRay wiederum will durch biologisch individualisierte, technologisch optimale Protonentherapie Krebserkrankungen besser heilen helfen. Bund und Land unterstützen das Team von Biologen, Physikern und Medizinern mit einer Millionen-Förderung. Bis 2015 soll eine weltweit einmalige Plattform zur patientenorientierten Strahlenforschung entstehen.

Die JADO Techologies GmbH im BioInnovationsZentrum entwickelt neue Therapeutika zur Behandlung von Entzündungen und Allergien. Diese sollen – so der Wirkungsmechanismus – Prozesse in der Zellmembran beeinflussen. Autologes Zelltransplantat heißt das Produkt der Uro Tiss GmbH Dresden. Mit ihm können Harnröhrenverengungen behandelt werden. Die Weltneuheit beziehen inzwischen führende urologische Kliniken Europas.

Biotechnologie nur in Dresden? Durchaus nicht. Ende 2011 stellte das „Handelsblatt" die Partec GmbH in Görlitz als Weltmarktführer bei Aids-Tests vor: „Vom ostsächsischen Unternehmenssitz aus werden die Aids-Tests in über 100 Länder verschickt – ein Großteil nach Afrika. Mittlerweile kommen bei drei Millionen von weltweit jährlich 7,4 Millionen Patiententests die Partec-Geräte zum Einsatz." Neuerungen in der Diagnostik sind seit 2000 Partecs Trümpfe. Jüngster Erfolg: Die Firma errang unter 4515 Produkten von 1800 Herstellern und Designern aus 58 Nationen den „red dot award" für Produktdesign. Das Siegergerät: ein Durchflusszytometriesystem für die Immunologie.

Erfreulicher Aufstand der Zwerge

Zwerge verändern die Welt. Das ist kein Fantasyfilm, sondern nanotechnologische Wirklichkeit seit Ende der 90er-Jahre. Das altgriechische „nános" heißt Zwerg und ist Namenspatron der Nanotechnologie. Im Kammerbezirk Dresden haben sich rund 80 Unternehmen und 40 Forschungs- und Entwicklungseinrichtungen der jungen Sparte verschrieben. Die Nanotechnologie gilt als Schlüsseltechnologie schlechthin für das 21. Jahrhundert. Sie ist das Kind gleich mehrerer Naturwissenschaften und durchdringt zahlreiche Branchen.

The BioMeT network bridges the gap to medicine and is part of the BioPolis complex. More than 200 partners from science, industry, associations, local authorities and state institutions are involved in the network, including the Max Planck Institute for Molecular Cell Biology and Genetics Dresden. Together with the TU Dresden, it has created the "Dresden International Graduate School for Biomedicine and Bioengineering". The project addresses a new generation of scientists: up to 300 post-graduate students work here on their doctorates in molecular cell and development biology, regenerative medicine, nanobiotechnology, biophysics and bioengineering. For the man on the street, these are all mysterious disciplines, but their findings and results are constantly driving forward towards new therapies.

From new bones to worldwide AIDS test

Dresden's Max Bergmann Centre for Biomaterials is investigating new implant materials. Together with TU Dresden and the Leibniz Institute for Polymer Research Dresden, it works on materials to replace bones and cartilage. The ZIK OncoRay Centre for Radiation Research in Oncology for its part wants to help improve the treatment of cancer with biologically individualised and technologically optimised proton therapy. Both federal and state government support the team of biologists, physicists and medical experts financially with millions of Euros. The intention is to create a globally unique platform for patient-oriented radiation research by 2015.

JADO Techologies GmbH in the BioInnovationCentre develops new therapies for inflammatory and allergic diseases with a mode of action that influences processes in the cell membrane. Autologous cell transplants are the focus of attention at Uro Tiss GmbH Dresden. The products are used to treat urethral stricture. The world novelty is meanwhile to be found in leading urological hospitals throughout Europe.

Biotechnology just in Dresden? Oh no, it goes way beyond the city boundaries. At the end of 2011, the "Handelsblatt" newspaper presented Partec GmbH in Görlitz as the world market leader for AIDS tests: "From company headquarters in East Saxony, the AIDS tests are sent out to more than 100 countries, with a large share going to Africa. Meanwhile the Partec devices are used for 3 million of the 7.4 million patient tests carried out in the world every year." New aspects on the diagnosis front have been the ace up Partecs' sleeve since 2000. The most recent success: the company received the "red dot award" for product design, competing against 4,515 products submitted by 1,800 manufacturers and designers from 58 different countries. The winning device is a flow cytometry system for immunology.

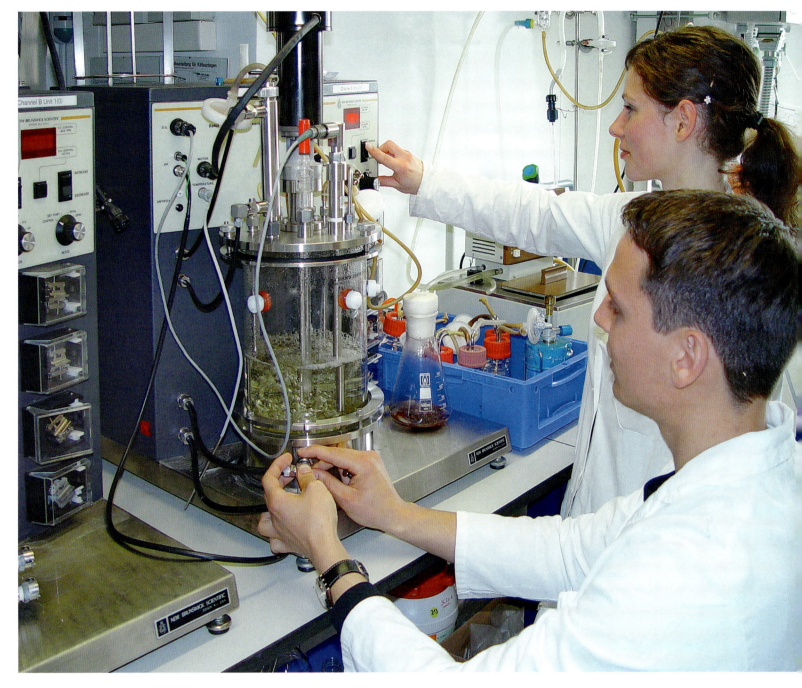

An der TU Dresden bekommt der wissenschaftliche Nachwuchs hervorragende Arbeitsbedingungen.

At the Technical University of Dresden, young scientists are offered outstanding working conditions.

Was gibt dem Zwerg solche Kräfte? Seine Winzigkeit. Ein Nanometer ist das Milliardstel eines Meters. In diesem Bereich nutzt die Nanotechnologie bekannte und neuartige Effekte allerkleinster Strukturen. Das olympische Motto „Höher, schneller, weiter" hat sie in „Kleiner, schneller, effizienter" abgewandelt. Dresden gilt als nanotechnologischer Standort der Weltspitze.

Mit Nano in die Produktion

Mitreißend ist das Tempo, mit dem sich interdisziplinäre Forschungsergebnisse in marktfähige Verfahren und Produkte umsetzen. „nano for production" heißt folgerichtig ein sächsischer Innovationscluster. In Regie des Dresdner Fraunhofer-Instituts für Werkstoff- und Strahltechnik (IWS) kooperieren 20 Forschungs- und Industriepartner. Ihre Themen sind Nanoschichten zur Oberflächenveredlung, Nanopartikel und Nanostrukturierung von Oberflächen.

Bei ultradünnen Schichten unter 100 Nanometern führt der Kammerbezirk Dresden international. Sie sind ein Schlüsselelement der Nanotechnik überhaupt. Ihre Einsatzbreite ist immens – von der Mikroelektronik und Optik über die Medizin bis zu Verschleißteilen im Maschinenbau. Die erstaunliche Steigerung der Speicherdichte von magnetischen Festspeicherplatten geht wesentlich auf die nur wenige Nanometer dicken Schutzschichten aus Kohlenstoff dieser Medien zurück.

In Dresden ist das bundesweite Kompetenzzentrum „Ultradünne funktionale Schichten" (Nano-CC-UFS) beheimatet. Es wird vom Fraunhofer IWS koordiniert. 51 Unternehmen, zehn Hochschulinstitute, 22 Forschungseinrichtungen und fünf Verbände haben in diesem Netzwerk ihre Kräfte gebündelt.

Superfein, intelligent und hochgeladen

Vorwärtsdrängende mittelständische Firmen greifen zügig neues Wissen auf. Die VDT Vakuumtechnik Dresden entwickelt und produziert Anlagen, die superfeine Beläge auf Kunststoff, Glas, Keramik und Metall zaubern. In der DDR gehörten die Vakuum-Experten zum Kombinat Carl Zeiss Jena. Privatisierung nach 1990, Integration in die METZ Holding Nürtingen, Kooperationen mit der Forschung vor Ort, exzellente Mitarbeiter – all das hat dem Unternehmen die Türen geöffnet, in Europa, den USA, Südkorea, Taiwan und Indien.

Mit „Biotemplating" hat die Namos GmbH Dresden – 1998 als Ausgründung der TU Dresden entstanden – eine revolutionäre Methode entwickelt, um Autoabgaskatalysatoren zu beschichten. Mittels Molekularbiologie designt sie Oberflächen im Nanometerbereich. „Namos Biotemplating bedeutet, dass wir die Intelligenz komplexer Biomoleküle nutzen, um in Katalysatoren Edelmetall genau dort zu platzieren, wo wir es brauchen", erläutert Geschäftsführer Dr. Jürgen Hofinger. Gegenüber herkömmlichen Methoden können bis zu 50 Prozent Edelmetall eingespart werden.

Positive uprising of the dwarfs

Dwarfs change the world. That's not a fantasy film but nanotechnological reality since the end of the 1990s. The Ancient Greek word "nános" means dwarf and has given its name to nanotechnology. In the Dresden chamber district, around 80 companies and 40 research and development institutions are dedicated to the young branch. Nanotechnology is seen as the key technology per se for the 21st century. It is the child of several scientific disciplines and pervades many branches.

What is the secret to the dwarf's success? His tininess. A nanometre is one billionth of a metre. This is the range in which nanotechnology uses the known and new effects of the tiniest structures. It has converted the Olympic slogan "higher, faster, further" into "smaller, faster, more efficient". Dresden is seen as one of the world's top places for nanotechnology.

Nano for production

Interdisciplinary research results are being converted into processes and products ready for the market at a stunning speed. It therefore makes sense for Saxony to have an innovation cluster called "nano for production". Here 20 research and industry partners work together under the auspices of the Fraunhofer Institute for Material and Beam Technology (IWS), looking at nano-coatings for surface treatment, nano-particles and nano-structuring of surfaces.

Dresden chamber district takes the international lead when it comes to ultrathin layers of less than 100 nanometres. These are a key element in nanotechnology, with a huge range of applications – from microelectronics and optics via medicine through to wear parts in mechanical engineering. The amazing increase in storage capacity on magnetic hard disks is primarily a result of the carbon protective layers on these media that are no more than a few nanometres thick.

Dresden is home to the national centre of excellence for "Ultrathin Functional Films" (Nano-CC-UFF), coordinated by the Fraunhofer IWS as a network pooling the strengths of 51 companies, ten university institutes, 22 research institutes and five associations.

Super-fine, intelligent and highly charged

Aspiring SME companies are quick to take up new know-how. VDT Vakuumtechnik Dresden develops and produces systems for conjuring superfine coatings on plastic, glass, ceramic and metal. In the GDR, the vacuum experts belonged to the Carl Zeiss Jena collective. Privatisation in 1990, integration in the METZ Holding Nürtingen, cooperation with local research activities, excellent employees – all this has opened doors for the company in Europe, the USA, South Korea, Taiwan and India.

Biotemplating is a revolutionary method developed by Namos GmbH Dresden, a spin-off from TU Dresden in 1998, for coating

Ein sächsisches Innovationscluster heißt „nano for production" und beschäftigt sich ganz gezielt mit der Umsetzung von Forschungsergebnissen in marktfähige Verfahren und Produkte.

Achtung! Die DREEBIT GmbH Dresden – 2006 von einem Zweierteam gegründet – schießt scharf. Mit Ionen. Ihre international patentierten Kanonen feuern hochgeladene Projektile auf Oberflächen, um extrem kleine Strukturen zu erzeugen oder zu vermessen. Sie geben beispielsweise der Strahlentherapie bei Krebs neue Chancen. Referenzanlagen stehen in Universitäten Deutschlands, Englands und Polens.

Nano – der Zwerg ist zum Riesen geworden. Woraus erwachsen seine unvergleichlichen Kräfte, mit denen er sich überall einmischt? Aus einer Region, die auch Bildungs- und Forschungshochburg ist.

A Saxonian innovation cluster is called "nano for production" and systematically focuses its efforts on turning research results into marketable techniques and products.

automotive exhaust gas catalytic converters. Molecular biology is used to design surfaces in the nanometre range. "Namos biotemplating means that we use the intelligence of complex biomolecules to ensure that precious metal is positioned exactly where it is needed in catalytic converters", is how Managing Director Dr. Jürgen Hofinger explains the process. This helps to save up to 50 percent precious metal compared to conventional methods.

Caution! DREEBIT GmbH Dresden – founded by a team of just two in 2006 – is a sharpshooter, using ions as ammunition. Their internationally patented guns fire highly charged projectiles onto surfaces to create or measure extremely small structures. They are used for example to give radiotherapy a new chance in the fight against cancer. Reference systems are in use at universities throughout Germany, England and Poland.

Nano – the dwarf has become a giant. Where does it get its strength from to be involved in so many different fields? From a region that is also an education and research stronghold.

Sprudelnde Quellen für Spitzenleistungen
Forschungspool von Weltrang

Philosoph Johann Gottlieb Fichte schrieb um 1800 klugen Leuten ins Stammbuch: „Der Gelehrte vergesse, was er getan hat, sobald es getan ist, und denke stets nur an das, was er noch zu tun hat." Der gebürtige Sachse selbst hatte sich vom begabten Webersohn aus Rammenau – zwischen Dresden und Bautzen gelegen – über die Stadtschule Meißen und ein Studium in Leipzig in den Olymp des deutschen Geistes hinaufgearbeitet.

Ein Junge aus dem nahen Kamenz wiederum stieg zum großen Dichter der Aufklärung auf. Er formulierte die Erfahrung all jener, die nach Wissen streben: „Der Blick des Forschers fand nicht selten mehr, als er zu finden wünschte." Pfarrerssohn Lessing nahm seinen Weg über die Fürstenschule St. Afra in Meißen. Womit wir mitten in der Gegenwart sind: St. Afra ist heute das Sächsische Landesgymnasium für die Hochbegabtenförderung. Eine von vielen Einrichtungen, die das Image der „fischelanten" Sachsen untermauern. Und weitere Talente und Kapazitäten anlocken.

Studieren an Deutschlands größter TU

In Sachsen studieren 110 000 junge Leute. Nach 1990 hatte sich die Hochschullandschaft neu strukturiert: Aus 22 staatlichen Bildungsstätten gingen vier Universitäten, ein universitäres Hochschulinstitut, fünf Kunsthochschulen und fünf Fachhochschulen hervor. Die Berufsakademie Sachsen unterhält sechs Studienakademien, darunter in Bautzen, Dresden und Riesa. Acht Spezial-Hochschulen haben private oder freie Träger. 50 außeruniversitäre Forschungseinrichtungen geben dem Land zusätzliches Profil. Überall entsteht Zukunft.

Welche Wissensquellen sprudeln im Kammerbezirk Dresden? Die Technische Hochschule Dresden ist mit 36 000 Studierenden und 8100 Mitarbeitern Deutschlands größte Technische Universität. Auf ihrer Webseite bekennt sie souverän Farbe: „Die TU Dresden ist eine der Spitzenuniversitäten Deutschlands und Europas: stark in der Forschung, erstklassig in der Vielfalt und der Qualität der Studienangebote, eng vernetzt mit Kultur, Wirtschaft und Gesellschaft." Ihre Geschichte reicht bis 1828 zurück. Neubauten wie das Hörsaalzentrum von 1998 und das Informatikgebäude von 2006 prägen ihr modernes Bild. 14 Fakultäten umfassen ingenieur- und naturwissenschaftliche Disziplinen, Geistes- und Sozialwissenschaften sowie die Medizin.

Flourishing sources for top achievements
World ranking research pool

Philosopher Johann Gottlieb Fichte wrote around 1800: "The scholar forgets what he has done as soon as he's done it and only thinks about what he still has to do." Born in Saxony, the gifted weaver's son from the town of Rammenau between Dresden and Bautzen worked his way from Meißen town school and studies in Leipzig to the Olympus of the German spirit.

A young man from near Kamenz in turn became the great poet of the Enlightenment. He expressed what everyone striving for knowledge experiences: "The researcher often saw more than he wanted to find." The path followed by pastor's son Lessing began at the Fürstenschule St. Afra in Meißen. Which brings us right back to the present day: today St. Afra is Saxony's state grammar school for the highly gifted. One of many facilities underlining the image of the "fischelant" (vigilant) Saxons, while also attracting other talents and capacities.

Studying at Germany's largest TU

110,000 young people study in Saxony. Following 1990, the whole university landscape was reorganised. 22 state educational establishments were turned into four straight universities, one international graduate school, five art colleges and five universities of applied science. Saxony Vocational College runs six academies, including Bautzen, Dresden and Riesa. There are eight private or free special universities of applied sciences. 50 non-university research institutes give the state an additional profile. And all of them work towards creating the future.

Which sources of know-how flourish in the Dresden chamber district? The Technical University Dresden has 36,000 students and 8,100 employees, making it Germany's largest technical university. The university shows its true colours in the portrait featured on its website: "The TU Dresden is among the top universities in Germany and Europe: strong in research, offering first-rate programmes with an overwhelming diversity, with close ties to culture, industry and society." Its history goes right

Die TU Dresden ist Deutschlands größte Technische Universität.

The Technical University of Dresden is Germany's largest technical university.

Rang zwei nimmt die Hochschule für Technik und Wirtschaft Dresden mit 5300 Studierenden ein. Die Hochschulen für Bildende Künste sowie für Musik „Carl Maria von Weber" sind das künstlerische Pendant. Im Umfeld bildet die Fachhochschule der Sächsischen Verwaltung Meißen den gehobenen Verwaltungs- und Justiznachwuchs aus. Evangelische Hochschulen in Dresden und Moritzburg erinnern an Sachsen als Mutterland der Reformation.

Reich an Kultur und Bildung

„Die Reiche" wurde einst die florierende Handelsstadt Zittau in der Oberlausitz genannt. Im 17. Jahrhundert brachte Pädagoge Christian Weise frischen Wind in ihre Mauern. Reich und frisch ist sie heute als Kultur- und Bildungsstadt Zittau, vor allem mit der Hochschule Zittau/Görlitz. Zittau und das 35 Kilometer entfernte Görlitz teilen sich den Campus für ihre 3700 Studie-

back to 1828, while new buildings such as the lecture centre from 1998 and the IT building from 2006 shape its modern face. 14 departments include among others engineering and natural science, humanities, social science and medicine.

Next in size is the HTW University of Applied Sciences Dresden with 5,300 students, with the colleges of art and music "Carl Maria von Weber" as artistic counterpart. Further afield, budding administration and legal employees are trained at the Saxon College of Administration in Meißen, while the Protestant Universities in Dresden and Moritzburg recall Saxony's role as the motherland of the Reformation.

Rich in culture and education

"The Rich" was once the attribute accorded to the flourishing trading town of Zittau in Oberlausitz. In the 17th century, educationalist Christian Weise brought a fresh breeze to the place.

Die Hochschule Zittau/Görlitz bildet heute rund 3700 Studierende in 37 Studiengängen an sechs Fakultäten aus.

Today, the Zittau/Görlitz University of Applied Sciences educates approximately 3,700 students in 37 degree courses at six departments.

renden. 37 Studiengänge an sechs Fakultäten machen die Hochschule für mehr als 100 Partner in 38 Ländern interessant.

„Werkstatt des universitären Denkens" – so nennt sich das Internationale Hochschulinstitut in Zittau, 1993 gegründet. Es bildet über 200 junge Leute in Masterstudiengängen und im Doktorandenstudium aus. Die Studenten kommen aus 15 Nationen, insbesondere aus den Nachbarländern Polen und Tschechien. Die akademischen Wurzeln an der Neiße reichen tief: 1779 wurde in Görlitz die Oberlausitzische Gesellschaft der Wissenschaften gegründet, heute eine der ältesten Gelehrtengesellschaften Mitteleuropas mit 200 in- und ausländischen Mitgliedern.

Die Köpfe zusammenstecken

Ein Wunderwerk der Miniaturkunst vor 1589 zeigt das Neue Grüne Gewölbe in Dresden: einen Kirschkern mit 185 Antlitzen. Für ein Ohrgehänge geschnitzt, könnte man ihn in der Gegenwart augenzwinkernd als Symbol für Spitzenforschung betrachten: Viele Fachleute stecken ihre Köpfe zusammen. Dresdens Forschungsleben sucht seinesgleichen. Elf Fraunhofer-Institute, drei Max-Planck-Institute, drei Leibniz-Institute und ein Helmholtz-Zentrum sind in Dresden heimisch geworden. Das sind keine Elfenbeintürme, sondern herausragende Forschungsstätten – praxisorientiert, wirtschaftsnah und umweltbewusst.

Den Kammerbezirk Dresden schmücken natürlich diese Namen. Aber ohne die sächsischen Vorzüge wären die Forschungsgrößen gar nicht an die Elbe gekommen. Ein Namenspatron – Gottfried Wilhelm Leibniz – war selbst Sachse. „Beim Erwachen hatte ich schon so viele Einfälle, dass der Tag nicht ausreichte, um sie niederzuschreiben", notierte er einmal.

Einfälle sind das Salz der Forschung geblieben. Heutige

Rich and fresh are also present-day attributes for Zittau as a culture and education town, particularly with Zittau/Görlitz University of Applied Sciences. Zittau and Görlitz 35 kilometres away share the campus for their 3,700 students. 37 degree courses at six departments make the university interesting for more than 100 partners in 38 countries.

"A workbench for European thought" – that's what the International Graduate School in Zittau calls itself, founded in 1993. It offers Masters and Doctorate courses to more than 200 young graduates. The students come from 15 nations, particularly from the neighbouring countries of Poland and the Czech Republic. The academic roots here on the river Neiße go very deep: the Oberlausitz Society of Knowledge was founded in Görlitz back in 1779. Today it is one of the oldest scholarly societies in Central Europe with 200 German and foreign members.

Putting their heads together

A miracle of miniature art dating back to before 1589 shows the Neues Grünes Gewölbe in Dresden: a cherry stone with 185 faces. Engraved for an earring, in this present day and age it could be playfully viewed as a symbol for cutting-edge research, where many experts put their heads together. Dresden's research life is beyond compare. Eleven Fraunhofer institutes, three Max Planck institutes, three Leibniz institutes and one Helmholtz centre have settled here in Dresden. These aren't ivory towers but outstanding research facilities: practical, close to business and aware of the environment.

These names naturally adorn the Dresden chamber district. But it took Saxony's positive attributes to bring them to the river Elbe in the first place. One of the institutes takes its name

Sprudelnde Quellen für Spitzenleistungen

Hörsaalgebäude auf dem Campus Zittau

Auditorium building on the Zittau campus

Am Fraunhofer-Institut für Werkstoff- und Strahltechnik in Dresden werden dünne Barriere- oder leitfähige Schichten mittels eines speziellen Verfahrens auf ebene Substrate aufgebracht. Im Bild: dünne Schichten für die Fotovoltaik.

At the Fraunhofer Institute for Material and Beam Technology in Dresden, thin barrier or conductive layers are applied to plane substrates by means of a special technique. In the image: thin layers used in the photovoltaic industry.

Arbeitsweisen verbinden die Ideen vieler. Den Slogan „Wissen schafft Brücken – Bildung verbindet Menschen" hat sich die TU Dresden als Motto gewählt. Sie gehört zu den leistungsstärksten Partnern vor Ort und weltweit. In Exzellenzclustern betreiben TU-Wissenschaftler international anerkannte Spitzenforschung. Exzellenz – dieses Wort ist dabei, in der modernen Welt Karriere zu machen: Exzellenzinitiative, Exzellenzcluster, Exzellenz-Universitäten ... Das lateinische Verb „excellere" bedeutet herausragen, sich auszeichnen.

from an original Saxon – Gottfried Wilhelm Leibniz, who once said: "When I woke up in the morning, I already had so many ideas that the day simply wasn't long enough to write them all down."

Ideas have remained the salt of research. Current working methods combine the ideas of many. The slogan "Knowledge builds bridges – education unites people" rounds off the mission statement of TU Dresden, one of the most efficient partners here at home in Dresden and all over the world. Scientists from the

Exzellenz gleich Intelligenz plus Teamgeist

Mit seiner Exzellenzinitiative seit 2005/06 fördert der Bund Spitzenleistungen an Hochschulen. Eine Förderlinie verbindet sich mit Exzellenzclustern, die Forschung zu jeweils einem Themenkomplex am Standort betreiben. Die TU Dresden ist zur Spitze der deutschen Wissenschaft aufgerückt: Sie gehört zu den elf Universitäten, die in der zweiten Phase der Exzellenzinitiative bis 2017 den Titel „Elite-Universität" führen dürfen. Und das als erste Hochschule in den neuen Bundesländern. Am 15. Juni 2012 nachmittags hatte Rektor Hans-Martin Steinhagen in der Alten Mensa unter Jubel die freudige Botschaft verkündet. Mit der Förderung habe die TU Dresden die Chance, auch international eine der angesehensten Universitäten zu werden. „Und ich verspreche, wir werden diese Chance nutzen!", sagte der glückliche Rektor. In den kommenden fünf Jahren erhält die Uni von Bund und Freistaat für ihre komplett bewilligten vier Teilanträge 172 Mio. Euro.

Schon in der ersten Förderrunde hatte sie sich als Einzige in den neuen Bundesländern durchsetzen können. Ihre Bewerbung mit dem Exzellenzcluster „From Cells to Tissues to Therapies" überzeugte. Von 2006 bis 2011 flossen jährlich 1,5 Mio. Euro in das Projekt. Als interdisziplinäres Forschungszentrum für Regenerative Therapien Dresden (CRTD) verbindet es wissenschaftlichen und medizinischen Fortschritt mit technologischem. Über 90 Gruppen forschen mit Industriepartnern an modernen Therapieverfahren, damit Patienten mit Leukämie, Diabetes, Herzkreislauferkrankungen und degenerativen Erkrankungen des Nervensystems besser geholfen werden kann. Als erstes Forschungszentrum in Deutschland rückt es adulte Stammzellen – Stammzellen nach der Geburt – in den Mittelpunkt, mit dem Ziel, neuartige regenerative Therapien zu testen und in vermarktbare Produkte umzuwandeln.

Dieses Exzellenzcluster erhält nun erneut Fördergelder. Das neue Eisen im Feuer heißt „Center for Advancing Electronics Dresden" (cfAED). Ein Exzellenzcluster, das elektronische Informationsverarbeitungssysteme weiterentwickeln will. Naturwissenschaftlicher Erkenntnisdrang soll mit der ingenieurwissenschaftlichen Fähigkeit, Probleme zu lösen, verschmelzen. Ein Pool von 57 Experten vereint kluge Köpfe der TU Dresden und Chemnitz, aus sieben Leibniz-, Max-Planck-, Fraunhofer- und Helmholtz-Einrichtungen. Elektrotechnik, Informatik, Materialwissenschaften, Physik, Chemie und Mathematik kommen salopp gesagt in einen Topf. Wie jedes schmackhafte Gericht mehr ist als die Summe seiner Zutaten, soll dieser Austausch zu grundlegenden Neuansätzen führen.

Wir wollen die Besten

Wie können die Besten zu uns kommen? „DRESDEN concept" wirbt um den Geist der Welt. 14 Partner um Initiator TU Dresden wollen die Stadt als einzigartiges Wissenschaftsnetzwerk

TU are involved in internationally acknowledged cutting-edge research in a whole range of excellence clusters. Excellence – a word that is enjoying a new career in the modern world: excellence initiative, excellence cluster, excellent universities ... it comes originally from the Latin verb "excellere" which means to excel, to be outstanding.

Excellence equals intelligence plus team spirit

Since 2005/06, the excellence initiative of the German government has been funding cutting-edge performance at universities, with a funding line connecting excellence clusters that pursue research into a certain issue at the specific site. TU Dresden has taken its place at the cutting edge of German society: it is one of the eleven universities permitted to call themselves "Elite University" in the second phase of the excellence initiative through to 2017, and the first university in the new federal states. The good news was announced on the afternoon of 15 June 2012 by Rector Hans-Martin Steinhagen in the Old Refectory. The funds coming with the new title give TU Dresden the chance to become one of the most prestigious universities on the international scale. "And I promise that we will use this chance", said the happy Rector. Over the next five years, the university will be receiving altogether 172 million Euro from the federal government and the Free State for its four sub-applications that were all fully approved.

Already in the first funding session, TU Dresden was the only applicant from the new states to win through. Its application with the excellence cluster "From Cells to Tissues to Therapies" convinced the panel, resulting in annual funds of 1.5 million Euro for the project between 2006 and 2011. The interdisciplinary Centre for Regenerative Therapies Dresden (CRTD) combines scientific and medical advances with technological progress. More than 90 groups work together with industrial partners to research into modern therapeutic procedures to provide better help and assistance to patients suffering from leukaemia, diabetes, cardiovascular diseases and degenerative diseases of the central nervous system. It is the first research centre in Germany to shift the focus to adult stem cells – non-embryonic stem cells – with the aim of testing novel regenerative therapies and turning them into products ready for marketing.

This excellence cluster is now receiving more funds. The new iron in the fire is called "Centre for Advancing Electronics Dresden" (cfAED) – an excellence cluster for advancing information processing systems. The scientific urge for knowledge is to be merged with the engineering capability of solving problems. A pool of 57 experts combines clever brains from the TUs in Dresden and Chemnitz, from seven Leibniz, Max Planck, Fraunhofer and Helmholtz institutes. To put it simply, electrical engineering, IT, materials science, physics, chemistry and mathematics are all getting put into the same pot. Just as every

schmackhaft machen. Qualität, Ganzheitlichkeit und Interaktion – so beschreibt der 2009 gegründete Verbund die Zukunftsstrategie. Die Mitstreiter wissen, wovon sie reden. Zwölf kommen von den Forschungsriesen Fraunhofer, Helmholtz, Max Planck und Leibniz aus den alten Bundesländern, die ab 1990 hier den fruchtbaren Boden entdeckten und die Forschungslandschaft mit erblühen ließen.

Finanzregen aus dem Freistaat hilft beim weiteren Gedeihen. Mit der 2007 gestarteten Landesexzellenzinitiative fließen bis 2013 rund 160 Mio. Euro in Sachsens Spitzenforschung. Zwei der fünf Projekte sind im Kammerbezirk Dresden angesiedelt: Das „European Centre for Emerging Materials and Processes Dresden" festigt den Ruf der sächsischen Metropole als ein führendes deutsches Zentrum der Materialforschung; das Gemeinsame Zentrum für Strahlenforschung in der Onkologie in Dresden entwickelt neuartige laserbasierte Geräte für Protonen- und Ionenstrahlen, die eine erheblich verbesserte Krebsbehandlung erwarten lassen.

Gute Beziehungen sind alles

Beziehungsgeflechte entscheiden über den Fortschritt im 21. Jahrhundert. Für diese intelligenten und nutzbringenden Systeme hat sich der Begriff Netzwerk eingebürgert. Die Dichte

tasty dish is more than the sum of its ingredients, the aim here too is for this exchange to lead to new fundamental approaches.

We want the best

How can we attract the best? "DRESDEN concept" woos the spirit of the world. 14 partners around the TU Dresden initiator want to make the city attractive as a unique science network. Quality, holistic approach and interaction were the attributes used to describe the future strategy set up in 2009. The stakeholders know what they're talking about. Twelve come from the research giants Fraunhofer, Helmholtz, Max Planck and Leibniz based in the old German states, having discovered the fertile ground available here following reunification in 1990 and now bringing the research landscape to life.

Funds from the Free State help the concept to flourish. The state excellence initiative launched in 2007 will have poured around 160 million Euro into Saxony's cutting-edge research by 2013. Two of the five projects are located here in the Dresden chamber district: the "European Centre for Emerging Materials and Processes Dresden" consolidates the reputation of Saxony's capital as a leading centre for German material research, while Dresden's Centre for Radiation Research in Oncology develops new laser-based systems for proton and ion radiation that are

Die Dichte von Forschung und Industrie in Sachsens Ballungszentren begünstigt die Lebenskraft von Netzwerken und forciert die Entwicklung von Verfahren und Produkten aus dem Hightechbereich.

The great density of research and industry in Saxony's centre favours the vital force of networks and expedites the development of processes and products coming from the high-tech sector.

von Forschung und Industrie in Sachsens Ballungszentren begünstigt die Geburt und Lebenskraft von Netzwerken, die Blutkreisläufe zwischen Wissenschaft und Wirtschaft, aber auch in und zwischen Branchen sind.

Viele Verbünde agieren vom Kammerbezirk Dresden aus, darunter Silicon Saxony, biosaxony, das Nanotechnologie-Kompetenzzentrum „Ultradünne funktionale Schichten", Organic Electronics Saxony (OES), das Netzwerk für innovative Oberflächentechnik und Anlagenbau (noa), die Verbundinitiative Maschinenbau Sachsen (VEMAS), die Verbundinitiative Industrielles Netzwerk Erneuerbare Energien Sachsen (EESA), der Materialforschungsverbund Dresden und die Verbundinitiative Automobilzulieferer Sachsen (AMZ).

expected to bring about considerable improvements in the treatment of cancer.

Good relations are the be-all and end-all

Networks are intelligent, beneficial systems of connections and relations that play a crucial role in 21st century progress. The density of research and industry in Saxony's conurbations encourages the birth and vitality of networks that pump life through science and industry and in and between individual branches.

Many networks use the Dresden chamber district as their base, including Silicon Saxony, biosaxony, the nanotechnology centre of excellence for "Ultrathin Functional Films", Organic Electronics Saxony (OES), the network for innovative surface technology and mechanical engineering (noa), the Initiative Mechanical Engineering Saxony (VEMAS), the Initiative Industrial Network Renewables in Saxony (EESA), the Material Research Association Dresden and the Initiative Automotive Suppliers Saxony (AMZ).

Von Arzneimittel bis Zeitmesser
Neue Chancen mit Tradition, Qualität und Vielfalt

Drugs, chronometers and much more besides
New chances with tradition, quality and diversity

Sachsen ist bunt und mannigfaltig. Auch der Kammerbezirk Dresden. Über die „Sechs Richtigen" hinaus besticht er mit einer Breite an Unternehmergeist, Schöpferkraft und Leistungsfähigkeit. Viele Traditionen wurden seit 1990 wieder aufgegriffen, andere neu begründet. Die Firmen haben sich untereinander und mit der Forschung vernetzt. Wer nach Sachsen kommt, hat sich nicht irgendeinen Standort ausgesucht, sondern will genau diese verdichtete Struktur von Wirtschaft und Kultur.

Klein, aber fein und wettbewerbsfähig – das trifft auf viele Mittelständler zu. Mit erlesener Kopf- und Handarbeit, hochmodernem Know-how und gefragten Spezialsortimenten fügen alle ihre schillernden Mosaiksteine zum Gesamtbild Sachsens hinzu. Große deutsche und ausländische Mutterkonzerne wiederum sind auf ihre Töchter stolz, die im Kammerbezirk Dresden leben. In Sachsen, wo die schönen Mädchen an den Bäumen wachsen – diese Redensart lässt sich wohl auch auf den Reiz beziehen, der von diesen Tochterunternehmen für das Umfeld ausgeht. Ein kleines Abc soll die Leistungsvielfalt beispielhaft veranschaulichen.

A wie Arzneimittel

... oder ASS (Acetylsalicylsäure). Dieses Derivat der Salicylsäure ist das meistangewandte Schmerzmittel, etwa als Aspirin erhältlich. Chemiker Dr. Friedrich von Heyden stellte Salicylsäure 1874 erstmals großtechnisch in Dresden, später in Radebeul her. Er begründete Deutschlands Pharmaindustrie. Beide Städte sind Pharmastandorte geblieben. GlaxoSmithKline Biologicals in Dresden gehört zu GlaxoSmithKline Deutschland. Die Mutter – ein weltweit führendes Gesundheitsunternehmen – hat die Tochter an der Elbe mit 50 Mio. Euro herausgeputzt. 600 Mitarbeiter entwickeln und produzieren Impfstoffe – zehn Prozent aller Impfstoffe, die in der Welt gebraucht werden. Traditionen führen bis 1908 zum bakteriologischen Labor von Karl August Lingner – Erfinder des Mundwassers Odol – und zum 1911 gegründeten Serumwerk Dresden zurück.

Nachfolger des Arzneimittelwerkes Dresden – größter DDR-Pharmahersteller mit 3000 Beschäftigten – ist die AWD.pharma GmbH & Co. KG in Radebeul. Sie gehört zur israelischen Teva Pharmaceutical Industries Ltd., einem weltweit führenden Generika-Konzern. Die Firma mit 300 Mitarbeitern bietet patentgeschützte Arzneimittel und preiswerte Generika an.

Saxony is a mixing pot of diversity. The same also goes for the Dresden chamber district. Over and beyond the "six winners", it stands out with the sheer diversity of enterprise, creative spirit and productivity. Following reunification in 1990, new life has flowed into many traditions while other new traditions have been founded. Companies have set up networks with each other and with the research sector. Those coming to Saxony have not made any old choice but aimed specifically for this compact structure of business and culture.

They may be small, but they've got what it takes and are competitive besides: skilled workmanship and exquisite brainwork, ultramodern know-how and coveted special assortments combine together to form the brilliant fragments in the mosaic that makes up Saxony. Large parent companies in Germany and abroad in turn are proud of their subsidiaries in the Dresden chamber district – here in Saxony, where pretty girls grow on trees – and flourishing subsidiaries enhance the charm of the area. Let's take a brief alphabetical look at some examples of what it has to offer.

A (D) for drugs

... and acetylsalicylic acid. This derivative of salicylic acid is the most used pain killer, available as aspirin, for example. It was in 1874 that chemist Dr. Friedrich von Heyden first produced salicylic acid on a large scale initially in Dresden and later in Radebeul. He was the founding father of Germany's pharmaceutical industry. Both Dresden and Radebeul remain pharmaceutical sites today. GlaxoSmithKline Biologicals in Dresden belongs to GlaxoSmithKline Deutschland. The parent company, one of the world's leading healthcare companies, has revamped the subsidiary on the river Elbe to the tune of 50 million Euro. 600 employees develop and produce vaccines – ten percent of all vaccines needed in the world. Traditions go back to 1908 to the bacteriological laboratory of Karl August Lingner

Bahntechnik aus dem Hause Bombardier auf den Straßen der sächsischen Landeshauptstadt

Railway technology by Bombardier on the streets of the Saxonian state capital

Auf das Therapiegebiet Urologie hat sich die unabhängige APOGEPHA Arzneimittel GmbH in Dresden spezialisiert. Als Apotheke 1882 gegründet, in der DDR enteignet, 1991 reprivatisiert und mit neuer Herstellungsstätte seit 1996, ist sie Medizinpartner weit über Deutschland hinaus bis Großbritannien, Japan und Südafrika.

Naturheilmittel der Marke „Bombastus" sind seit 1904 begehrt. Die heutige Bombastus-Werke AG in Freital stellt Nahrungsergänzungsmittel, Fertigarzneien, homöopathische Präparate, Kosmetika und ätherische Öle her. Außerdem ist die Firma einer der größten deutschen Teeproduzenten.

B wie Bahntechnik

Großauftrag der Deutschen Bahn: Bis 2014 wird Bombardier in Görlitz 16 vierteilige Doppelstockwagen für die Regionalzugflotte in Schleswig-Holstein bauen. Für den kanadischen Weltkonzern ist die Neißestadt das Kompetenzzentrum für Doppelstockzüge. Die 1160 Beschäftigten fertigen auch Wagenkästen für Flugzeuge und U-Bahnen. Die Fähigkeiten der

– inventor of Odol mouthwash – and to Dresden serum factory founded in 1911.

The successor of Arzneimittelwerke Dresden – the largest pharmaceutical manufacturer in the GDR with 3,000 employees – is AWD.pharma GmbH & Co. KG in Radebeul. It belongs to the Israeli firm Teva Pharmaceutical Industries Ltd., one of the world's leading generic drug companies. The firm with a workforce of 300 employees offers patented medicines and low-cost generic drugs. The independent company APOGEPHA Arzneimittel GmbH in Dresden has specialised in urology therapy. Founded as a pharmacy in 1882, expropriated by the GDR, reprivatised in 1991 and with new production facilities since 1996, it acts as medical partner on a global scale from Germany via the United Kingdom and Japan to South Africa.

Natural remedies in the "Bombastus" brand have been popular since 1904. Today's Bombastus-Werke AG in Freital produces food supplements, finished drugs, homoeopathic preparations, cosmetics and ethereal oils. The company is also one of Germany's largest tea producers.

Görlitzer manifestieren sich ab 1849 in der hiesigen Eisenbahn-Wagenbau-Anstalt. Später wurden Doppelstockwagen ihr internationales Markenzeichen. Heute gehört das Werk mit eigenem Entwicklungszentrum zu Bombardier Transportation. Gemeinsam mit Siemens und Fiat haben die Görlitzer einen Hochgeschwindigkeitszug mit Neigetechnik entwickelt.

Bombardier auch in Bautzen: Was dort 1878 mit dem Bau von Pferdebahnwagen begann, ist heute Weltspitze. Das Werk mit 850 Mitarbeitern gehört zu den größten Straßenbahnherstellern. Schon 1930 hatten die Sachsen mit dem „Großen Hecht" in Dresden Straßenbahnbaugeschichte geschrieben. Die zeitgemäßen Nachfolger aus Bautzen sind die variantenreichen Flexity-Straßenbahnen. Sie befördern Fahrgäste in Australien, Deutschland, England, den Niederlanden, Spanien, Polen und der Türkei.

C wie Chemieindustrie

Wer in Sachsen „fit" sagt, der meint nicht nur frische körperliche Verfassung. „fit" spült Geschirr. Für die Ostdeutschen ist es das Spülmittel schlechthin. Retter der DDR-Marke war 1993 der Mannheimer Chemiker Dr. Wolfgang Groß. Er gründete am Produktionsstandort Zittau-Hirschfelde die fit GmbH, erweiterte das Sortiment um Putz- und Waschmittel auf heute rund 60 Produkte. Für „fit Grüne Kraft" und „Rei Grüne Kraft" vergab Sachsen den Umweltpreis 2011. Dr. Wolfgang Groß wurde zu Sachsens „Unternehmer 2011" gekürt. „Heute ist die fit GmbH nicht nur Marktführer in Ostdeutschland, sondern hat sich u. a. mit der Übernahme verschiedener westdeutscher Traditionsmarken eine feste Position im gesamtdeutschen und internationalen Markt erarbeitet", hieß es in der Begründung.

Neben Charleston, Kalkutta, Köln, Pilsen oder Zhangjiagang hört sich der Ortsname Nünchritz unspektakulär an. Die Gemeinde bei Meißen gehört aber zu den weltweit 20 Standorten der Wacker Chemie AG. 1998 übernahm der Münchner Konzern das ortsansässige Chemiewerk, investierte 1,4 Mrd. Euro und schuf 1400 Arbeitsplätze. Jährlich verlassen 130 000 Tonnen Silicone das Werk. Eine weitere Anlage produziert hochreines polykristallines Silicium für die Solarindustrie.

F wie Fahrzeugbau

Das „Autoland Sachsen" repräsentieren die Weltmarken BMW, Porsche und Volkswagen. Rückgrat ihrer Ansiedlungen sind 750 Zulieferer, Ausrüster und Dienstleister sowie 50 universitäre und außeruniversitäre Forschungseinrichtungen. Sie alle agieren in Nachfolge von Autopionier August Horch, der 1904 in Zwickau seine „Motorwagenwerke" gegründet hatte. In Sachsen ist die Autoindustrie mit einem Viertel des Gesamtumsatzes stärkste Kraft des verarbeitenden Gewerbes. Der Kammerbezirk Dresden bringt etwas Besonderes ein: die Gläserne Manufaktur in Dresden.

B (R) for railway engineering

Big order for Deutsche Bahn: by 2014, Bombardier in Görlitz will be making 16 four-part double-deck coaches for the regional train fleet in Schleswig-Holstein. Here on the river Neiße, the Canadian global corporation has established a centre of excellence for double-deck trains. The 1,160 employees also produce body elements for airplanes and underground trains. The skills of the local population were revealed from 1849 on in the local railway engineering workshop. Later on, double-deck coaches became its international trade mark. Today the factory with its own development centre is part of Bombardier Transportation. The experts here in Görlitz have worked together with Siemens and Fiat to develop a high-speed tilting train.

Bombardier is in Bautzen too: starting from modest beginnings in 1878 with the production of horse-drawn rail wagons, today the company is one of the best of its kind in the world. The factory with 850 employees is one of the biggest tram manufacturers. Already back in 1930, the Saxons wrote tram history in Dresden with the "Großer Hecht" (Big Pike). Modern-day successors from Bautzen are the Flexity trams, carrying passengers in Australia, Germany, England, the Netherlands, Spain, Poland and Turkey.

C for the chemical industry

If you say "fit" in Saxony, you don't mean physical fitness. "fit" rinses the dishes. For the East Germans, it is washing up liquid per se. The GDR brand was saved in 1993 by chemist Dr. Wolfgang Groß from Mannheim. He founded fit GmbH at the production site in Zittau-Hirschfelde and expanded the assortment by adding cleaning agents and detergents so that today the company offers 60 products. The products "fit Grüne Kraft" and "Rei Grüne Kraft" received Saxony's Environment Prize in 2011, while Dr. Wolfgang Groß was declared Saxony's "Entrepreneur of the Year 2011". The reasons stated among others: "Today, fit GmbH is not just market leader in East Germany but has also established a firm position for itself on the German and international market by including various traditional West German brands."

The name Nünchritz doesn't sound very spectacular compared to Charleston, Calcutta, Cologne, Pilsen or Zhangjiagang. But the municipality near Meißen is one of the 20 worldwide sites of Wacker Chemie AG. In 1998, the local chemical plant was taken over by the parent company in Munich, who invested 1.4 billion Euro and created 1,400 jobs. Every year, 130,000 tons of silicone leave the factory, while another facility produces high-purity polycrystalline silicon for the solar industry.

Vielfalt in Breite und Tiefe: 750 Zulieferer, Ausrüster und Dienstleister bilden das Rückgrat der sächsischen Automobilindustrie.

Variety in both breadth and depth: 750 sub-contractors, suppliers and service providers form the backbone of the Saxonian automotive industry.

F (A) for automotive engineering

"Car state Saxony" is represented by the world brands BMW, Porsche and Volkswagen, backed up by an established infrastructure with 750 suppliers, OEMs and service providers together with 50 university and non-university research institutions. They are all successors to car pioneer August Horch, who had founded his "Motorwagenwerke" (motor car works) in Zwickau back in 1904. In Saxony today, the automotive sector is the strongest force on the manufacturing sector, generating one quarter of total turnover. The Dresden chamber district has a special contribution to make in this respect, with the Gläserne Manufaktur (glass car factory) in Dresden.

Since 2001, VW has been producing its luxury Phaeton car here on Großer Garten just ten minutes' walk from the historic city centre. The futuristic production facility with its 40 metres high glass tower combines high-tech and craftsmanship – the latter also living up to the tradition of engineer Emil Hermann Nacke, who built Saxony's very first car (the "Coswiga") in 1990 in nearby Coswig, together with Dresden's coach-builder Carl Heinrich Gläser, whose company became synonymous for luxury car bodies made for convertibles during the 1920s. "Making cars in the living room" was the headline appearing in the Süddeutsche Zeitung newspaper on the 10th jubilee of VW's

VW stellt am Großen Garten – zehn Gehminuten von der Altstadt entfernt – seit 2001 sein Oberklasse-Fahrzeug Phaeton her. Die futuristische Fertigungsstätte mit 40 Meter hohem Glasturm vereint Hochtechnologie und Handarbeit. Letztere auch in der Tradition von Ingenieur Emil Hermann Nacke, der 1900 im nahen Coswig mit der „Coswiga" das erste sächsische Auto überhaupt baute, und des Dresdner Kutschenbauers Carl Heinrich Gläser, dessen Firma in den 1920er-Jahren zum Synonym für Luxuskarossen für Cabriolets wurde. „Autobau im Wohnzimmer" titelte die Süddeutsche Zeitung zum zehnjährigen Jubiläum der VW-Manufaktur. Man wähne sich dort eher in der guten Stube als in einem Industriebetrieb. 500 Beschäftigte in weißen Overalls komplettierten 2011 über 11 000 Fahrzeuge. Auch touristisch profitiert Dresden: Acht von zehn der betuchten Kunden holen ihr Fahrzeug vor Ort ab, über 100 000 Besucher besichtigen jährlich die transparente Montage.

Der kleine Bruder der Automobilmanufaktur Dresden GmbH ist Melkus Sportwagen GmbH. Das Dresdner Familienunter-

Fortsetzung Seite 98

Continued on page 98

MFT Motoren und Fahrzeugtechnik GmbH

Information

Gründungsjahr: 1992

Mitarbeiter: ca. 150

Produkt- und Leistungsspektrum:
Komponentenfertigung
- Nockenwellen
- Ausgleichswellen
- Pleuel
- Halterungen für Motor und Getriebe
- Kurbel- und Pumpengehäuse

Konstruktion und Montage von
- speziellen Prototypen
- Werkzeugen und Vorrichtungen

Year founded: 1992

Employees: approx. 150

Range of products and services:
component manufacturing
- camshafts
- balance shafts
- connecting rods
- engine and transmission mounts
- crank and pump housing

design and manufacture of
- special prototypes
- tooling and fixtures

MFT Motoren und Fahrzeugtechnik GmbH, Cunewalde

MFT Motoren und Fahrzeugtechnik GmbH

Mit der Erfahrung aus sechs Jahrzehnten Verbrennungsmotorenbau hat sich MFT Motoren und Fahrzeugtechnik zu einem anerkannten Hersteller anspruchsvoller Fahrzeugkomponenten spezialisiert: Nockenwellen, Ausgleichswellen, Pleuel, Halterungen für Motor und Getriebe sowie Kurbel- und Pumpengehäuse.

Neben der Teilefertigung umfasst das Leistungsangebot von MFT auch die Montage kompletter Baugruppen sowie die Konstruktion und Herstellung spezieller Prototypen, Werkzeuge und Vorrichtungen.

Wie aus Ideen Resultate werden – Qualität aus der Oberlausitz.

MFT Motoren und Fahrzeugtechnik GmbH

With the experience of six decades of internal combustion engine MFT Motoren und Fahrzeugtechnik had developed in a recognized manufacturer of sophisticated vehicle components: camshafts, balance shafts, connecting rods, engine and transmission mounts and crank and pump housing.

In addition to the production of parts includes the services by MFT the assembly of complete modules and the design and manufacture of special prototypes, tooling and fixtures.

Turning ideas into results: quality from Oberlausitz.

www.mft-cunewalde.de

nehmen in dritter Generation gründet sich auf die Motorsportbegeisterung und Fahrzeugbaukunst von Heinz Melkus. Von 1950 bis 1977 nahm er in eigenen Gefährten an mehr als 200 Rennen teil und wurde sechsmal DDR-Meister. Seit 2006 setzen die 15 Melkus-Mitarbeiter auf kleinste Serien: Jährlich entstehen unter ihren Händen 25 hoch individuell gefertigte Sportwagen.

Kabelbäume, Getriebe, Bremsen, Verglasung, Innenverkleidung... Einzelteile und Baugruppen für Autos aus Sachsen werden von 60 000 Beschäftigten in mittelständischen Firmen gefertigt. Die Verbundinitiative Automobilzulieferer Sachsen (AMZ) hilft seit 1999, Kooperationen zu knüpfen und neue Produkte einzuführen. Die FEP Fahrzeugelektrik Pirna GmbH stellt jährlich eine Milliarde Schalter, Steckverbindungen, Kabelführungen und weitere Teile für Abnehmer in gut 50 Ländern her. Die TD Deutsche Klimakompressor GmbH in Straßgräbchen bei Kamenz produziert einzigartige Klimakompressoren mit geringem Geräusch- und Vibrationslevel.

Rollende Apartments kommen aus Neustadt in der Sächsischen Schweiz. Die CAPRON GmbH fertigt Reisemobile, Alkoven-Modelle und Caravans. 2005 hatten die Branchenriesen Hymer AG in Bad Waldsee und Dethleffs GmbH & Co. KG in Isny im einstigen Landmaschinenwerk eine hochmoderne Produktionsstraße aufgebaut. Viele Anhänger hat die STEMA Metallleichtbau GmbH in Großenhain: Jeder vierte Pkw-Anhänger in Deutschland stammt aus dem Betrieb. Zu den 8000 Fahrzeugen pro Monat gehören Kasten-, Motorrad- und Bootstransporter.

G wie Gesundheitswirtschaft

Arthur Schopenhauer – der in Dresden sein philosophisches Hauptwerk schrieb – kannte den Wert des Wohlbefindens: „Gesundheit ist nicht alles, aber ohne Gesundheit ist alles nichts." Der moderne Gesundheitsmarkt bietet dem Menschen die Güter und Dienstleistungen, mit denen er seine Gesundheit bewahren oder wiederherstellen kann. Die Gesundheitswirtschaft ist eine Wachstumsbranche. Die Plattform „Gesundheitswirtschaft in Sachsen" unterstützt die Akteure dabei, effektiver zusammenzuarbeiten und neue wissenschaftliche Erkenntnisse schneller umzusetzen. Zu den Initiatoren gehört das Gesundheitsökonomische Zentrum der TU Dresden.

Auf dem Gesundheitsmarkt vermischen sich Medizin, Pharmaindustrie, Maschinen- und Anlagenbau, Bio- und Nanotechnologie, Ernährungswirtschaft und Tourismus. Die Medizintechniker etwa bringen mit mehr als 100 Mittelständlern in Sachsen das größte Potenzial ihrer Art in den neuen Ländern ein – von der hochmodernen Diagnose und Therapie bis hin zu weltweit gefragten Verbrauchsmaterialien.

Die Alpha Plan GmbH in Radeberg entwickelt Technologien für medizinische Einwegartikel und Filtrationssysteme. Bei Dialysesystemen führt sie international. Die TUR Therapietechnik GmbH Dresden fertigt medizinische Geräte, darunter für die Reiz-

Gläserne Manufaktur. It's more like being in the parlour than in an industrial factory. In 2011, 500 employees in white overalls completed more than 11,000 vehicles. Dresden also profits in terms of its tourist trade: eight of ten of the well-heeled customers come in person to collect their vehicle, while more than 100,000 visitors come to see the transparent assembly line every year.

The Automobilmanufaktur Dresden GmbH has a smaller brother – Melkus Sportwagen GmbH. The Dresden family company now being run by the third generation arose from the racing passion and automotive engineering skills of Heinz Melkus. Between 1950 and 1977, he took part in more than 200 races in vehicles he had made himself, and was GDR champion six times. Since 2006, the 15 Melkus employees have focused on mini-series: every year, their skilled hands produce 25 highly individual custom-made sports cars.

Cable harnesses, gear systems, brakes, window elements, interior trim – individual parts and assemblies for cars from Saxony are made by 60,000 employees in SME firms. The Initiative Automotive Suppliers Saxony (AMZ) has been busy since 1999 in linking cooperation possibilities and introducing new products. FEP Fahrzeugelektrik Pirna GmbH makes a billion switches, connectors, cable routings and other parts every year for customers in a good 50 countries. TD Deutsche Klimakompressor GmbH in Straßgräbchen near Kamenz produces unique air-conditioning compressors with a low noise and vibration level.

Rolling homes come from Neustadt in Saxon Switzerland. CAPRON GmbH produces motor homes, alcove models and caravans. In 2005, branch giants Hymer AG in Bad Waldsee and Dethleffs GmbH & Co. KG in Isny set up a state-of-the-art production line in the former agricultural machinery factory. STEMA Metallleichtbau GmbH in Großenhain produces every fourth car trailer found on German roads. The 8,000 vehicles made every month include box trailers, motorbike transport trailers and boat trailers.

G (H) for health

Arthur Schopenhauer – who wrote his main philosophical work in Dresden – knew the value of well-being: "Health is not everything, but without health, everything is nothing." The modern health-care market offers people the goods and services for preserving or restoring their health. The health-care branch is a growth branch. The platform "Health-Care in Saxony" supports the players in working together more efficiently and implementing new scientific findings more swiftly. The initiators include the Health Economics Centre of TU Dresden.

The health-care market combines medicine, the pharmaceutical industry, machine and plant construction, bio- and nanotechnology, the food industry and tourism. Medical engineers for example in more than 100 SME companies in Saxony con-

Die sächsische Glasindustrie ist vor allem auf Nischenprodukte spezialisiert, zum Beispiel auf technische Gläser.

First and foremost, the Saxonian glass industry is specialised on niche products, for instance on technical glass.

strom-, Ultraschall- und Schröpftherapie. Die Großbuchstaben im Firmennamen erinnern an das Transformatoren- und Röntgenwerk mit 3500 Beschäftigten, einem planwirtschaftlichen Tausendsassa mit Produktionen vom Fahrstuhl bis zum Herzschrittmacher. Die MEGADENTA Dentalprodukte GmbH in Radeberg geht Zahnärzten in über 50 Ländern zur Hand, darunter mit Abformwerkstoffen und Lichtpolymerisationsgeräten.

G wie Glas

Um 1930 galt die Lausitz als Europas größte Glasregion. In der DDR war „Lausitzer Glas" der Name eines Kombinates mit Sitz in Weißwasser, rund 20 Betrieben und 19 000 Beschäftigten. Es konzentrierte die ostdeutsche Blei-, Wirtschafts- und Behälterglasproduktion. Nach der Wende zerfiel die Glasindustrie, einige Betriebe riskierten den Neustart. Die Glasherstellung im Kammerbezirk Dresden ist stark geschrumpft, mit Spezialsortimenten aber am Markt gut vertreten. In Weißwasser selbst, wo 1872 die erste Glashütte und 1996 ein Glasmuseum eröffnet

Fortsetzung Seite 103

tribute the greatest potential of their particular kind in the new German states – from state-of-the-art diagnosis and therapy through to consumables in global demand.

Alpha Plan GmbH in Radeberg develops technologies for disposable medical articles and filtration systems, and leads the international field for dialysis systems. TUR Therapietechnik GmbH Dresden produces medical devices, for instance for stimulation current, ultrasound and cupping therapy. The large letters in the company name recall the transformer and X-ray factory with 3,500 employees, an all-rounder under the socialist regime with a production range extending from lifts to pacemakers. MEGADENTA Dentalprodukte GmbH in Radeberg assists dentists in more than 50 countries with products such as impression compounds and light polymerisation devices.

G for glass

In 1930, Lausitz was Europe's largest glass region. In the GDR, "Lausitzer Glas" was the name of a collective based in Weißwasser with around 20 factories and 19,000 employees. This was the heart of East German lead, industrial and con-

Continued on page 103

fit GmbH

Die Geschichte der fit GmbH beginnt 1954 in Chemnitz mit dem Markennamen fit-flüssig. Ein Jahr später kam fit Spülmittel auf den Markt; erhältlich zunächst als Pulver, später auch flüssig in der Glasflasche. 1967 wurde eine neue Produktionsanlage in Hirschfelde bei Zittau gebaut, mit der auch die unverkennbare Flasche in Form des Roten Turms in Chemnitz eingeführt wurde.

Nach der Wiedervereinigung machte das Unternehmen zunächst eine schwere Zeit durch, schaffte es aber mit Mut und Erfindungsreichtum Marktanteile und Akzeptanz zurückzuerobern. 1993 schließlich kaufte der Chemiker Dr. Wolfgang Groß das Werk. Seine unternehmerische Weitsicht und bedeutende Investitionen in die Modernisierung und in den Aufbau neuer Produktionsanlagen sicherten der fit GmbH eine neue Zukunft. Seitdem konnte der Umsatz bis heute nahezu versiebenfacht werden. 2011 wurde Dr. Wolfgang Groß in Sachsen als „Unternehmer des Jahres" ausgezeichnet.

Das Motto der fit GmbH lautet seit über 50 Jahren: „Weniger versprechen, mehr halten." Davon profitieren nicht nur die Verbraucher, sondern auch die Natur. Alle Produkte des Unternehmens überzeugen dank modernster Forschung mit hervorragender Wasch- und Spülleistung. Gleichzeitig wird streng darauf geachtet, dass jedes Produkt ökologisch sinnvoll hergestellt wird. Schadstoffemissionen werden so gering wie möglich gehalten, der Energieverbrauch bei der Produktion gesenkt und innovative Fertigungsverfahren helfen dabei, Abfall zu verringern – zum Beispiel mit der wasserlöslichen Folie für Geschirrspültabs.

Seit 2008 werden viele Produkte auf Basis nachwachsender Rohstoffe hergestellt. fit Grüne Kraft Spülmittel, Tabs, Haushaltsreiniger und Rei Grüne Kraft Waschmittel reinigen zuverlässig auf Basis von Zitronensäure oder Palmöl, sind phosphatfrei und vollständig biologisch abbaubar. Dass dies der richtige Weg ist, zeigen die Fakten: Jeder zehnte deutsche Haushalt verlässt sich auf die Erfahrung der fit-Experten in Sachen Sauberkeit, und viele fit-Produkte tragen das Europäische Umweltzeichen.

fit Spülmittel Original in der 500-ml-Flasche ist 2011 – wie schon 2010 – Deutschlands meistverkaufte Spülmitteleinzelvariante und damit zugleich stolzer Träger des Labels Top-Marke 2011.

fit GmbH

The history of fit GmbH begins in 1954 in Chemnitz with the brand name fit-flüssig. One year later, fit washing up detergent was launched, initially as a powder and later on also as a liquid in a glass bottle. In 1967 a new production facility in Hirschfelde near Zittau was constructed, also heralding the launch of the unmistakable bottle shaped like the Red Tower of Chemnitz.

After reunification, the company went through a difficult phase at first, before recovering market shares and acceptance with courage and inventiveness. It was in 1993 that chemist Dr. Wolfgang Groß eventually purchased the factory. His entrepreneurial foresight paired with significant investment in modernisation and in setting up new production facilities ensured a new future for fit GmbH. Since then, turnover has multiplied nearly sevenfold through to today. In 2011, Dr. Wolfgang Groß received the award as Saxony's "Entrepreneur of the Year".

For more than 50 years, the motto of fit GmbH has been "promise less and do more". This is beneficial not just to consumers but also to nature. Thanks to state-of-the-art research, all the company's products stand out with convincing washing and rinsing performance. At the same time, strict attention is paid to ecologically sound manufacturing of every product. Harmful emissions are kept to a minimum, energy consumption during production is reduced and innovative manufacturing procedures help to reduce waste – for example with the water-soluble foil for dishwasher tabs.

Since 2008, many products have been made on the basis of renewable raw materials. fit Grüne Kraft washing up liquid, tabs, household cleaning agents and Rei Grüne Kraft detergent clean reliably on the basis of citric acid or palm oil, are free of phosphates and fully biodegradable. Facts and figures show that this is the right approach. One in ten German households relies on the experience of fit's experts when it comes to cleanness, and many fit products bear the European ecolabel.

As already in 2010, fit Original washing up liquid in the 500 ml bottle is Germany's top selling individual washing up liquid variant in 2011 and thus also proudly bears the label Top Brand 2011.

Information

Gründungsjahr: 1993

Mitarbeiter: 160

Produktspektrum:
Wasch-, Putz- und Reinigungsmittel, die unter den Markennamen fit, *Kuschelweich*, *Sunil*, *Rei*, *Rei in der Tube* sowie *Sanso* bundesweit vertrieben werden

Umsatz: ca. 106 Mio. Euro in 2011

Year founded: 1993

Employees: 160

Range of products:
washing and cleaning agents sold nationwide under the brand names fit, *Kuschelweich*, *Sunil*, *Rei*, *Rei in der Tube* and *Sanso*

Turnover: approx. 106 million Euro in 2011

fit GmbH
Zittau

Information

Gründungsjahr: 1956
Mitarbeiter:
das EZG arbeitet deutschlandweit mit
- 6 Dipl.-Ingenieuren
- 3 Dipl.-Ökonomen
- 10 kaufmännischen Mitarbeitern
- 18 Meistern
- 50 Monteuren
- 3 Helfern
- 20 Auszubildenden

Produkt- und Leistungsspektrum:
- Eletrotechnik
- elektronische Sicherheitstechnik
- Gebäudekommunikation
- Antennen- und SAT-Anlagen
- Netzwerkverkabelung
- Zählerschrankbau
- Handel und Service mit Hausgeräten
- Service für E-Motoren und E-Werkzeuge
- Berufsausbildung

Year founded: 1956
Employees:
EZG works throughout Germany with
- 6 engineering graduates
- 3 economics graduates
- 10 commercial staff
- 18 masters
- 50 fitters
- 3 helpers
- 20 apprentices

Range of products and services:
- electrical engineering
- electronic security systems
- building communication
- aerials and SAT systems
- network cabling
- meter cabinet construction
- sales and servicing of domestic appliances
- servicing of electric motors and electric tools
- vocational training

Elektro Zentrum Großenhain EZG eG
Großenhain

Elektro Zentrum Großenhain EZG eG

Das Unternehmen geht zurück auf das Jahr 1956 und wurde damals von vier Handwerksmeistern und fünf Gesellen unter dem Namen „Produktionsgenossenschaft des Handwerks PGH 1. Mai Elektro-Radio-Fernsehen" gegründet. Nach der politischen Wende erfolgte 1991 durch genossenschaftlichen Wahlmodus die Umwandlung zum Elektro Zentrum Großenhain EZG eG.

Heute präsentiert sich die Firma als ein bundesweit tätiger Anbieter von anspruchsvollen Montage- und Serviceleistungen im elektrotechnischen Bereich. Besonderen Wert legt das Unternehmen auf die laufende fachliche Aus- und Weiterbildung. In der firmeneigenen Lehrwerkstatt werden durchschnittlich 20 Lehrlinge ausgebildet.

Die Referenzliste des Unternehmens verdeutlicht, dass das Elektro Zentrum Großenhain längst über den Status einer regionalen Elektrofirma hinausgewachsen ist.

Elektro Zentrum Großenhain EZG eG

The company goes back to 1956, when it was founded by four master craftsmen and five journeymen under the name "Produktionsgenossenschaft des Handwerks PGH 1. Mai Elektro-Radio-Fernsehen" (Skilled Crafts Production Cooperative PGH 1st of May, Radio, Television and Electrical Engineers). Following reunification in 1991, the company was reorganised under its current name Elektro Zentrum Großenhain EZG eG.

Today the firm is a nationwide provider of top quality installation and support services in the field of electrical engineering. Special attention is paid to on-going initial and advanced vocational training, including on average 20 apprentices in the company's own training facility.

The company's reference list clearly shows that Elektro Zentrum Großenhain has meanwhile achieved a status far above that of a regional electrical contractor.

wurde, führt die Stölzle Lausitz GmbH die Tradition fort. Bis zu 35 Millionen bleifreie Kristallgläser für die moderne Tischkultur vor allem in der Gastronomie gehen jährlich in alle Welt.

Die TELUX Spezialglas GmbH in Weißwasser entwickelt und produziert technische Gläser, darunter Spezialglaskolben für Hochdruckentladungslampen. Ein weiteres Produkt sind Alumosilicatglasröhren für die Fahrzeug-Frontbeleuchtung. Bei diesen Spezialglasrohren hat TELUX weltweit die Nase vorn. Vom Fensterglas zum Hightech-Werkstoff ist die Polartherm Flachglas GmbH vorangeschritten. Aus NRW verlagerte sie ihren Hauptsitz für vier Produktionsstätten nach Großenhain. Isolierglas, Innenraumglas, komplette Fenster-, Türen- und Fassadenelemente – die Firma bietet mit wärme- und schalldämmenden Gläsern der Architektur neue Gestaltungsspielräume. So hat das Unternehmen bereits für den Carlton Tower Dubai, den Flughafen Kopenhagen und Rolls-Royce gearbeitet.

Das Glaswerk Freital der internationalen Gruppe Preiss-Daimler stellt für höchste Ansprüche der Lebensmittelindustrie Behälterglas her. Die Spirituosen-, Wein- und Saftflaschen werden bis zu 70 Prozent aus Altglasscherben produziert. Das Werk mit Wurzeln bis 1818 zählt mit seiner Schmelzleistung zu den kleinsten Glashütten Deutschlands. Der Vorteil: Es kann schnell und flexibel auf Kundenwünsche aus dem In- und Ausland reagieren.

H wie Handwerk

VW hat in Dresden den Manufaktur-Begriff wieder salonfähig gemacht. „Manus" ist im Lateinischen die Hand, „factura" die Herstellung. Die Übergänge zum traditionellen Handwerk sind fließend. „Verachtet mir die Meister nicht und ehrt mir ihre Kunst!", mahnte ein gebürtiger Sachse, Komponist Richard Wagner. In Sachsen bestehen knapp 60 000 Handwerksbetriebe mit 420 000 Arbeitsplätzen. Fast jeder vierte Erwerbstätige im Freistaat arbeitet im Handwerk. Die Firmendichte pro 1000 Einwohner liegt mit 14,2 Betrieben über dem bundesdeutschen Mittel.

Mit Können, Fleiß, Traditionssinn und Innovationsgeist bereichern im Kammerbezirk Dresden rund 22 500 Handwerksfirmen in mehr als 90 Innungen Sachsens Wirtschaft. Bäcker, Bauhandwerker, Elektrotechniker, Dachdecker, Fleischer, Friseure, Kfz-Handwerker, Maler, Klempner, Metallbauer, Tischler, Zimmerer... Mit ihrer Wertschöpfung sorgen sie lokal und regional für Fortentwicklung, Beschäftigung und Lebensqualität. Sie sind nimmermüde Dienstleister für die Bürger. Einige Gewerke bewähren sich als zuverlässige und flexible Partner der Industrie.

Die Handwerkskammer Dresden ehrt und vermehrt ihre Meister: 2012 sind weitere 400 bis 450 Absolventen hinzugekommen. „Die Meisterausbildung sichert die Qualität im Handwerk, aber auch Beschäftigung und Wachstum für die sächsische Wirtschaft", sagt HWK-Präsident Claus Dittrich. Seit der Wende

tainer glass production. After reunification, the glass branch fell apart, with just a few companies daring to go for a new start. Glass production in the Dresden chamber district has declined considerably in size, but is still well represented with special products on the market. In Weißwasser itself, where the first glass works began operation in 1872 and a glass museum was opened in 1996, Stölzle Lausitz GmbH keeps the tradition going. Up to 35 million lead-free crystal glasses for modern dining culture leave the factory every year, intended primarily for the world's catering industry.

TELUX Spezialglas GmbH in Weißwasser develops and produces technical glass, including special glass bulbs for high-pressure discharge lamps, and also aluminosilicate glass tubes for vehicle front lights. TELUX leads the global market for these special glass tubes. The production range of Polartherm Flachglas GmbH has advanced from window glass to high-tech solutions. The company from NRW relocated its headquarters for four production sites to Großenhain. Here it makes insulating glass, interior glass, complete window, door and facade elements, together with heat-insulating and sound-proofing glass solutions that offer architects new scope for design. The company has already produced glass for example for Carlton Tower Dubai, Copenhagen Airport and for Rolls-Royce.

Glaswerk Freital belongs to the international Preiss-Daimler Group and makes container glass to meet the strict requirements of the food industry. Bottles for spirits, wine and juice are made up to 70 percent from fragments of used glass. The glass factory with roots going back to 1818 is one of the smallest of its kind in Germany, with the advantage that it is in a position to react quickly and flexibly to customer requests from Germany and abroad.

H (S) for skilled crafts

VW in Dresden has made manufacturing respectable again. "Manus" is the Latin word for hand and "factura" means production. The transitions to the traditional skilled crafts are fuzzy. "Do not scorn the masters and honour their skill!", warned composer Richard Wagner who was born in Saxony. Saxony has just about 60,000 skilled crafts companies with 420,000 employees. Nearly one in four of the gainfully employed in the Free State works in the skilled crafts. The company density of 14.2 companies per 1,000 residents is above the German average.

Around 22,500 skilled crafts firms enrich the Dresden chamber district with skill, diligence, a sense of tradition and innovation, belonging to more than 90 guilds in Saxony's economy. Bakers, builders, electrical engineers, roofing engineers, butchers, hairdressers, car mechanics, painters, plumbers, metalworkers, cabinetmakers, carpenters... The added value they contribute to the economy provides progress, employment and quality of life on a local and regional scale. They are the never-

Das sächsische Handwerk ist einer der wichtigsten Wirtschaftsfaktoren und sichert Tausende Arbeitsplätze.

Saxonian craftsmanship is one of the most important economic factors and secures thousands of jobs.

haben im Kammerbezirk insgesamt 14 200 Absolventen ihren Meisterbrief erworben.

Sachsens Handwerker widmen sich auch seltenen Fertigungen und Produkten. Die Stuhlbauer in der Stuhlbauerstadt Rabenau, die erzgebirgischen Holzkünstler in Dippoldiswalde, die Pfefferküchler in Pulsnitz, die Kunstblumenhersteller in Sebnitz und die Töpfer in Neukirch gehören zu ihnen.

K wie Kosmetik

Die Kinderzahncreme Putzi ist eine Ost-Legende. Sie schmeckte auch. 1990 wurde aus der VEB Elbe-Chemie die Dental-Kosmetik GmbH & Co. KG. Rund 20 Zahncremes und Mundwasser – darunter Putzi mit „sehr gut" von Öko-Test – verlassen die modernen Produktions-, Abfüll- und Verpackungsanlagen in Dresdens Neustadt. Stammvater ist Ottomar von Mayenburg: Er erfand 1907 in Dresden die Chlorodont, die erste Zahncreme, die maschinell hergestellt und in Metalltuben abgefüllt wurde. In den 1920er-Jahren war sie die führende Weltmarke.

tiring service providers for the local population, while others prove their worth as reliable and flexible partners for industry.

Dresden Chamber of Skilled Crafts honours its master craftsmen and ensures that they increase in number: in 2012, a further 400 to 450 had completed their qualifications. "The master craftsman qualification assures quality in the skilled trades, while also securing employment and growth for Saxony's economy", says Claus Dittrich, President of the Chamber of Skilled Crafts. Since reunification, 14,200 candidates have acquired the master craftsman qualification in the Dresden chamber district.

Saxony's skilled craftsmen also devote their time and energy to rare skills, products and processes, including chair-making in Rabenau, the wood-carving traditions of the Erzgebirge mountains in Dippoldiswalde, gingerbread in Pulsnitz, artificial flowers in Sebnitz and pottery in Neukirch.

Besonders im Bereich der Naturkosmetik haben sächsische Unternehmen Maßstäbe gesetzt.

Particularly in the field of natural cosmetics, Saxonian companies have set standards.

Die Kosmetikmarke „Charlotte Meentzen" verbindet sich seit 1930 mit Dresden und seit 2002 mit der neuen Produktionsstätte in Radeberg. Der 1991 reprivatisierte Familienbetrieb gilt als Wegbereiter der Naturkosmetik in Deutschland. Dazu nutzt heute die Charlotte Meentzen Kräutervital Kosmetik GmbH neueste Erkenntnisse der Naturwissenschaften. Das Familienunternehmen Kappus aus Offenbach gab 1990 dem Konsumseifenwerk Riesa – mit Tradition seit 1910 und größter DDR-Seifenproduzent – eine neue Perspektive: Die Kappus Seifen GmbH Riesa & Co stellt Seifen, Körperlotionen, Gels und Duschbäder her, darunter die patentierte Schwimmseife.

„Li-iL" ist keine chinesische, sondern eine Ur-Dresdner Firma. 1910 kombinierte Gründer Richard Carl Pittlik die Begriffe „Lithium" – Trägerstoff für ätherische Öle – und „Ilatium" – Wirkungsprinzip von außen nach innen – miteinander. Heute steht die familiengeführte Li-iL GmbH Arzneimittel und Arzneibäder mit rund 130 Produkten der Marke „Dresdner Essenz" für die medizinische Wirksamkeit von Heilkräuterextrakten.

Fortsetzung Seite 111

K (C) for cosmetics

Putzi children's toothpaste is a legend of the east. It's one that tastes good too. In 1990, the state-owned VEB Elbe-Chemie was turned into Dental-Kosmetik GmbH & Co. KG. Around 20 toothpaste and mouthwash products leave the modern production, filling and packaging lines in Dresden's Neustadt, including Putzi with the "very good" rating by the consumer organisation Öko-Test. The progenitor is Ottomar von Mayenburg, who invented Chlorodont in Dresden in 1907: this was the first toothpaste to be produced by machine and filled in metal tubes. It was the world's leading brand during the 1920s.

The "Charlotte Meentzen" cosmetics brand has been associated with Dresden since 1930, and since 2002 with the new production facility in Radeberg. The family company reprivatised in 1990 is seen as the pioneer of natural cosmetics in Germany. To this end, today Charlotte Meentzen Kräutervital Kosmetik GmbH uses the very latest scientific findings. In 1990,

Continued on page 111

Veritas Sachsen GmbH

Vollautomatische Spritzgießmaschinen und Facharbeiter gewährleisten Qualität auf höchstem Niveau.

Fully automatic injection moulding machines and skilled workers warrant quality on the very highest level.

Information

Gründungsjahr/Umfirmierung:
1914 Pyrotechnische Fabrik,
1930 Umfirmierung Ostsächsische Gummiwerke,
2012 Umfirmierung Veritas Sachsen GmbH und Neubau

Mitarbeiter: 130 (2012)

Standorte: Polenz und Neustadt in Sachsen

Produkt- und Leistungsspektrum:
- komplexe Mehrkomponenten-Systeme
- technische Form- und Verbundteile aus Gummi sowie Gummi-Metall-Verbindungen und Gummi-Kunststoff-Verbindungen
- Montage von Baugruppen

Kundenspektrum:
Automobilindustrie, Maschinenbau, Elektroindustrie und andere Branchen

Year founded/renaming:
1914 pyrotechnical factory,
1930 renamed as Ostsächsische Gummiwerke,
2012 renamed as Veritas Sachsen GmbH and new-build

Employees: 130 (2012)

Sites: Polenz and Neustadt in Saxony

Range of products and services:
- complex multi-component systems
- technical mouldings and composite parts of rubber and rubber-metal combinations and rubber-plastic combinations
- assembly of component groups

Customer range:
automotive industry, machine construction, electrical industry and other branches

Veritas Sachsen GmbH
Neustadt

Veritas Sachsen GmbH

Die Veritas Sachsen GmbH in Polenz und Neustadt bei Dresden verfügt über eine jahrzehntelange Erfahrung in der Verarbeitung elastomerer Werkstoffe. Technische Formteile aus Gummi sowie Gummi-Metall- und Gummi-Kunststoff-Verbindungen sind die Kernkompetenzen.

Die von der Veritas AG im Juli 2010 übernommene Ostsächsische Gummiwerke GmbH in Neustadt firmiert seit dem 1. März 2012 als Veritas Sachsen GmbH. Der neue Name ist äußeres Zeichen der erfolgreichen Integration des sächsischen Gummiverarbeiters in den hessischen Konzern. Aufgrund des Wissens um die Gummi- und Kunststofftechnik engagierte sich die Veritas AG im Gewerbegebiet von Neustadt mit einer Gesamtinvestition von über 40 Mio. Euro. Auf einem rund 20 000 Quadratmeter großen Konversionsareal entsteht eine neue Produktionshalle mit einer Fläche von 6000 Quadratmetern, die in mehreren Bauabschnitten um das Doppelte vergrößert werden kann. Der erste Spatenstich für den Neubau erfolgte am 30. September 2011.

Das neue Fertigungswerk ist mit den modernsten Injektions- und Transfermaschinen ausgestattet. In der neuen Fabrik wird die Veritas Sachsen GmbH komplexe Mehrkomponenten-Spritzgießteile und vormontierte Systeme für die Automobilindustrie produzieren.

Alle Produkte werden individuell und auftragsbezogen nach Kundenspezifikation gefertigt. Das Neustädter Werk fungiert auch als interner Zulieferer im weltweiten Produktionsnetzwerk der Veritas-Gruppe.

Die Veritas Sachsen GmbH arbeitet konsequent kundenorientiert: angefangen von der Erstberatung über die Entwicklung von Musterserien bis hin zum Endprodukt. Die Stärken des Unternehmens sind seine große Flexibilität, die unbedingte Liefertreue und der erfahrene Mitarbeiterstamm. Mit einer Basis von derzeit über 1000 Werkzeugen können auch Kleinserien wirtschaftlich hergestellt werden. Die Veritas Sachsen GmbH ist nach ISO/TS 16949 zertifiziert und gehört zur Firmengruppe Veritas mit Sitz in Gelnhausen.

Die Veritas AG, 1849 gegründet, ist ein global agierender Automobilzulieferer. Zum Produktportfolio zählen innovative Leitungssysteme zum Transport von Kraftstoff, Öl und anderen Fluiden. Zum Kundenkreis gehören alle europäischen Automobilhersteller sowie deren Zulieferer.

Veritas Sachsen GmbH

Veritas Sachsen GmbH in Polenz and Neustadt near Dresden, offers decades of experience in processing elastomers. The company's core competencies consist in technical mouldings made of rubber together with rubber-metal and rubber-plastic combinations.

Following the takeover in July 2010 by Veritas AG of the former Ostsächsische Gummiwerke GmbH in Neustadt, as of March 1, 2012 the company is now called Veritas Sachsen GmbH. The new name clearly indicates the successful integration of the Saxon rubber processing firm in the Veritas Group based in the German state of Hesse. With its know-how in rubber and plastics engineering, Veritas AG has committed capital expenditure of more than 40 million Euro at its site in Neustadt commercial estate. Premises covering 20,000 square metres are being used to construct a new production plant measuring 6,000 square metres which offers space for gradual expansion until twice its size. The groundbreaking ceremony for the new-build took place on September 30, 2011.

The new production site is equipped with state-of-the-art injection moulding and transfer machinery. The new factory will be used by Veritas Sachsen GmbH to produce complex multi-component injection moulding parts and premounted systems for the automotive industry.

All parts are individually custom-made to customer specifications. Veritas Neustadt site also acts as internal supplier in the global production network of the Veritas Group.

Veritas Sachsen GmbH takes a consistently customer-oriented approach, starting from initial consultations through the development of pilot series to the final product. The strengths of the company consist in great flexibility, absolute delivery reliability and its experienced workforce. Even small series can be produced economically, based on currently more than 1,000 tools. Veritas Sachsen GmbH is certified to ISO/TS 16949 and belongs to the Veritas Group with headquarters in Gelnhausen.

Veritas AG, founded in 1849, is a global automotive supplier. The product portfolio includes innovative line systems for transporting fuel, oil and other fluids. The customer base is made up of all European automotive producers and their suppliers.

Mitras Composites Systems GmbH

Erste Qualitätskontrolle nach der Entnahme aus der Presse

First quality control after removing from the press

Information

Gründungsjahr: 1962
Mitarbeiter: 161
Leistungsspektrum:
Full-Service-Dienstleistungen bei der Entwicklung und Herstellung von faserverstärkten Kunststoffen
zertifiziert nach DIN EN ISO 9001:2008 und Energiemanagement nach ISO 50001

Year founded: 1962
Employees: 161
Range of services:
full range of services for the development and production of fibreglass reinforced plastics
certified to DIN EN ISO 9001:2008 and energy management to ISO 50001

Mitras Composites Systems GmbH
Radeburg

Mitras Composites Systems GmbH

Mitras Composites Systems GmbH ist ein dynamisch wachsendes Unternehmen und einer der europäischen Marktführer in der Verarbeitung von glasfaserverstärkten, duroplastischen Kunststoffen auf Polyesterharzbasis.

Die Fertigung erfolgt in den drei Technologien: Heißpressen, Spritzgießen und der Sondertechnologie Spritzprägen. Dazu stehen zwölf Pressen bis 1000 Tonnen Schließkraft und acht Spritzgießmaschinen bis zu 1300 Tonnen Schließkraft zur Verfügung. Mitras Composites Systems ist so in der Lage, Klein- wie Großserien zu fertigen und kann aufgrund einer hochflexiblen Logistik auf Kundenbedürfnisse rasch reagieren.

Eine leistungsfähige und innovative Entwicklungsabteilung betreut alle Kunden von der Produktidee bis zur Einführung in die Serienproduktion. Dabei profitiert die Mitras nicht nur von der mehr als 50-jährigen Erfahrung in der Formteilgestaltung und Duroplastverarbeitung, sondern auch von ihren hoch motivierten Mitarbeitern, den modernen Maschinen und Anlagen sowie der günstigen Lage in der unmittelbaren Nähe von Dresden.

Zielmärkte von Mitras Composites sind die Branchen Energieverteilung, Telekommunikation, industrielle Anwendungen und Medizintechnik. Zu den Kunden gehören namhafte Konzerne und mittelständische Unternehmen, mit denen teilweise langfristige Partnerschaften bestehen.

Mitras Composites Systems GmbH

Mitras Composites Systems GmbH is a dynamically growing company and one of Europe's market leaders in the processing of fibreglass reinforced thermoset plastics based on polyester resin.

Three technologies are used in the production process: compression moulding, injection moulding and the special technology injection-compression moulding. To this end, the company has twelve presses with clamping forces up to 1,000 tonnes and eight injection moulding machines with clamping forces up to 1,300 tonnes. This puts Mitras Composites Systems in a position to produce both small and bulk series, while always being able to respond swiftly to customer requirements, thanks to its highly flexible logistics.

An efficient, innovative development department looks after all customers, from the initial idea until the start of series production. Here Mitras benefits not just from more than 50 years of experience in the design of mouldings and the processing of thermoset plastics, but also from its highly motivated workforce, the modern machinery and equipment, and the favourable location in the direct vicinity of Dresden.

The company's target markets consist of energy distribution, telecommunications, industrial applications and medical technology. The customer base includes renowned companies and medium-sized firms, with long-standing partnerships existing in some cases.

Vollautomatisierter Spritzprozess

Fully automated injection process

Projektplanung

Project planning

DIW Mechanical Engineering GmbH & Co. KG
Mit technischen Dienstleistungen die Produktionsprozesse beim Kunden perfekt zu unterstützen und kontinuierlich zu verbessern – das ist das Ziel der DIW Mechanical Engineering GmbH & Co. KG.

Den Standort in Radebeul gibt es bereits seit mehr als 20 Jahren. 1990 gründete die Stuttgarter DIW mit wenigen Mitarbeitern eine Außenstelle. Das Leistungsangebot in den ersten Jahren beschränkte sich auf die Instandhaltung von Werkzeugmaschinen. Heute sind wir – als DIW Mechanical Engineering GmbH & Co. KG – innerhalb des Firmenverbundes der DIW ein eigenständiges Unternehmen und ein starker Partner der Industrie, wenn es um Outsourcing-Projekte im Bereich der Technischen Dienstleistungen geht. Rund 400 Mitarbeiterinnen und Mitarbeiter setzen sich mit Engagement und Können jeden Tag für die optimale Kundenlösung ein.

Ob Anlagen- und Komponentenmontage, OEM-Service für Werkzeugmaschinen, Retrofit, Instandhaltung, De- und Remontage oder Werksverlagerungen – mit einem umfassenden Portfolio bietet die DIW Komplett-Dienstleistungen entlang des Lebenszyklus einer Produktionsanlage.

Unser Schwerpunkt liegt bei Kunden aus dem Maschinenbau. Wir sind aber auch in anderen Industrien zu Hause. Zum Beispiel unterstützen wir seit vielen Jahren Unternehmen im Bereich Aerospace. Auch in den Branchen Optik und Halbleiter ist die DIW mit Instandhaltungsleistungen in der Produktion ein anerkannter Dienstleister. Unsere Flexibilität und Vielseitigkeit hat uns geholfen, auch wirtschaftlich schwierige Zeiten zu meistern.

Die DIW verfügt über ein breit gefächertes Know-how und alle notwendigen Zertifizierungen und Zulassungen.

Verantwortungsvolles Handeln und die kontinuierlich hohe Qualität unserer Dienstleistungen – dafür steht die DIW.

DIW Mechanical Engineering GmbH & Co. KG
The goal of DIW Mechanical Engineering GmbH & Co. KG is to perfectly support and continuously optimize the customer's production processes by providing technical services.

The location in Radebeul has existed for over 20 years. In 1990, DIW in Stuttgart founded a

DIW Mechanical Engineering GmbH & Co. KG

branch office there which back then employed only a few employees. In the first years, the scope of services was limited to machine tool maintenance. Today, DIW Mechanical Engineering GmbH & Co. KG is a separate enterprise of DIW and a strong service provider to the industry when it comes to outsourcing technical services. Every day, about 400 employees are committed to delivering the perfect customer solution.

Whether it be equipment and component assembly, OEM services for machine tools, retrofits, maintenance, disassembly and reassembly or plant relocations, with its comprehensive range of services DIW offers its customers complete services throughout the entire life cycle of production facilities.

Our focus is in the field of mechanical engineering. We also service many different industries. For example, we have been providing services to customers in the aviation industry for many years. DIW is also an acknowledged provider of production maintenance services for the optics and semiconductor industry. Our flexibility and the diversity of services has helped DIW getting through economically difficult times.

DIW has experience and diverse industrial expertise as well as all required certificates and permits.

DIW is committed to operating responsibly and providing high-quality services at all times.

Information

Gründungsjahr: 2007

Mitarbeiter: ca. 400

Leistungsspektrum:
- Anlagen- und Komponentenmontage
- OEM-Service für Werkzeugmaschinen
- Retrofit
- Instandhaltung nach DIN 31051
- Werksverlagerungen
- Services in den Branchen Optik und Halbleiter

Standorte/Locations:
- Radebeul
- Chemnitz
- Bad Muskau
- Jena
- Langenau
- Ahrensburg

Year founded: 2007

Employees: approx. 400

Range of services:
- equipment and component assembly
- OEM services for machine tools
- retrofits
- maintenance pursuant to DIN 31051
- plant relocations
- services for the optics and semiconductor industry

DIW Mechanical Engineering GmbH & Co. KG
Radebeul

Information

Gründungsjahr: 2004

Mitarbeiter: ca. 140

Leistungsspektrum:
· funktionelle Oberflächenveredelung von Aluminium, Titan, Kupfer und seinen Legierungen, CrNiSt-Werkstoffen, Sonderwerkstoffen, hochfesten Stählen und Faserverbundwerkstoffen (CFK, GFK) für die Bereiche Luftfahrt und Industrie
· vielfältige mechanische, galvanische, chemische, anodische und organische Behandlungsverfahren
· langjähriger Partner der Luftfahrtindustrie (QSF-A/B)

Year founded: 2004

Employees: approx. 140

Range of services:
· functional surface treatment of aluminium, titanium, copper and its alloys, CrNiSt materials, special materials, high-strength steel and composites (CRP, GRP) for the aviation sector and industry
· wide range of mechanical, electroplating, chemical, anodic and organic treatment processes
· long-standing partner of the aviation industry (QSF-A/B)

Nehlsen-BWB Flugzeug-Galvanik
Dresden GmbH & Co. KG
Dresden

Die herkömmliche Galvanotechnik ist eine der innovativsten Technologien und verlängert die Lebensdauer von Metallteilen.

Conventional electroplating is one of the most innovative technologies for prolonging the service life of metal parts.

Nehlsen-BWB Flugzeug-Galvanik Dresden GmbH & Co. KG

Die am Flughafen Dresden-Klotzsche ansässige Nehlsen-BWB Flugzeug-Galvanik Dresden GmbH & Co. KG ist ein Hightechunternehmen der Oberflächenschutz-Branche, das seit etwa 50 Jahren am Standort existiert. Der frühere Betriebsteil der ehemaligen Flugzeugwerft Dresden gehört heute zur Schweizer BWB-Gruppe.

Über den Schwerpunkt Luftfahrttechnik hinaus wissen auch viele Betriebe des Maschinenbaus, der Fahrzeug- und Elektroindustrie sowie der Halbleiterindustrie das umfassende Leistungsangebot zu schätzen. Die Nehlsen-BWB Flugzeug-Galvanik ist damit einer der führenden Anbieter hochwertiger, funktioneller Beschichtungen für die verschiedensten technischen Anwendungszwecke.

Die größte Stärke von Nehlsen-BWB ist das Engagement seiner Mitarbeiter. Sie sind die treibende Kraft des Unternehmens. Ihre fachlichen Fertigkeiten und Fähigkeiten sind der Motor für die Sicherung einer fachgerechten spezialisierten Produktion und damit Grundvoraussetzung zur Sicherung der hohen Qualität, die die Kunden erwarten können.

Dazu fördert Nehlsen-BWB seine Mitarbeiter in besonderer Weise – fördert Ideenreichtum und Kreativität, selbstständiges Denken und Handeln und investiert jährlich hohe Summen in die fachliche Aus- und Weiterbildung.

In den vergangenen Jahren ist es der Geschäftsführung und den engagierten Mitarbeitern gelungen, das Unternehmen zum führenden Zulieferer für Oberflächenschutz im Luftfahrtbereich mit der bundesweit größten luftfahrtzertifizierten Verfahrenspalette (DIN ISO 9001:2008 (QMS); EN 9100) zu entwickeln.

Nehlsen-BWB Flugzeug-Galvanik Dresden GmbH & Co. KG

The high-tech company in the surface treatment branch has been based at its site near Dresden-Klotzsche airport for about 50 years. Formerly a division of Dresden Aircraft Works, today the company belongs to the Swiss BWB Group.

Going over and beyond the aviation industry, today many other companies involved in machine construction, automotive engineering, the electrical industry and the semiconductor sector appreciate the comprehensive range of services provided by the company. Nehlsen-BWB Flugzeug-Galvanik is thus one of the leading providers of top quality functional coatings for many different technical applications.

Workforce commitment is the great strength of Nehlsen-BWB. The employees are the driving force in the company. Their professional skills and capabilities are the motor that safeguards skilled, specialised production and provides the basic prerequisite for assuring the high quality that customers can expect.

To this end, Nehlsen-BWB supports its workforce by fostering inventiveness and creativity and encouraging employees to think and act for themselves, while investing large amounts in initial and advanced vocational training every year.

In recent years, the management and committed workforce have succeeded in making the company one of the leading suppliers of surface treatment in the aviation sector with Germany's largest range of aviation-certified processes (DIN ISO 9001:2008 (QMS); EN 9100).

Eine lückenlose Qualitätskontrolle ist für alle bei Nehlsen-BWB bearbeiteten Metallteile selbstverständlich.

Total quality control is a matter of course for all metal parts treated at Nehlsen-BWB.

K wie Kunststoff

Kunststoffe sind Alleskönner für Haushalts- und Elektroindustrie, Fahrzeug-, Maschinen- und Anlagenbau, Medizin- und Telekommunikationstechnik. Das freut die Oberlausitz als Kerngebiet: 90 Betriebe mit 3500 Beschäftigten vertreten ein Viertel der sächsischen Kunststoffindustrie. Knopffabriken waren vielfach ihr Ursprung. Im Netzwerk „Oberlausitzer Kunststoff" tauschen sie sich zu Know-how, Qualität und Ausbildung aus. Forschungspartner sind die Hochschule Zittau/Görlitz, die brandenburgische Hochschule Lausitz, Einrichtungen im tschechischen Liberec und die TU Dresden.

Nicht nur Heimwerkers Freund ist die KEW Kunststofferzeugnisse GmbH in Wilthen mit ihren Dübeln. Auch technische Formteile, Prototypen und Baugruppen werden kundengerecht entwickelt und gefertigt. Die Firma J. Brühl Design in Schmeckwitz lackiert mit Robotern Kunststoffe und Metalle für die Autoindustrie. Die Plastic Concept GmbH in Neusalza-Spremberg stattet die Innenräume von Automobilen – darunter von Porsche, VW und MAN – mit Baugruppen aus. Flaschen, Dosen und weitere Hohlkörper für Lebensmittel, Arzneimittel, Kosmetik und Farben kommen aus der TPK Technoplast GmbH Großröhrsdorf. In Dresden stellt die Plasticard-ZFT GmbH Plastik- und Chipkarten in Auflagen zwischen 20 und 100 000 Stück in jährlich bis zu 6000 Drucklayouts her.

L wie Luft- und Raumfahrt

Dresden hat deutsche Luftfahrtgeschichte geschrieben. 1958 rollte die vierstrahlige „152" aus der Flugzeugwerft im Stadtteil Klotzsche, das erste deutsche Düsenverkehrsflugzeug. Diese ingenieurtechnische Leistung fiel dem sozialistischen Wirtschafts- und Bündnissystem zum Opfer: 1961 kam das Aus für die eigenständigen Ambitionen. Die Marktwirtschaft beflügelte die Träume der Flugzeugbauer neu: Die Elbe Flugzeugwerke GmbH – Nachbar des Flughafens – ist seit 2000 ein Unternehmen der European Aeronautic Defence and Space Company (EADS), Europas größtem Luft- und Raumfahrtkonzern. 1100 Mitarbeiter rüsten die Innenräume der Airbus-Familie mit hochwertigen Leichtbaukomponenten aus – von Deckenpaneelen bis zu schussfesten Cockpittüren. Außerdem bauen sie Airbus-Passagierflugzeuge zu Frachtflugzeugen um und warten die gesamte Airbus-Flotte.

In Sachsens Luft- und Raumfahrtindustrie sind 4600 Mitarbeiter tätig. Sie stellen Flugzeugteile, Spezialwerkstoffe und Spezialtextilien her. Wärme-, Kälte-, Schall- und Brandschutz für Luftfahrzeuge – bei Isolationssystemen gehört die OLUTEX Oberlausitzer Luftfahrttextilien GmbH in Seifhennersdorf zu den Weltmarktführern. Die Nehlsen-BWB Flugzeug-Galvanik Dresden GmbH & Co. KG veredelt Metalloberflächen von der Unterlegscheibe bis hin zu sicherheitsrelevanten Bauteilen. Das Kompetenzzentrum Luft- und Raumfahrttechnik Sachsen/

the family company Kappus from Offenbach offered a new perspective for Konsumseifenwerk Riesa; with traditions going back to 1910, this had been the largest soap producer in the GDR. Today, Kappus Seifen GmbH Riesa & Co produces soaps, body lotion, gels and shower gels, including the patented floating soap.

"Li-iL" doesn't come from China: this is an original Dresden company. In 1910, company founder Richard Carl Pittlik combined the word "lithium" as carrier medium for ethereal oils and "ilatium" which describes the principle of action from the outside inwards. Today the family-run Li-iL GmbH Arzneimittel und Arzneibäder with around 130 products in the "Dresdner Essenz" brand stands for the medical efficacy of medicinal herb extracts.

K (P) for plastic

Plastics are all-rounders for the domestic appliance and electrical industry, automotive engineering, machine and plant construction, medical and telecommunications technology and much more besides. This is good for the Oberlausitz as a core area for plastics: 90 companies with 3,500 employees represent one quarter of Saxony's plastics industry. In many cases, their origins go back to button factories. In the Oberlausitz Plastics Network, they share know-how, quality and training. Their research partners are Zittau/Görlitz University of Applied Sciences and Lausitz University of Applied Sciences, together with institutions in Liberec in the Czech Republic and TU Dresden.

KEW Kunststofferzeugnisse GmbH in Wilthen with its plugs and dowels serves not just DIY fans. The company also develops and produces technical mouldings, prototypes and components according to customer specifications. J. Brühl Design in Schmeckwitz uses robots to apply coatings to plastics and metals for the automotive industry. Plastic Concept GmbH in Neusalza-Spremberg installs components and assemblies in vehicle interiors, for Porsche, VW and MAN, among others. Bottles, cans and other hollow bodies for food products, drugs and medicines, cosmetics and paints come from TPK Technoplast GmbH Großröhrsdorf. In Dresden, Plasticard-ZFT GmbH produces plastic and chip cards in quantities between 20 and 100,000 every year with up to 6,000 print layouts.

L (A) for aviation and aerospace

Dresden wrote German aviation history. In 1958, the four-engine "152" aircraft left the factory in Dresden-Klotzsche as Germany's first passenger jet. This engineering achievement fell victim to the socialist economic and alliance system, with no scope for independent ambitions from 1961 onwards. The return of the market economy put new life into aviation dreams: since 2000, Elbe Flugzeugwerke GmbH next-door to the airport

Porzellankunst aus Meißen ist ein weltweites Gütesiegel und Markenzeichen.

Porcelain art from Meißen is a global trademark and seal of quality.

Thüringen e. V. mit Sitz in Dresden hilft Fertigungs-, Dienstleistungs- und Forschungspotenziale beider Bundesländer zu vernetzen. Expertennachwuchs bildet das Institut für Luft- und Raumfahrttechnik der TU Dresden aus.

P wie Porzellan

Bei blauen Schwertern denkt niemand ans Fechten. Die gekreuzten Waffen – handgemalt in Blau unter der Glasur – sind seit 1731 verbindliches Zeichen der heutigen weltbekannten Luxus- und Lifestylemarke „Meissener Porzellan". Die Staatliche Porzellan-Manufaktur Meissen GmbH nennt für Philosophie und Sortiment drei Säulen: „MEISSEN Fine Art" mit limitierten traditionellen Kunstwerken für Sammler, „MEISSEN Joaillerie" mit hochwertigen Schmuckstücken und „MEISSEN Home" mit exklusiver Wohnkultur.

1710 hatte die sächsische Hofkanzlei viersprachig die Erfindung des ersten europäischen Porzellans und die Gründung einer Porzellan-Manufaktur verkündet. Dem Abenteurer und vermeintlichen Goldmacher Johann Friedrich Böttger war – angetrieben von August dem Starken – die Schöpfung dieses Luxusgutes geglückt. Inzwischen befindet sich die Fertigungsstätte im Stadtteil Triebischtal.

Eine Erfolgsstory im 19. Jahrhundert: Carl Gottlieb Thieme bemalte zunächst in seinem Dresdner Geschäft angekauftes Weißporzellan auf kunstvolle Art, ab 1872 brannte er in Potschappel nahe der Residenzstadt seinen eigenen Scherben. Seine Kreationen mit üppiger Blumenornamentik verkauften sich gut, später in alle Welt und bis zum englischen Königshaus.

has become part of the European Aeronautic Defence and Space Company (EADS), Europe's largest aviation and aerospace company. 1,100 employees fit top quality lightweight components to the interiors of bullet-proof cockpit doors. They also convert Airbus passenger jets to freight aircraft and perform maintenance work on the whole Airbus fleet.

Saxony's aviation and aerospace industry has 4,600 employees, making aircraft parts, special materials and special textiles. OLUTEX Oberlausitzer Luftfahrttextilien GmbH in Seifhennersdorf is one of the world market leaders for heat/cold/sound/fire protection for aircraft and all kinds of insulation systems. Nehlsen-BWB Flugzeug-Galvanik Dresden GmbH & Co. KG treats metallic surfaces from washers through to safety-relevant parts. The centre of excellent Aviation and Aerospace Technology Saxony/Thuringia based in Dresden helps to network production, service and research potential in both federal states. The Institute of Aerospace Engineering at TU Dresden provides specialised training for the up-and-coming generation of young experts.

P for porcelain

No-one thinks of fencing when they see blue swords. The crossed weapons – hand-painted in blue under the glaze – have been the binding symbol of today's world-famous luxury and lifestyle brand "Meissen Porcelain" since 1731. Staatliche Porzellan-Manufaktur Meissen GmbH bases its philosophy and assortment on three pillars: "MEISSEN Fine Art" with limited traditional works of art for collectors, "MEISSEN Joaillerie"

Sieht nicht nur gut aus, fühlt sich auch gut an – Wäsche von Thieme aus Großröhrsdorf

Not only does it look good, it feels good too – underwear and sleepwear by Thieme from Großröhrsdorf

Unternehmergeist und Kunstsinn des Gründers inspirieren heute die Sächsische Porzellan-Manufaktur Dresden GmbH mit Sitz in Freital, zu dem Potschappel gehört. Seit der Wende erlebt die Marke „SP Dresden" eine Renaissance: Der auf 12 500 Stücke angewachsene Formenschatz begeistert Kenner in 25 Ländern.

T wie Textilien

Ein bunter R 16/3 schwebt zur Erde. Er bringt den Springer sicher und genau ans Ziel. Mit diesem Sportfallschirm hat die Deutsche Fallschirmsport-Nationalmannschaft schon über 30 Weltmeistertitel errungen. Das Präzisionsgerät stellt die SPEKON Sächsische Spezialkonfektion GmbH in Seifhennersdorf her. Seit über 70 Jahren werden in dem Oberlausitzort Fallschirme gefertigt, heute für Kunden weltweit. Technische Textilien, gewebte und veredelte Spezial- und Nischenprodukte sind ein Merkmal des Kammerbezirkes Dresden.

Fortsetzung Seite 115

with top-quality jewellery and "MEISSEN Home" with exclusive home decor.

In 1710, the Saxon court announced the invention of Europe's first porcelain in four languages, with the founding of a porcelain manufactory. Driven by August the Strong, the adventurer and alleged gold-maker Johann Friedrich Böttger succeeded in creating this luxury good. Meanwhile the production facility is located in Triebischtal.

A 19th century success story: initially Carl Gottlieb Thieme purchased white porcelain to paint it with artistic motifs in his shop in Dresden. As from 1872, he fired his own products in Potschappel near the city. His creations with luxuriant ornamental flower designs sold well and were eventually exported all over the world, even to the English Royal Family. The founder's entrepreneurial spirit and appreciation of art still inspires Sächsische Porzellan-Manufaktur Dresden GmbH today, based in Freital which now also includes Potschappel. Reunification brought a renaissance for the brand "SP Dresden", with the range of meanwhile 12,500 shapes appreciated by enthusiastic connoisseurs in 25 countries.

T for textiles

A colourful R 16/3 floats to earth, bringing the jumper safely and precisely to the target. Germany's national parachuting team has used this sport parachute to win more than 30 world championship titles. The precision parachute is produced by SPEKON Sächsische Spezialkonfektion GmbH in Seifhennersdorf. Parachutes have been made here in the Oberlausitz for more than 70 years and today for customers all over the world. Technical textiles together with woven and refined special and niche products are just one of the characteristics of Dresden chamber district.

Although the GDR's textile industry collapsed after reunification, including production facilities in the Oberlausitz, today Saxony is still one of the centres of Germany's textile and clothing industry, together with North Rhine-Westphalia, Baden-Württemberg and Bavaria. The Free State accounts for about two thirds of the workforce and branch turnover in East German companies. Since 2006, the initiative "SACHSEN! TEXTIL!" has helped to safeguard a strong position for the Saxon branch, particularly on the growth market for technical textiles.

Continued on page 115

MICRO-EPSILON Optronic GmbH

Baugruppenmontage

Component assembly

MICRO-EPSILON Optronic GmbH
MICRO-EPSILON Optronic ist ein mittelständisches Unternehmen der MICRO-EPSILON Gruppe. Seit seiner Gründung 1993 ist das sächsische Werk auf die Entwicklung und Herstellung von optoelektronischen Sensoren und Systemen für das berührungslose Messen vorwiegend geometrischer aber auch anderer physikalischer Größen spezialisiert.

Die Produkte von MICRO-EPSILON Optronic nutzen dabei verschiedenste Wirkprinzipien, welche mit den Kompetenzen in Optikdesign, Laser- und LED-Beleuchtungen, Bildsensoren, Spektrometrie sowie der digitalen Signalverarbeitung realisiert werden. Die Opto- und Mikroelektronik erfüllen hier höchste Ansprüche in der präzisen Weg- und Abstandsmessung und der spektralen Farbmessung. Das „Micro" im Unternehmensnamen deutet dabei auf den Fokus der Messsysteme für kleine Dimensionen hin, welche hochgenau und blitzschnell erfasst werden.

Innerhalb der Unternehmensgruppe nimmt die MICRO-EPSILON Optronic aufgrund ihrer überdurchschnittlich großen Entwicklungsabteilung eine besondere Position als Kompetenzzentrum für die optische Messtechnik ein. Dies wird auch durch die enge Zusammenarbeit mit sächsischen und überregionalen Forschungseinrichtungen unterstützt. Das gute Betriebsklima spornt zu ständigen Höchstleistungen an, welche Maßstäbe in der Branche setzen.

Der gute Rückhalt in der MICRO-EPSILON Gruppe ermöglicht eine Serienfertigung auf höchstem Niveau sowie Sonderlösungen in mittleren Stückzahlen, aber auch OEM-Lösungen für Global Player.

MICRO-EPSILON Optronic GmbH
MICRO-EPSILON Optronic is an SME firm in the MICRO-EPSILON Group. Since it was founded in 1993, the Saxon plant has specialised in the development and production of optoelectronic sensors and systems for contact-free measurement of primarily geometric but also other physical parameters.

The MICRO-EPSILON Optronic products work according to many different principles and are produced with the company's expertise in optic design, laser and LED lighting, image sensors, spectrometry and digital signal processing. Here, opto- and micro-electronics fulfil the strictest demands of precise displacement and distance measurement, together with spectral colour measurement. The "micro" in the company name clearly indicates how the systems focus on measuring small dimensions with high precision at high speed.

MICRO-EPSILON Optronic with its larger than average development department plays a special role in the Group as the centre of excellence for optical measuring technology. This is also supported by close cooperation with research institutions in Saxony and further afield. The good working climate provides the right stimulating basis for constant first-rate achievements which in turn set standards in the branch.

The excellent backing provided by the MICRO-EPSILON Group facilitates bulk production on the highest standard together with customised solutions in medium quantities, as well as OEM solutions for global players.

Information

Gründungsjahr: 1993
Mitarbeiter: 70
Leistungsspektrum:
Entwicklung und Herstellung von optoelektronischen Sensoren und Systemen für industrielle Anwendungen
Standorte:
Die MICRO-EPSILON Unternehmensgruppe umfasst heute 20 erfolgreiche Unternehmen in Deutschland, Europa, USA und China.

Year founded: 1993
Employees: 70
Range of products:
development and production of optoelectronic sensors and systems for industrial applications
Locations:
The MICRO-EPSILON Group today has 20 successful companies in Germany, Europe, the USA and China.

MICRO-EPSILON Optronic GmbH
Dresden-Langebrück

Obwohl die großen DDR-Textilbetriebe – darunter in der Oberlausitz – nach der Wende zusammengebrochen sind, gehört Sachsen heute neben Nordrhein-Westfalen, Baden-Württemberg und Bayern weiterhin zu den deutschen Zentren der Textil- und Bekleidungsindustrie. Über zwei Drittel der Beschäftigten und des Branchenumsatzes der ostdeutschen Unternehmen entfallen auf den Freistaat. Die Verbundinitiative „SACHSEN! TEXTIL!" trägt seit 2006 dazu bei, der sächsischen Branche eine starke Position zu sichern, vor allem auf dem Wachstumsmarkt Technische Textilien.

Zwei Standbeine hat sich ein 100 Jahre altes Familienunternehmen in Großröhrsdorf geschaffen: Unterwäsche und Nachtwäsche stellt die Thieme Fashion GmbH her, technische Textilien produziert die E. Richard-Thieme GmbH, darunter Schutztechnik, Gurte und Bänder. Aus der Oberlausitzstadt kommen schon seit drei Jahrhunderten textile Bänder aller Art. Auch die F. A. Schurig GmbH & Co KG setzt mit Bändern für Verpackung, Dekoration, Floristik und Technik diese Tradition fort. Spezialist für Arbeits- und Schutzbekleidung wiederum ist die Großröhrsdorfer F. W. Kunath GmbH, seit fünf Generationen familiengeführt.

Im Oberlausitzer Textilort Großschönau überzeugt die Frottana Textil GmbH & Co. KG mit flauschig-kuscheligem Frottee. Der Hersteller von Handtüchern, Bademänteln und Badteppichen hat einzigartige Wurzeln: 1856 stand im Ort der erste Frottierwebstuhl überhaupt in Deutschland.

Dolce & Gabbana in Italien, Triumph in der Schweiz und Wolford in Österreich schätzen Spitzen und Spitzenstoffe aus Dresden. Betriebstradition seit 1884, modernste Technologien, kreative Ideen und umweltbewusste Produktion – mit diesen Vorzügen haben sich die 45 Mitarbeiter der Dresdner Gardinen- und Spitzenmanufaktur GmbH international als Zulieferer weit nach vorn gearbeitet. Von 100 Tonnen Spitze jährlich exportieren sie die Hälfte.

Z wie Zeitmesser

Eine 7200-Einwohner-Stadt im Müglitztal, einst Fundort von Silbererz, eine Postmeilensäule von 1734. Was ist daran Besonderes? Der Name: Glashütte. Der Ort im Osterzgebirge ist das Zentrum der deutschen Uhrmacherkunst. Über zehn Manufakturen tragen den exzellenten Ruf Glashütter Uhren in alle Welt. Für Glanz und Perfektion stehen Marken wie A. Lange & Söhne, Glashütte Original, Nomos Glashütte, Mühle-Glashütte oder WEMPE Chronometerwerke. Die Stadt wirbt mit dem Slogan „Hier lebt die Zeit". Und von ihr mehr als 1000 Menschen in den Unternehmen.

1845 gründete Ferdinand Adolph Lange mit königlich-sächsischem Kredit seine Feinuhrmacherei mit arbeitsteiliger Fertigung. Bald kamen weitere Uhrmacherbetriebe hinzu. 1878 öffnete die Deutsche Uhrmacherschule Glashütte ihre Pforten. Die Historie des mechanischen Uhrenbaus widerspiegeln über 400 einzigartige Exponate im Deutschen Uhrenmuseum Glashütte.

A family company in Großröhrsdorf that looks back on 100 years of history has created two mainstays for its business: underwear and nightwear are produced by Thieme Fashion GmbH, while E. Richard-Thieme GmbH produces technical textiles, including safety and protection solutions, straps and belts. Textile belts of all kinds have been coming from the Oberlausitz for three hundred years. F. A. Schurig GmbH & Co KG also continues this tradition with belts and ribbons for packaging, decoration, floral and technical use. On the other hand, workwear and protective clothing is the speciality of F. W. Kunath GmbH, a Großröhrsdorf family company meanwhile being run by the fifth generation.

In the Oberlausitz textiles town Großschönau, Frottana Textil GmbH & Co. KG supplies its customers with soft, fluffy terry towelling products. The manufacturer of towels, dressing gowns and bath mats has unique roots, as the site of Germany's very first terry weaving loom in 1856.

Dolce & Gabbana in Italy, Triumph in Switzerland and Wolford in Austria love lace and lace fabrics from Dresden. A company tradition going back to 1884, state-of-the-art technology, creative ideas and eco-friendly production – these are the advantages that the 45 employees of Dresdner Gardinen- und Spitzenmanufaktur GmbH have put to their advantage to come to the front of the field as international suppliers, exporting half of the 100 tons of lace produced each year.

Z (C) for chronometer

A small town in Müglitztal with 7,200 residents, once the site of silver ore and a posting milestone dated 1734. What's so special about all that? The name: Glashütte. The town in the Erzgebirge mountains is the heart of the German art of watchmaking. More than ten manufactories export the excellent reputation of Glashütte watches all over the world. Brilliance and perfection are embodied by brands such as A. Lange & Söhne, Glashütte Original, Nomos Glashütte, Mühle-Glashütte or WEMPE Chronometerwerke. The town slogan is "Time lives here". And it provides work for more than 1,000 employees in the companies.

In 1845, Ferdinand Adolph Lange founded his precision watchmaking firm based on the division of labour, with a loan from the Saxon court. He was soon joined by other watchmakers. In 1878, the German watchmakers school opened its doors in Glashütte. The history of mechanical watchmaking is reflected in more than 400 unique exhibits on display in Glashütte's German Watchmaking Museum.

Lange Uhren GmbH goes back to its progenitor. Its watches in the luxury brand Lange & Söhne are eulogised as "horological oeuvres of flawless beauty". Whiplash precision index adjuster, screwed gold chatons, three-quarter plate and fuse and chain are just some of the traditional elements. Up to 556 individual parts are put together with utmost precision under a magnifying glass to create an exquisite masterpiece. LANGE 1 was the

Von Hand werden die wichtigsten Arbeitsschritte für die Fertigung der Modelle „Glashütte Original" ausgeführt.

The main stages in production of the "Glashütte Original" models are performed by hand.

Auf den Stammvater geht die Lange Uhren GmbH zurück. Sie preist ihre Uhren der Luxusmarke Lange & Söhne als „uhrmacherische Meisterwerke von makelloser Schönheit". Schwanenhals-Feinregulierung, verschraubte Goldchatons, Dreiviertelplatine, Kette und Schnecke gehören zu den traditionellen Merkmalen. Mit Lupe und Feingefühl werden bis zu 556 Teile zu einem kunstvollen Zeitmesser zusammengesetzt. Das Meisterstück LANGE 1 markierte den Neustart der Uhrmacherdynastie nach der Wiedervereinigung.

Per Hand werden auch die wichtigsten Arbeitsschritte für die Modellreihen von „Glashütte Original" der Glashütter Uhrenbetrieb GmbH – ein Unternehmen der Swatch-Gruppe – ausgeführt. Ihr Vorläufer war ein DDR-Großbetrieb, der vorwiegend Alltagsuhren für Abnehmer in Ost und West herstellte. Heute fertigt die Traditionsfirma hochkomplizierte und hochfein veredelte mechanische Uhren für einen weltweiten Kundenkreis. Ein Meisterwerk ist der PanoRetroGraph, der erste mechanische Zeitmesser der Welt, der vorwärts und rückwärts zählen kann. Mühle – seit fünf Generationen steht der Name für präzises Messen. 1869 begründete Robert Mühle die Mühle-Glashütte GmbH nautische Instrumente und Feinmechanik. Nach 1945 war er alleiniger ostdeutscher Hersteller von Zeigerwerken für Druck- und Temperaturmessgeräte. 1994 begann der Wiederaufstieg als renommierte Manufaktur für Marinechronometer, Schiffsuhrenanlagen und mechanische Armbanduhren. ■

very first watch produced after reunification, marking the start of a new watchmaking dynasty.

The main stages in production of the "Glashütte Original" models by the Swatch Group subsidiary Glashütter Uhrenbetrieb GmbH are also performed by hand. Its precursor was a large GDR-concern that predominantly manufactured everyday watches for customers in both the East and the West. Today the tradition-steeped company manufactures highly complex and highly-refined mechanical watches for a global clientele. A masterpiece is the PanoRetroGraph, the first mechanical timekeeper on earth that is capable of counting both down and up.

Mühle is a name that has been synonymous for precision measurement for five generations. In 1869, Robert Mühle founded Mühle-Glashütte GmbH as a precision engineering company for nautical instruments. After 1945, this was East Germany's only manufacturer of hands and dials for barometers and thermometers. As from 1994, the company gradually restored its reputation as a renowned manufactory for marine chronometers, marine time pieces and mechanical wristwatches. ■

„Der Sachse liebt das Reisen sehr"
Tourismus als Wirtschaftsfaktor

Sachsens inoffizielle Hymne heißt „Sing, mei Sachse, sing". Mit ihr hat der Leipziger Kabarettist Jürgen Hardt 1979 seinen reiselustigen Landsleuten ein selbstironisches Denkmal gesetzt. „Der Sachse liebt das Reisen sehr", verkündete er zu einer Zeit, als die Sachsen nur bis „nunder nach Bulgarchen... die Welt beschnarchen" konnten. Jetzt fahren die Sachsen überall hin, und sie lieben alle Reisenden sehr, die zu ihnen kommen.

Die TMGS – Tourismus Marketing Gesellschaft Sachsen mbH, zu deren Gesellschaftern die IHK Dresden gehört, rührt am internationalen Markt die Trommel für Sachsen als „Land von Welt". Ihre Top-Themen sind Kunst und Kultur, Städtetourismus, Familienurlaub, Vitalurlaub & Wellness und Aktivurlaub.

Zum Tagesausflug und Urlaub im Kammerbezirk Dresden laden die Landeshauptstadt und vier große Feriengebiete ein: Sächsische Schweiz, Osterzgebirge, Sächsisches Elbland und Oberlausitz. Gemeinsam mit der TMGS setzen sich die Dresden Marketing GmbH, die Tourismusverbände Sächsische Schweiz-Osterzgebirge und Sächsisches Elbland, die Marketing-Gesellschaft Oberlausitz-Niederschlesien mbH, viele regionale und lokale Partner sowie private Unternehmen und Anbieter für das Gästewohl ein.

Beliebter als je zuvor

„Tourismus bringt Dresden 20 000 Jobs." Unter dieser Überschrift auf Seite eins vermeldeten die „Dresdner Neuesten Nachrichten" am 23. Februar 2012 einen Rekord: 2011 hätten so viele Touristen wie noch nie die sächsische Landeshauptstadt besucht. Mit knapp 3,8 Millionen Übernachtungen sei ein Plus von 7,6 Prozent gegenüber 2010 zu verzeichnen. Ein Aufwärtstrend, der eine ganze Branche boomen lasse: „20 000 Vollarbeitsplätze bringt der Tourismus der Landeshauptstadt. Die Netto-Umsätze der Branche betragen 500 Mio. Euro. Damit ist der Tourismus drittwichtigster Arbeitgeber." Das Beispiel illustriert die Wirtschaftskraft eines florierenden Tourismus.

Zugegeben, Dresden ist mit internationaler Bekanntheit, bedeutenden Sehenswürdigkeiten, geballter Geistes- und Industriekraft privilegiert. Im Städteranking des Wirtschaftsmagazin „Capital" für das Jahr 2011 war die ostdeutsche Wachstumsperle erstmals unter den Top Ten vertreten. Doch Dresden ist kein Sonderfall, sondern Teil der Erfolgsgeschichte des sächsischen Tourismus seit 1990.

Auch Sachsen ist beliebter denn je. Es verbuchte 2011 ein touristisches Rekordjahr: 17,3 Millionen Übernachtungen. Damit

"The Saxons love to travel"
Tourism as an economic factor

Saxony's unofficial anthem goes "Sing, my Saxon, sing", used in 1979 by cabaret artist Jürgen Hardt from Leipzig as an ironic memorial to the avid travelling passion of the local population. "The Saxons love to travel", he announced back in those days when the only place they could go was down to Bulgaria. Today, Saxons can go where they want in the world, and they also love welcoming travellers who come to see what Saxony has to offer.

Saxony's tourism marketing company is called TMGS – Tourismus Marketing Gesellschaft Sachsen mbH. Its shareholders include Dresden CCI, and its tasks include making sure the international market knows all about what Saxony has to offer tourists as a "country of the world". The key attributes include art and culture, city tours, family holidays, spas & wellness as well as active holidays.

Together with the state capital itself, the Dresden chamber district offers four main holiday areas for day trips and as holiday destinations: these are Saxon Switzerland, the Eastern Erzgebirge mountains, the Saxon Elbe valley and Oberlausitz. TMGS works together with Dresden Marketing GmbH, the tourism associations for Saxon Switzerland, the Eastern Erzgebirge and the Saxon Elbe valley as well as the Marketing-Gesellschaft Oberlausitz-Niederschlesien mbH, and many regional and local partners together with private companies and service providers to look after the well-being of guests, tourists, visitors and travellers.

More popular than ever before

"Tourism brings Dresden 20,000 jobs." This heading on page one of the "Dresdner Neueste Nachrichten" on 23 February 2012 was followed by the announcement of a record: in 2011, more tourists than ever before had visited Saxony's state capital. Just around 3.8 million overnight stays achieved an increase of 7.6 percent compared to 2010 in an upwards trend that lets a whole branch boom: "Tourism brings 20,000 full-time jobs to the state

wurde erstmals, seit die touristische Beherbergung statistisch erhoben wird, die 17-Millionen-Marke überschritten. Auch die Gästeankünfte erreichten mit 6,7 Millionen eine neue Bestmarke. Damit liegt Sachsen unter den 16 Bundesländern im guten Mittelfeld. Sächsische Schweiz, Sächsisches Elbland und Oberlausitz verbuchten zusammen 1,4 Millionen Ankünfte und 4,3 Millionen Übernachtungen, rund 203 000 Ankünfte und über 160 000 Übernachtungen mehr als im Jahr 2000. Nach Ankünften pro 100 Einwohner berechnet, liegt der Kammerbezirk Dresden mit 205 über dem sächsischen Mittel von 159.

Einträglich und dynamisch

Tourismus schafft Einkommen, Beschäftigung und spült Steuern in die kommunalen Kassen. 7,2 Mrd. Euro lassen sich die Übernachtungsgäste und Tagestouristen jährlich ihre Aufenthalte in Sachsen kosten. Die klassische Querschnittsbranche lässt viele am Erfolg teilhaben, vor allem das Gastgewerbe, die Dienstleister und den Einzelhandel. Im Freistaat leben über 217 000 Menschen direkt oder indirekt vom Tourismus. Er ist der zweitgrößte Arbeitgeber in Sachsen und trägt 5,2 Prozent zum

Drei Dresdner Wahrzeichen: Reiterstandbild von König Johann von Sachsen, Katholische Hofkirche und das Residenzschloss mit seinen einmaligen kulturhistorischen Sammlungen

Three famous landmarks in Dresden: the equestrian statue of King John of Saxony, the Catholic Court Church and Dresden Castle, with its unique cultural and historical collections

capital, with the branch generating net turnover of 500 million Euro. This makes tourism the third most important employer." The example illustrates the economic power of a flourishing tourism industry.

Admittedly, Dresden is privileged with international popularity and major tourist attractions together with a thriving industry and accumulated brainpower. For the first time in 2011, the business magazine "Capital" put the East German "boomtown" among the Top Ten in its city ranking. But Dresden is not an exception to the rule but part of the success story of tourism in Saxony since 1990.

Saxony in general is also more popular than ever before,

„Der Sachse liebt das Reisen sehr"

Die Elbe bei Königstein

The River Elbe at Königstein

Volksvermögen bei. Seine Dynamik im Wandel der Trends sucht seinesgleichen.

Schauen, genießen, aktiv sein, chillen – Urlauber wollen alles und zunehmend vieles kombiniert. Die Sachsen bleiben bei den Gästewünschen auf dem Laufenden und dabei zugleich die Alten – als nette Menschen. In allen Befragungen der vergangenen Jahre haben die Touristen die freundliche, hilfsbereite Art ihrer Gastgeber gelobt. Seit 1990, als der Tourismus noch Fremdenverkehr hieß, ist Sachsen in die neue Rolle als attraktives Reiseland hineingewachsen.

Gab es zur Wende gerade einmal 4800 Betten in Dresden, so sind es 2012 rund 21 000. Dort und im gesamten Freistaat ist

notching up a record tourism year in 2011 with 17.3 million overnight stays. This was the first time it had topped the 17-million mark since they started keeping tourism statistics. 6.7 million guest arrivals was also a new record, putting Saxony in a good mid-field position among all 16 federal states. Saxon Switzerland, Saxon Elbe valley and Oberlausitz together accounted for 1.4 million arrivals and 4.3 million overnight stays, which is around 203,000 more arrivals and over 160,000 overnight stays more than in 2000. With 205 arrivals per 100 residents, the Dresden chamber district is well over the Saxon average of 159.

Lucrative and dynamic

Tourism creates revenues and employment while generating taxation income for the local councils. Overnight guests and day-trippers spend 7.2 billion Euro when staying in Saxony every year. Many are able to share in the success of the classic cross-sectoral branch, including above all the hotel and catering trade, service providers and the retail sector. More than 217,000 people live directly or indirectly from tourism in the

eine moderne touristische Infrastruktur entstanden. Hotels, Straßen, Nahverkehr, Einkaufszentren... Allein die Zahl der Beherbergungsbetriebe hat sich seit 1991 um das 2,4-fache auf mehr als 2100 erhöht.

Nachholbedarf, unerfüllte Träume und Service-Q

In den 1990er-Jahren hieß es zunächst: Kapazitäten schaffen. Üppige Fördermittel katapultierten Neues und Schönes, hie und da Entbehrliches in die Landschaft. DDR-Ferienheime wurden rekonstruiert, moderne Hotels und Freizeitstätten gebaut. Um 1998 war der Beherbergungsmarkt weitgehend gesättigt. Einige Träume platzten, etwa der von Bettenauslastungen um die 50 bis 60 Prozent. Sie liegt derzeit bei 36 Prozent. Gleichwohl: Der touristische Start ins 21. Jahrhundert gelang.

Die Ostdeutschen entdeckten alte Reiseziele neu. Die Berliner beispielsweise fuhren zum Skifahren wieder ins Erzgebirge oder zum Wandern in die Sächsische Schweiz. Sachsens Anbieter stellten sich zunehmend besser auf den turbulenten Reisemarkt mit schnell wechselnden Trends ein. Sie wissen, dass Sachsen im globalen Überangebot „nur" ein Kurzreiseland ist, mit durchschnittlicher Verweildauer der Gäste von 2,2 Tagen. Sie orientieren sich auf neue Zielgruppen wie Kultur- und Städtereisende, Aktiv- und Wellness-Urlauber. Sie setzen auf Qualität.

Sachsen gehört zu den Wegbereitern der „ServiceQualität Deutschland". Die Initiative befähigt die Anbieter, ihre Unternehmen noch gästefreundlicher zu gestalten und mit anderen touristischen Leistungsträgern in Ort und Region wirksamer zu vernetzen. Bis Ende 2011 haben im Freistaat 269 Unternehmen – davon 170 aus dem Kammerbezirk Dresden – das gleichnamige Qualitätssiegel errungen, das alle drei Jahre verteidigt werden muss.

Deutschlands Nummer 1

Sachsen besuchen – warum überhaupt? Unser Canaletto-Blick hat Schönes und Einzigartiges angedeutet. Laut Umfragen sind sich die Touristen einig: Sachsen ist das Kulturreiseziel Nummer eins in Deutschland. Nicht allein das Historische und Neue Grüne Gewölbe in Dresden offerieren Meisterwerke der Schatzkunst, ganz Sachsen ist eine Schatzkammer. 500 Museen und Gedenkstätten der Geschichte und Künste, eine herausragende Architektur von der Romanik bis zum Dekonstruktivismus, rund 70 Burgen, Schlösser und Gärten, eine dichte Theater-, Orchester- und Ensemblestruktur mit erlesenen Spielstätten, über 40 renommierte Festivals... Besonderer Reiseanreiz liegt in der jeweiligen inspirierenden Atmosphäre, in der Freude, Professionalität und Leidenschaft der Gastgeber, die sich mit Sachsens Schätzen verbinden – ob mit dem Grünen Gewölbe als eine der reichsten Kunstkammern Europas oder dem Internationalen Folklorefestival „Łužica/Lausitz", das 2013 zum zehnten Mal stattfindet.

Free State, making it the second largest employer in Saxony. Tourism contributes 5.2 percent to public wealth, while its dynamic response to changing trends is second to none.

What do holidaymakers want? To see the sights, have a good time, enjoy some exercise and chill-out – all this and more, and frequently all combined. The Saxons keep pace with all the new developments, while remaining true to themselves – as nice people. All surveys of recent years featured praise from the tourists for their friendly, helpful hosts. Since the early days of tourism in 1990, Saxony has grown into its new role as an attractive travel destination.

Compared to the 4,800 beds available in Dresden at the time of reunification, in 2012 there are 21,000 on offer. Dresden and the whole Free State has seen the development of a modern tourism infrastructure. Hotels, roads, local public transport, shopping malls – since 1991, the number of establishments offering accommodation has increased by 2.4 fold to more than 2,100.

Catching up, unfulfilled dreams and Service-Q

The key focus in the 1990s was to create capacities. Abundant funds saw many new, attractive and in some cases even expendable facilities shooting up throughout the state. GDR holiday homes were rebuilt, modern hotels and leisure amenities constructed. By around 1998, the accommodation market had practically reached saturation point. Some dreams remained unfulfilled, for example to see a 50 to 60 percent level of bed occupancy. Instead, this is currently on a level of 36 percent. Even so, the tourism branch started well in the 21st century.

The East Germans rediscovered old holiday destinations. People from Berlin for example rediscovered the Erzgebirge mountains for skiing or Saxon Switzerland for walking. Saxony's providers also proved more capable of adapting to the swiftly changing trends on the turbulent tourism market. They know that in the glut of global tourism, Saxony is "only" a short-break destination with guests staying for an average of 2.2 days. Now their attention focuses on new target groups such as culture and city trip visitors, or those seeking exercise or wellness. They advocate quality.

Saxony is one of the pioneers of "Service Quality Germany". The initiative enables providers to make their companies even more hospitable and to work together in a network with other local and regional tourist service providers and organisations in the interests of greater efficiency. By the end of 2011, 269 companies in the Free State including 170 from the Dresden chamber district had received the Service Quality Germany seal of quality, with a re-audit carried out every three years.

Der Elberadweg – hier in Meißen – gehört zu den reizvollsten und schönsten Radwanderrouten in Deutschland.

The River Elbe cycle track – here in Meißen – is one of the most attractive and beautiful cycle routes in Germany.

Die Semperoper befindet sich am Theaterplatz – im historischen Stadtkern von Dresden.

The Semper opera is situated in the Theaterplatz (theatre square) – in the historical city centre of Dresden.

„Eines schickt sich nicht für alle! / Sehe jeder, wie er's treibe..." Die Verse weisen Goethe geradezu als Lehrmeister für modernes Tourismusmarketing aus. Weiterentwicklung geschieht dort, wo Unternehmen, Kommunen und private Vermieter ihre Alleinstellungsmerkmale noch besser erkennen und herausstellen. Die Frage ist einfach: Was kann ich anbieten, was der Gast woanders nicht hat?

Auch ideenreiche Kooperationen helfen, Flagge zu zeigen. „Oberlausitz per Bus" ist ein solches gelungenes Netzwerk. Tourismusunternehmen dieser Region bieten zusammen mit der einheimischen Marketinggesellschaft Reiseideen für die internationale Bustouristik an. Sie wissen, wie Busreiseveranstalter ticken, was die Busreisenden erwarten. Die IHK Dresden gehörte 2001 zu den Projektinitiatoren und begleitet seither die Gemeinschaft. Deren aktueller – inzwischen sechster – Katalog umfasst nahezu 60 Angebote.

Preis für Kreativität und Strategie für morgen

Erfolg der IHK Dresden auf der Internationalen Tourismusbörse Berlin (ITB) 2012: Vom Ostdeutschen Sparkassenverband erhielt sie den Marketing-Award „Leuchttürme der Tourismuswirtschaft". Ihre Geschäftsstelle Zittau wurde für nachhaltige und kreative Personalarbeit ausgezeichnet. Seit 21 Jahren arbeitet sie

Germany's Number 1

Visit Saxony – what for? Our Canaletto view revealed plenty of attractive and unique things to do and see. Surveys indicate a general consensus among tourists that Saxony is Germany's Number One cultural destination. It's not just the Historisches and Neues Grünes Gewölbe in Dresden that offers a treasure trove of art: in fact, the same goes for the whole of Saxony. The state offers 500 museums and monuments to history and the arts, outstanding architecture from the Romanesque to Deconstructivism, around 70 castles, palaces and gardens, plenty of theatres, orchestras and ensembles with exquisite venues, more than 40 renowned festivals. Cultural travellers will find a special appeal in each specific inspiring atmosphere, in the joy, passion and professional approach of the hosts associated with Saxony's treasures – whether the Grünes Gewölbe as one of Europe's richest art chambers or the International "Łužica/Lausitz" Folk Festival which is being held for the 10th time in 2013.

"But one thing does not suit everyone; each should see what he can do..." These words by Goethe can be taken as textbook teaching for modern tourism marketing. Advancement and further development will happen wherever companies, local authorities and private providers are more aware of their USPs and ensure that these are the focus of attention. The question is quite simple: What do I have to offer that the guest can't get elsewhere?

Imaginative cooperation also helps to keep the flag flying. "Oberlausitz by bus" is just one such successful network. Tourism companies in this region have joined forces with the local marketing company to offer a versatile range of ideas for international bus tourism. They know how bus tour operators work and what bus and coach travellers want. Dresden CCI was one of the initiators of the project in 2001 and has kept an eye on the activities ever since. The current catalogue – meanwhile in the 6th edition – contains nearly 60 different ideas and suggestions.

Prize for future-oriented creativity and strategy

Success for the CCI Dresden at the ITB Berlin 2012 (the world's leading travel trade show): it received the marketing award "Lighthouse of the tourism branch" from the East German Savings Bank Association, while the Zittau branch received an award for sustainable and creative HR management. For 21 years now, it has been working together with the CEFPPA hotel management school in Alsace, with 150 young Saxons attending the international courses to complete their training as chefs, restaurant and hotel managers. The branch also encourages youngsters in the local hotel and catering trade to pursue initial and advanced training with the Czech neighbours at the Turnov hotel management school.

Pulverturm GmbH & Co. KG
www.pulverturm-dresden.de

Ob herzhaft oder süß – alle Backwaren werden stets frisch in der Heeresbäckerei zubereitet.

Whether savoury or sweet, all baked products always come fresh from the army bakery.

Information

Angebot:
- Erlebnisgastronomie im Herzen von Dresden in historischem Ambiente
- 400 Plätze
- täglich geöffnet von 11:00 bis 1:00 Uhr
- Außenterrasse
- spezielle Arrangements auf Anfrage
- saisonale Küche
- Catering-Service

Services:
- themed restaurant with historic atmosphere at the heart of Dresden
- capacity for 400 guests
- open every day from 11 a.m. to 1 a.m.
- outside terrace
- special arrangements on request
- seasonal cuisine
- catering service

Pulverturm GmbH & Co. KG
Dresden

Pulverturm an der Frauenkirche

Das Gewölberestaurant „Pulverturm" befindet sich im historischen Zentrum Dresdens, direkt neben der weltberühmten Frauenkirche. Das Restaurant bietet seinen Gästen 400 Plätze in verschiedenen Gewölben wie „Russische Stube", „Marschall de Saxe Zimmer" und „Türkisches Gewölbe", die an bedeutende geschichtliche Ereignisse erinnern. Serviert werden die zahlreichen Spezialitäten und rustikalen Leckereien stilecht von Mägden und Grenadieren.

Pulverturm at Frauenkirche

The Pulverturm vault restaurant is located in the historical centre of Dresden, right next to the world-famous Frauenkirche. The restaurant can accommodate 400 guests in various vaults, called among others "Russian Room", "Marshall de Saxe Room" and "Turkish Vault", in memory of significant events in history. The numerous specialities and rustic delights are served in style by maids and grenadiers in historic costumes.

---

mit der Hotelfachschule CEFPPA im Elsass zusammen. In deren internationaler Klasse konnten so schon über 150 junge Sachsen eine Lehre zum Koch, Restaurant- und Hotelfachmann absolvieren. Zudem fördert die Geschäftsstelle die Aus- und Weiterbildung des hiesigen Gastronomienachwuchses beim tschechischen Nachbarn in der Hotelfachschule Turnov.

Sächsischer Tourismus – wohin geht die Reise? Der Kurs ist klar: Die Staatsregierung verabschiedete 2011 eine Tourismusstrategie bis 2020. Fast 30 touristische Partner hatten deren Erarbeitung fachlich begleitet, darunter die IHK Dresden. Bis zum Beginn des neuen Jahrzehnts werden jährliche Übernachtungszahlen von 18 bis 19 Millionen angepeilt. Laut Strategie soll Sachsen „als hochwertiges Reiseziel mit hoher Produktqualität und authentischer, stilvoller, weltoffener Lebensart auf dem nationalen und internationalen Markt positioniert und weiter profiliert sowie die Position als Kulturreiseziel Nummer eins in Deutschland gefestigt werden".

Staatliche Fördermittel werden jene Destinationen – Reiseziele – erhalten, die wirtschaftlich, ideenreich und gemeinschaftlich ihre Anziehungskraft stärken. Behaupten im Wettbewerb – hat es Jürgen Hardt nicht schon erahnt? „Der Sachse dud nich gnietschen, der Sachse singt 'n Liedschen!"

Saxony's tourism: where's the journey going? The course has been clearly laid out. In 2011 the state government adopted a tourism strategy for 2020. Nearly 30 tourism partners had been involved in elaborating the strategy, including the CCI Dresden. By the start of the new decade, a target of 18 to 19 million has been set for the annual statistics for overnight stays. According to the strategy, Saxony is to be positioned "as a top quality travel destination offering high product quality with an authentic, stylish, cosmopolitan way of life that can stand its own on the national and international market, working constantly at improving its image and profile while consolidating its position as Germany's number one culture destination".

State funds will be made available to those destinations that enhance their appeal with a profitable, imaginative and cooperative approach. Surviving in the face of competition – that brings us back to Jürgen Hardt, who tells us that "Saxons don't moan and grumble, they sing a song!"

Kein schöner Land
Ein unverwechselbarer Lebens- und Kulturraum

„Der Spiegel" fragte im Heft 15/2012: Was ist Heimat? Die Titelseite der Sachsen-Ausgabe zeigte das heutige Dresden aus dem Blickwinkel Canalettos, mit rastenden Radlern im Vordergrund. Heimat. Ein Wirtschaftsstandort, ein Reiseland ist für Tausende Menschen immer auch Heimat. Jeder empfindet „seine" Heimat anders. Der Blick aus dem Zimmer, Berge, Treppen, der Baum, der Arbeitsweg, alte Häuser, das Industriewerk, ein Bachlauf, Wahrzeichen, Gerüche, Spracheigenheiten...

Gebürtige Sachsen werden die Gegend, in der sie jeweils leben, wiederum anders wahrnehmen als Neu-Sachsen, die im Kammerbezirk Dresden sesshaft geworden sind, von neuen Lebenschancen angezogen. Fremd Empfundenes und Anheimelndes mögen sich bei ihnen noch mischen. Vielleicht aber haben sie ihr Zuhause auch schon als Heimat angenommen. Schön ist sie jedenfalls.

Zwischen Barock und Beta-Zellen

Dresden, über 529 000 Einwohner, 99 Stadtteile und Ortschaften, um 1206 erstmals erwähnt, von Johann Gottfried Herder 1802 als „ein Deutsches Florenz" bezeichnet, heute Kultur-, Wirtschafts-, Wissenschafts-, Einkaufs- und Einkehrstadt. Unter den deutschen Großstädten dehnen sich nur Berlin, Hamburg und Köln weiter aus. 62 Prozent der Stadtfläche sind grün, darunter die Elbwiesen und der Große Garten.

Wer Dresden sagt, der meint Barock. Am Neustädter Markt funkelt August der Starke als mächtiger Goldener Reiter. Seine Prunkbauten haben der Stadt diesen Ruf verschafft. Der Dresdner Barock ging sogar als eigene Spielart in die Kunstgeschichte ein. Das Barocke – das seltsam Geformte – macht heute nur einen Teil der Stadtarchitektur aus, wenngleich den bedeutendsten: Frauenkirche, Zwinger, Kathedrale, Brühlsche Terrasse, Bürgerhäuser... Beim Residenzschloss mischen sich die Stile von der Romanik bis zum Historismus. Die Semperoper ist Neorenaissance, das Albertinum Neoklassizismus, das Militärhistorische Museum – mit dem „Dresdner Keil" von US-Stararchitekt Daniel Libeskind – Historismus, das Deutsche Hygiene-Museum Reformarchitektur, der Kulturpalast Moderne und der Ufa-Kristallpalast Dekonstruktivismus.

Ein Freund Dresdens ist mit dem erneuten Aufblühen der Stadt eng verbunden: Nobelpreisträger Günter Blobel. 1994 gründete der US-amerikanische Biochemiker in New York den Förderverein „Friends of Dresden". Dieser unterstützt seither die Rekonstruktion historischer Gebäude und vergibt seit 2010 die inter-

No place more beautiful
Unmistakable living space and culture area

The weekly news magazine "Der Spiegel" asked in its issue 15/2012: "What is homeland?" The front page of the Saxony issue showed present-day Dresden from Canaletto's angle, with cyclists taking a break in the foreground. Homeland. A business place or a tourist destination that attracts thousands is always also homeland. Everyone sees "their" homeland in a different way. The view from their room, mountains, steps, the tree, the way to work, old houses, the industrial factory, a stream bed, landmarks, smells, local dialects...

Those born in Saxony will see the area where they live differently from new arrivals who have come here to settle, attracted by the new chances offered by the Dresden chamber district. They may still feel a mixture of strangeness and homely cosiness. But maybe they also see their new home as their homeland. It is certainly a beautiful place to call home.

Between Baroque and beta cells

Dresden: population of more than 529,000, 99 districts and suburbs, first mentioned around 1206, called "Germany's Florence" by Johann Gottfried Herder in 1802, today a place for culture, business, science and shopping, with plenty of places to pop in for refreshments. Berlin, Hamburg and Cologne are the only other German cities to expand more. 62 percent of the city's surface area are green, including the Elbe meadows and the Großer Garten (Great Garden).

The name Dresden conjures up pictures of Baroque architecture. A statue of August the Strong takes pride of place on Neustädter Markt as a mighty Golden Rider. It is his impressive buildings that gave the city its architectural reputation. Dresden Baroque even has its place as a variety of its own in art history. Today, Baroque – "the irregularly shaped" – only accounts for part of the city architecture, even though it covers the most important buildings: Frauenkirche, Zwinger, Cathedral, Brühlsche Terrasse, town houses... The Residenzschloss (royal castle) offers a mixture of styles from the Romanesque to Historicism. The Semperoper is neo-Renaissance, the Albertinum neo-

Der Zwinger in Dresden wurde unter Kurfürst Friedrich August I. im frühen 18. Jahrhundert erbaut und ist eines der schönsten und bedeutendsten Bauwerke des Barock.

The Zwinger in Dresden was constructed in the name of elector Friedrich August I in the early 18th century and is one of the most beautiful and significant buildings of the baroque era.

nationale Auszeichnung „Dresden-Preis". Für den Wiederaufbau der Frauenkirche spendete Günter Blobel selbst 820 000 Euro seines Stockholmer Preisgeldes von 1999. Mit seinem Namen kann sich auch Dresdens Wissenschaft schmücken. Er ist Ehrensenator der TU Dresden. Dort experimentieren Forscher beispielsweise mit Betazellen zur Diabetesbehandlung.

Die Zuneigung des Wissenschaftlers zu Dresden wurzelt tief: Anfang 1945 hatte der Neunjährige auf der Flucht aus Schlesien das noch unversehrte Dresden durchquert, das ihn tief beeindruckte. Am 13. Februar sah er rund 30 Kilometer entfernt am Himmel die Stadt brennen. Günter Blobels Engagement – auch im Gedenken an seine vor Kriegsende getötete Schwester – gehört zu den Taten unzähliger Menschen, die Sachsens Metropole in die erste Reihe der Kulturstädte Europas zurückgeführt haben. Die Frauenkirche ist inzwischen – laut Umfrage des Deutschen Tourismusverbandes – der Deutschen zweitbeliebteste Sehenswürdigkeit nach dem Kölner Dom.

Wer Dresden besucht, weiß nicht, was er zuerst machen soll. Das barocke „Pflichtprogramm" absolvieren? Der Sixtinischen Classicism, the Military History Museum – with the "Dresden Wedge" by US star architect Daniel Libeskind – Historicism, the German Hygiene Museum is Reform architecture, the Kulturpalast Modern Age and the Ufa-Kristallpalast Deconstructivism.

One friend of Dresden is closely related to the renewed flourishing of the city: Nobel Prize winner Günter Blobel. In 1994, the American biochemist founded the "Friends of Dresden" in New York. Since then, the association has been supporting the reconstruction of historical buildings, and has awarded the international Dresden Prize every year since 2010. Günter Blobel himself donated 820,000 Euro from his Nobel Prize money in 1999 to the reconstruction of the Frauenkirche. Dresden's science life can also lay claim to his name: he is honorary senator of TU Dresden, where researchers conduct experiments for example with beta cells for treating diabetes.

The scientist's affection for Dresden goes very deep: in early 1945, he passed through the still unharmed city as a nine-year old refugee fleeing from Silesia, and was deeply impressed by what he saw. On 13 February, from a distance of about 30 kilometres he saw the city burning in the sky. Günter Blobel's commitment, also in memory of his sister who was killed before the end of the war, is just one example of the deeds by countless people who have put Saxony's metropolis back among Europe's top-ranking cultural cities. A survey by the German Tourism Association shows that the Frauenkirche is meanwhile the second favourite tourist site for the German population after Cologne Cathedral.

Das Elbsandsteingebirge ist eines der touristischen Highlights Ostsachsens.

The Elbsandstein mountains is one of the tourist highlights of East Saxony.

Madonna in die Augen schauen? Auf der Einkaufsmeile Prager Straße bummeln? Mit einem Raddampfer zum Blauen Wunder – Stahlbrücke von 1893 – fahren? Durch das Szene- und Gründerzeitviertel Neustadt schlendern? Mit der ältesten Schwebebahn der Welt auf die Loschwitzer Elbhänge aufsteigen? Im 6000 Hektar großen Stadtwald Dresdner Heide wandern?

Kletterfelsen und Glückauf

Landkreis Sächsische Schweiz-Osterzgebirge, über 251 000 Einwohner, 19 Städte und 20 Gemeinden. Das dreigeteilte Wappen symbolisiert den Elbverlauf, die einstige Zugehörigkeit zur Markgrafschaft Meißen mit einem Löwen und die Bergbau-

Visitors to Dresden don't know where to start: the obligatory "Baroque tour" first of all? Look deep into the eyes of the Sixtine Madonna? Stroll along Prager Straße with its shops? Take a paddle steamer to the Blue Miracle – steel bridge dated 1893? Saunter through the trendy Neustadt with its Wilhelminian quarter? Take the world's oldest overhead railway up to the Loschwitz slopes along the river Elbe? Amble through the 6,000 city hectare forest called Dresdner Heide?

Climbing and mining

The rural district Sächsische Schweiz-Osterzgebirge covers Saxony Switzerland and the East Erzgebirge mountains. It has

Blick von der Dresdner Bergbahn hinunter auf die Loschwitzer Brücke, im Volksmund nur „Blaues Wunder" genannt

View from the Dresden mountain railway down to the Loschwitz Bridge, commonly referred to as "Blaues Wunder" (blue miracle)

Die Festung Königstein ist eine der größten Bergfestungen in Europa und liegt auf dem gleichnamigen Tafelberg.

The fortress of Königstein is one of the largest mountain fortresses in Europe and is situated on the table mountain known by the same name.

tradition mit Schlägel und Eisen. Pirna ist Verwaltungssitz. Große Kreisstädte sind zudem Dippoldiswalde, Freital und Sebnitz. Östlich grenzt der Landkreis an den tschechischen Ústecký kraj, den Kreis Ústí. Rote und Wilde Weißeritz im Osterzgebirge vereinen sich zur Weißeritz, einem Elbzufluss. Die Elbe ist die Lebensader des Landkreises. Die A 17 verbindet Sächsische Schweiz und Osterzgebirge verkehrstechnisch.

Anmutige Elbemäander, vielgestaltige Felsen, üppige Pflanzen- und Tierwelt. Ein erhebendes Gefühl ergreift den Wanderer im Elbsandsteingebirge. „Willkommen im Märchenland" – so hat der regionale Tourismusverband sein Urlaubsmagazin 2012 betitelt. Übertrieben? Offensichtlich nicht. Schon Caspar David Friedrich, Carl Gustav Carus und weitere Maler der deutschen Romantik haben ähnlich empfunden. In Höhen und Schluchten, grotesken Steingebilden, mystischen Wäldern und fantastischen Weitblicken sahen sie einen Spiegel der menschlichen Seele.

Das Wandern ist des Malers Lust… Der 112 Kilometer lange „Malerweg" – 2007 als schönster Wanderweg Deutschlands ausgezeichnet – führt rechts der Elbe durch den Nationalpark Sächsische Schweiz, linksseitig durch offene Landschaft. Stadt Wehlen, Kurort Rathen, Schmilka, die Festung Königstein und die Pirnaer Altstadt sind Stationen. Für schmale, steile Gebirgswege über Leitern und Stiegen empfiehlt sich trittsicheres Schuhwerk. Schaustück auf der Tour ist der 381 Meter hohe, frei stehende Falkenstein. 1864 bestiegen ihn erstmals Turner aus dem nahen Schandau und begründeten damit das sportliche

a population of more than 251,000 with 19 towns and 20 municipalities. The three-part coat of arms symbolises the course of the river Elbe, the former affiliation with Meißen margraviate featuring a lion, and the mining tradition with mallet and iron. Pirna is the administrative centre. Other large district towns also include Dippoldiswalde, Freital and Sebnitz. To the east, the rural district borders on Ústecký kraj, the Ústí district in the Czech Republic. Here in the East Erzgebirge mountains, the Rote and Wilde Weißeritz merge to form the Weißeritz, a tributary of the river Elbe. The Elbe is the lifeline of the rural district, while the A 17 motorway connects Saxon Switzerland and the East Erzgebirge mountains in terms of traffic.

The river Elbe meanders charmingly through rocks and cliffs of many different shapes amid luxuriant plant and animal wildlife. Walkers in the Elbsandstein mountains enjoy a truly uplifting experience. "Welcome to fairyland" was the title given to the 2012 holiday magazine of the regional tourism association. Exaggerated? Apparently not. Just a reflection on what Caspar David Friedrich, Carl Gustav Carus and other painters of the German Romantic period also felt, seeing a mirror of the human

Altenberg war früher eine Bergbaugemeinde, heute ist der Ort vor allem als internationales Wintersportzentrum (Bob- und Rodelbahn) bekannt.

Altenberg used to be a mining community. Today, first and foremost, the city of Altenberg is well-known as an international winter sport centre (bobsled and toboggan run).

Klettern überhaupt. Mit 1100 Kletterfelsen ist das Elbsandsteingebirge heute ein Eldorado für alle, die an schroffem Gestein hoch hinauf wollen.

Tief hinab führt das Besucherbergwerk „Vereinigt Zwitterfeld zu Zinnwald" im Osterzgebirge. Der Bergmannsgruß „Glückauf" – im Erzgebirge entstanden – begleitet die Touristen in den Tiefen-Bünau-Stollen von 1686. Im Raum Altenberg-Geising-Zinnwald wurde von 1420 an bis ins 20. Jahrhundert die bedeutendste Zinnlagerstätte Mitteleuropas abgebaut. Die Bergbauzeugnisse sind heute viel besichtigte Technische Denkmale. Die Einheimischen leben vor allem vom Tourismus, von der Wanderlust in der warmen, von Pisten und Loipen in der kalten Jahreszeit. Erholungsorte wie Kipsdorf, Rehefeld, Schellerhau und Bärenstein gehören mittlerweile zu Altenberg.

Die Berg- und Sportstadt liegt an der B 170 Richtung Nordböhmen und Prag. Internationalen Ruf hat ihre Rennschlitten- und Bobbahn erlangt, eine der modernsten der Welt. Auch mutige Touristen können hinter Bobpiloten den Eiskanal hinunterzischen. Wer's weniger rasant mag, kann das Georgenfelder Hochmoor auf Knüppelpfaden begehen oder sich an der Talsperre Malter erholen. Campingplätze, Strandbäder und Waldseilgarten haben die knapp Hundertjährige ansehnlich geliftet.

Wein und Weltruf

Landkreis Meißen, über 251 000 Einwohner, zehn Städte und 23 Gemeinden. Große Kreisstädte sind neben dem Verwaltungssitz Meißen Coswig, Großenhain, Radebeul und Riesa. Das Wappen bildet einen schwarzen Löwen mit roter Zunge ab. Der

soul in the heights and gorges, grotesque stone formation, mysterious forests and fantastic wide views.

Painters love to walk... the 112 kilometre-long "Painter's Path", declared Germany's loveliest footpath in 2007, goes through the Saxon Switzerland national park on the right bank of the Elbe and through open landscape on the left bank, passing the town of Wehlen, Rathen spa, Schmilka, Königstein fortress and Pirna old town. Sturdy shoes are recommended for narrow, steep mountain paths with steps and ladders. The highlight of the tour is the 381 metres high free-standing rock named Falkenstein. It was climbed for the first time in 1864 by climbers from nearby Schandau, who thus launched climbing as a sport. The Elbsandstein mountains offer 1,100 rocks and cliffs for climbing, an Eldorado for all those who love scrambling up craggy slopes.

The visitor's mine "Vereinigt Zwitterfeld zu Zinnwald" in the Eastern Erzgebirge takes visitors down into the depths of the earth. The miner's greeting "Glückauf" which originated here in the Erzgebirge accompanies tourists down to the deep Bünau mining gallery dated 1686. Central Europe's most important tin deposits were mined here between Altenberg, Geising and Zinnwald from 1420 right up into the 20th century. Today the mines are popular technical monuments for tourists to visit. Tourism is also the main livelihood of the local population, with the many footpaths tempting walkers in the summer months together with the slopes and cross-country skiing trails for skiers in the winter. Altenberg meanwhile also includes health resorts such as Kipsdorf, Rehefeld, Schellerhau and Bärenstein.

The mountain and sport town is located on the main road B 170 heading for North Bohemia and Prague. Its luge and bob

Die Weine vom Weingut Schloss Proschwitz sind bei Kennern und Feinschmeckern begehrt und beliebt.

The wines of the winery Schloss Proschwitz are highly coveted and very popular with both wine connoisseurs and gourmets.

Meißner Löwe war das Herrschaftssymbol der Wettiner als Meißner Markgraf mit Sitz auf der Albrechtsburg.

Sachsen ist von Meißen aus in die Welt getreten. Eine Ausstellung in der Albrechtsburg zeichnet die Geschichte nach, auch die der Felsenburg selbst. 929: hölzerne Verteidigungsanlage, 1471: Deutschlands erstes Schloss, 1710: Porzellanproduktion bis 1863. Im Areal steht der Meißner Dom mit Ursprung im 13. Jahrhundert. Besucherscharen drängen zu beiden Bauwerken den Burgberg hinauf. Die DDR hatte die historischen Häuser am Hang dem Verfall preisgegeben. Heute sind sie Kleinode. Auch ins Triebischtal strömen die Touristen. Das berühmte Porzellan wird seit 150 Jahren nunmehr dort gebrannt und verziert. Das Haus MEISSEN eröffnet jährlich 280 000 Touristen eine Erlebniswelt mit Schauwerkstätten und hochkarätiger Sammlung.

Wie begrüßt man einen Prinzen? Am besten mit einem Glas Wein aus dessen eigenem Weingut. Dr. Georg Prinz zur Lippe bewirtschaftet mit 50 Mitarbeitern das Weingut Schloss Proschwitz. Sein Weinberg liegt rechts der Elbe gegenüber der Altstadt. „Das Flaggschiff des sächsischen Weinbaus hält Kurs und bestätigt auch in diesem Jahr seine Spitzenposition im Anbaugebiet", schreibt das Fachmagazin „Der Feinschmecker" mit Blick auf die 900 besten Weingüter Deutschlands 2012.

run has acquired an international reputation as one of the most advanced in the world. Brave tourists can also race down the ice channel behind a bob pilot. Those who prefer less speed can try the paths on Georgenfelder Hochmoor or simply relax at Malter reservoir. Camp sites, beaches and a forest rope garden are among some of the attractive additions that have helped to modernise this 100-year old facility.

Wine and world renown

Meißen rural district has a population of over 251,000, ten towns and 23 municipalities. In addition to the administrative centre Meißen, other large district towns include Coswig, Großenhain, Radebeul and Riesa. The coat of arms shows a black lion with a red tongue. The Meißen lion was the heraldic symbol of the House of Wettin as margrave of Meißen, based on the Albrechtsburg.

It was Meißen that led Saxony out into the world. An exhibition in der Albrechtsburg illustrates the history, including that of the Felsenburg itself. 929: wooden defence structure, 1471: Germany's first palace, 1710: porcelain production until 1863. It also includes Meißen Cathedral that dates back to the 13th century. Both buildings attract visitors up to the Burgberg to have a look. The GDR let the historical houses on the slopes fall into disrepair. Today they are little gems. Triebischtal also pulls in the tourists. This is where the famous porcelain has been fired and decorated for what is now more than 150 years. The House of MEISSEN opens its doors to 280,000 tourists every year, offering them a world of experience with demonstration workshops and a first-class collection.

Feine sächsische Lebensart, hier ist sie zu Hause auf Schloss Wackerbarth in Radebeul.

The fine Saxonian way of life can be experienced here at Castle Wackerbarth in Radebeul.

Schloss Proschwitz ist das älteste und größte Weingut Sachsens. Der Prinz hatte das enteignete Familienanwesen ab 1990 zurückgekauft. „Ich wohnte damals oben im Weinberghäuschen auf einem Feldbett mit einer Luftmatratze", erinnert er sich. Mit Weinbergwanderungen, Gartenseminaren, Weinabenden und Konzerten verknüpft Schloss Proschwitz heute sächsische Weinbautraditionen mit reichem Kulturleben. Sein Besitzer – Spross eines der ältesten Adelshäuser Deutschlands – steht exemplarisch für 22 Weinerzeuger und Weinbaugemeinschaften im zweitkleinsten deutschen Weinbaugebiet. Alle verbindet Fachkunde, Heimatliebe und die Sächsische Weinstraße mit vielen Besichtigungs-, Einkehr- und Reiseangeboten, darunter die jährlichen Tage des offenen Weingutes.

„Sächsisches Elbland" hat der ansässige Tourismusverband die Region getauft, die zum Großteil im Landkreis Meißen liegt. Er wirbt für Meißen und sächsischen Rebensaft ebenso wie für weitere Kulturperlen, darunter Schloss Moritzburg, Klosterpark Altzella und Schloss Heynitz. In eine heimelige Ecke führt Udo Lindenbergs „Sonderzug nach Pankow". Die deutsche Nachkriegsversion des US-Klassikers swingte: „Entschuldigen Sie, fährt dieser Zug nach Kötzschenbroda?" Der sanierte Dorfanger Altkötzschenbroda – heute Teil Radebeuls – ist mit Cafés,

How do you welcome a prince? Preferably with a glass of wine from his own vineyard. Dr. Georg Prinz zur Lippe runs Schloss Proschwitz vineyard with 50 employees, located on the right bank of the river Elbe opposite the old town centre. "The flagship of Saxon wine-growing remains on course and confirms its leading position in the district yet again this year", writes "Der Feinschmecker" trade magazine in its review of the 900 best vineyards in Germany in 2012.

Schloss Proschwitz is Saxony's oldest and largest vineyard. The Prince had repurchased the expropriated family estate back in 1990. "Back then I lived on a camp bed with a lilo in the vineyard hut", he remembers. Today, Schloss Proschwitz offers vineyard walks, garden seminars, wine evenings and concerts to combine Saxon wine-growing traditions with a rich cultural life. The owner, scion of one of Germany's oldest noble families, is just one of the 22 wine growers and wine-growing consortiums in Germany's second smallest wine-growing area. They all combine professional knowledge, a love of their homeland and the Saxon Wine Road with much to see and do and lots of wine to taste and try, including the annual day of the Open Vineyard.

"Saxon Elbland" is the name that the local tourism association has given the region located mainly in Meißen rural district. The association promotes Meißen and Saxon wine together with other cultural pearls including Schloss Moritzburg, Klosterpark Altzella and Schloss Heynitz. In a cosy corner we find a village featured in a German post-war version of the "Chattenooga Choo Choo", where among others the text goes "Entschuldigen Sie, fährt dieser Zug nach Kötzschenbroda?"

Das barocke Jagdschloss Moritzburg erhebt sich auf einer künstlichen Insel.

The baroque hunting lodge Moritzburg is situated on an artificial island.

Galerien, Geschäften und Pensionen ein Schmuckkästchen. In der DDR hatte sein Totalabriss gedroht. Übrigens ist es von dort nicht weit in die Villa „Shatterhand", das heutige Karl-May-Museum.

Dom und Dreiländereck

Landkreis Bautzen und Landkreis Görlitz – die Oberlausitz, zusammen über 592 000 Einwohner, 29 Städte und 88 Gemeinden. Große Kreisstädte sind neben beiden Verwaltungssitzen Bischofswerda, Kamenz, Hoyerswerda und Radeberg sowie Löbau, Niesky, Weißwasser und Zittau. Das Wappen der Bautzener Region zeigt eine Zinnenmauer, das der Görlitzer Region vereint den Niederschlesischen Adler, den Böhmischen Löwen und die Oberlausitzer Zinnenmauer. Symbole eines alten Siedlungsraums, der politisch lange relativ selbstständig und mit den Nachbarn Niederschlesien und Nordböhmen wirtschaftlich und kulturell verschwistert war.

Rěčiće serbsce? Das heißt: Sprechen Sie Sorbisch? In der Oberlausitz lebt eine nationale Minderheit, das westslawische Volk der Sorben. Zu den 40 000 Sorben in Sachsen – vor allem zwischen Kamenz, Hoyerswerda und Bautzen zu Hause – gehört Ministerpräsident Stanislaw Tillich. Er lebt mit seiner Familie in

(sorry, does this train go to Kötzschenbroda?). The rehabilitated village green in Altkötzschenbroda, now part of Radebeul, is today a picturesque treasure trove with cafés, galleries and shops as well as bed-and-breakfast establishments. The GDR had threatened to demolish the whole village. By the way, from here it's not far to "Shatterhand Villa", the museum dedicated to German adventure novel writer Karl May.

Cathedral and three-country triangle

Bautzen rural district and Görlitz rural district make up the Oberlausitz with a population of more than 592,000, 29 towns and 88 municipalities. Together with Bautzen and Görlitz as administrative centres, large district towns include Bischofswerda, Kamenz, Hoyerswerda and Radeberg together with Löbau, Niesky, Weißwasser and Zittau. The coat of arms for the Bautzen region shows a battlement wall, while the Görlitz coat of arms combines the eagle of Lower Silesia, the lion of Bohemia and the battlement wall of Oberlausitz – symbols of an old settlement area that for a long time was relatively independent in political terms, with close economic and cultural ties with its neighbours in Lower Silesia and North Bohemia.

Rěčiće serbsce? That means: do you speak Sorbian? There's a national minority living here in the Oberlausitz: the West Slavic people of the Sorbs. The 40,000 Sorbs living in Saxony, primarily between Kamenz, Hoyerswerda and Bautzen, also include Minister President Stanislaw Tillich, who lives with his family in Panschwitz-Kuckau. Sorbian culture and customs have enriched the cohabitation of Sorbs and Germans for centuries.

Panschwitz-Kuckau. Sorbische Kultur und Bräuche bereichern seit Jahrhunderten das Zusammenleben von Sorben und Deutschen. Ostereierverzieren, Osterreiter in Frack und Zylinder, sorbische Trachten, Sorbisches Museum, Deutsch-Sorbisches Volkstheater... Zweisprachige Orts- und Straßenschilder signalisieren im Alltag das Miteinander von Sprachen und Menschen.

Bautzen – 1002 erstmals erwähnt – ist die historische Hauptstadt der Oberlausitz. Ihre Altstadt ist als Flächendenkmal geschützt. Wahrzeichen ist die Alte Wasserkunst am Spreelauf. Neben Pisa hat auch Bautzen einen schiefen Turm: Der Reichenturm am Kornmarkt neigt sich auf 56 Meter Höhe 1,44 Meter nach Nordwest. Der Dom St. Petri bewährt sich seit der Reformation als Simultankirche – als ältestes Gotteshaus in Deutschland für katholische und evangelische Gläubige gleichermaßen.

Der Dom gehört zur „Via Sacra". Sie durchzieht das Dreiländereck grenzübergreifend. Ein überlieferter Name? Keineswegs. Die „Heilige Straße" war ein touristisches EU-Projekt Mitte der 2000er-Jahre, das sich inzwischen mit 16 Stationen auf deutscher, polnischer und tschechischer Seite mit Leben erfüllt hat. „Nach der EU-Erweiterung wollten wir den Blick auf diese alte europäische Region lenken. Und das mit ihren historischen Stärken, nämlich bedeutenden, ja einmaligen sakralen Bauwerken und Kunstschätzen", sagt Historiker Dr. Volker Dudeck aus Zittau, der Spiritus Rector der Route. Auch das Große und Kleine Zittauer Fastentuch – deutschlandweit einzigartige religiöse Textilwerke – gehören dazu. Zittau profitiert von ihnen am internationalen Reisemarkt als „Stadt der Fastentücher".

Traditional Easter egg decorations, Easter riders in tails and top hats, Sorbian national costumes, Sorbian Museum, German-Sorbian Theatre... Bilingual place-names and road signs exemplify the cohabitation of languages and people in everyday life.

Bautzen, mentioned for the first time in 1002, is the historical capital of the Oberlausitz. All the old town centre is protected as a heritage area. The landmark of Bautzen is the Old Water Tower on the river Spree. And just like Pisa, Bautzen also has a leaning tower on Kornmarkt which with a height of 56 metres leans 1.44 metres to the northwest. Since the Reformation, St. Petri Cathedral has preserved its role as a simultaneous church: this is the oldest church in Germany for both Catholic and Protestant congregations.

The Cathedral is on the "Via Sacra" which passes through the three-country triangle on a cross-border course. An old traditional name? Not at all! The "Holy Road" was a tourism project launched by the EU in the first decade of the new millennium which has meanwhile been brought to life with 16 stations on the German, Polish and Czech sides of the respective borders. "We wanted to use the opportunity provided by the EU enlargement to focus attention on this old European region, with its historical assets consisting of significant and even unique sacred buildings and art treasures", says historian Dr. Volker Dudeck from Zittau and spiritus rector of the route. These also include the Large and Small Zittau Lenten Veil, unique religious textiles in Germany. Zittau benefits accordingly in the international travel market with its claim as being the "Town of Lenten Veils".

Der Naturpark Zittauer Gebirge nahe der deutsch-tschechischen Grenze ist heute eine beliebte Ferienregion.

Today, the natural preserve "Zittauer Gebirge", which is located in close proximity to the German-Czech border, is a popular holiday region.

Der Reichenturm in Bautzen

The Reichenturm (Rich Tower) in Bautzen

Kann man die Oberlausitz eine Wunderkammer nennen? Krabat jedenfalls, den Otfried Preußlers Kinderbuch berühmt gemacht hat, stammt aus einer sorbischen Volkssage und geradewegs aus Schwarzkollm bei Hoyerswerda. Wundersam ist auch das Heilige Grab in Görlitz. Die mittelalterliche Pilgerstätte gilt als historisch getreuer als ihr Jerusalemer Vorbild in der Gegenwart. Der Muskauer Park an der Neiße – angelegt von Hermann Fürst von Pückler-Muskau – gehört als Gartenkunstwerk zum UNESCO-Welterbe. Kleine Wunder verkörpern die Umgebindehäuser. Sie vereinen Block- und Fachwerkbau unter einem Dach. Diese in Europa einmalige Volksarchitektur hat sich konzentriert nur im hiesigen Raum erhalten. Nicht als riesiges Freilichtmuseum, sondern als Lebensraum mit sanierten Häusern zum Wohnen, Arbeiten und Erholen. Koreawissenschaftler Dr. Albrecht Huwe von der Universität Bonn etwa baut in Eibau ein Gebäude aus dem 18. Jahrhundert denkmalgerecht aus. Als Pensionär will er sich dort ansiedeln und seinen Lebenstraum von einer Pferdepension erfüllen.

Is Oberlausitz a chamber of marvels? Krabat, the figure that made Otfried Preußler's children's book famous, comes from a Sorbian folk tale straight out of Schwarzkollm near Hoyerswerda. Marvellous also describes the Holy Grave in Görlitz. The mediaeval place of pilgrimage is said to be historically more accurate that the present-day role model in Jerusalem. Muskauer Park on the river Neiße created by Hermann Prince of Pückler-Muskau with its lovely gardens has been declared a UNESCO world heritage site. The half-timbered houses themselves are also little marvels, in a style of architecture that can only be found in such concentrated form here in this particular area – and not as a huge open-air museum but as real renovated houses for living, working and relaxing. Korean scientist Dr. Albrecht Huwe from Bonn University for example is renovating a listed 18th century building in Eibau: once he has retired, he wants to settle there and fulfil his life's dream of running a horse boarding establishment.

Coaching für die Zukunft
Die IHK Dresden stärkt Vertrauen und Zuversicht

Am 22. Juli 1862 schrieben die „Dresdner Nachrichten": „Gestern fand die Konstituierung der Dresdner Handels- und Gewerbekammer in dem Saale des Innungsgebäudes, Kreuzgasse Nr. 17, unter Leitung des Regierungsrates Stelzner statt." Mit ihrer Gründung schlug die Geburtsstunde der heutigen IHK Dresden. Das Gewerbegesetz von Sachsens König Johann hatte damals den Weg frei gemacht. Eine Laune der Geschichte wollte es, dass sich just 158 Jahre zuvor in der Kreuzgasse August der Starke spontan in Gräfin Cosel verliebt hatte, als deren Elternhaus brannte. Womit ihre Zeit als langjährige Mätresse des Kurfürsten begann.

Als Handwerksmeister, Fabrikanten und Kaufleute ihre Kammer gründeten, ging ihnen anderes durch den Kopf: Sie organisierten ihre Selbstverwaltung und Selbsthilfe, um in der Zeit stürmischer Industrialisierung ihre Interessen gemeinschaftlich zu vertreten. Die IHK Dresden vertritt heute ebenso die Belange der regionalen Wirtschaft gegenüber Politik und Verwaltung, nur dass nicht mehr Dampfkraft und aufkommende Elektrizität das Tempo bestimmen, sondern die Hochtechnologien.

Boxring und Hürdenlauf

Mit der Neugründung am 29. Mai 1990 übernahm die IHK Dresden den Staffelstab der demokratisch gesinnten Altvorderen, nachdem die zwei deutschen Diktaturen im 20. Jahrhundert die Autonomie der Körperschaft weitgehend ausgelöscht hatten. Die IHK-Mitgliedschaft im Kammerbezirk Dresden ist seither Spiegel der aufstrebenden Wirtschaft. Seit 1992 hat sich die Zahl der Mitgliedsunternehmen mehr als verdoppelt – auf fast 97 000 im 150. Gründungsjahr.

Der Mitgliederrekord spornt an. 2012 mag's die IHK Dresden sportlich. „Für Unternehmen immer in Bewegung – seit 1862!" heißt der Jubiläumsslogan. In einer Imagekampagne symbolisieren Boxhandschuhe, Hürdenparcours, Start-Ziel-Flagge, Stoppuhr, Laufschuhe und Schiedsrichterpfeife die Disziplinen, in denen sie ihre Stärken als Teamplayer ausspielt. Konzentration, Ehrgeiz, Zielstrebigkeit, Willensstärke und Ausdauer sind Eigenschaften, die Unternehmer erfolgreich machen. Die Parallele zu sportlichen Leistungen lag nahe. Damit war die Idee für die IHK-Kampagne gefunden.

Coaching for the future
Dresden CCI reinforces trust and confidence

On 22 July 1862, the "Dresdner Nachrichten" wrote: "Yesterday the constituting meeting of Dresden Chamber of Trade and Industry was held in the Hall of the Guild Building, Kreuzgasse No. 17, chaired by Councillor Stelzner." This was the hour of birth of the CCI Dresden. The ground had been prepared by the Business Act of King Johann of Saxony. It's just one of those quirks of history that just 158 years previously, it was in Kreuzgasse again where August the Strong fell in love with Countess Cosel whose home burnt down. This was the start of her long career as the Elector's mistress.

But when the master craftsmen, manufacturers and merchants founded their Chamber, they had other ideas in mind. They organised their own self-administration and self-help philosophy for collaborative representation of their interests in the time of stormy industrialisation. Today the CCI Dresden similarly represents the interests of regional business and industry in its dealings with administration and the political sector, only that today the pace is dictated by high-tech rather than steam power and burgeoning electricity.

Boxing and hurdles

On 29 May 1990, the CCI Dresden was refounded, taking up the baton of its democratic predecessors following two German dictatorships in the 20th century that had extensively extinguished the autonomy of the corporation. Since then, the CCI membership in Dresden has mirrored the aspiring economy. The number of member companies more than doubled between 1992 and 2012, now counting nearly 97,000 in the 150th year since the year in which it was initially founded.

The membership record acts as an incentive. For 2012, the CCI Dresden has chosen an athletic approach. "Constantly on the move for its companies – since 1862!" is the jubilee slogan. The image campaign uses boxing gloves, hurdles, a starting/finishing line flag, stopwatch, running shoes and referee's whistles to symbolise the disciplines where its strengths as a team player

Hauptsitz der Industrie- und Handelskammer in Dresden-Dobritz, Langer Weg

Headquarters of the Chamber of Commerce and Industry and the educational centre in Dresden-Dobritz, Langer Weg

Von null auf hundert

Die 150-Jährige signalisiert Vitalität, Sportsgeist und Trainerqualitäten. Die Kammer kämpft für ihre Mitglieder im politischen Ring. Sie hilft ihnen beim Start über die ersten Hürden hinweg. Die IHK-Profis spurten mit ihnen auf den Zielgeraden bei Bildung, Innovation und Umweltschutz. Sie trauen sich auf neue Wege querfeldein und streiten bei (Rechts-)Gerangel für Fairplay.

Sportlich begann es schon im Umbruchjahr 1990. Das politische und wirtschaftliche System im Osten veränderte sich rasant. Die auferstehende sächsische Unternehmerschaft nahm die Geschwindigkeit auf. Für den gemeinsamen Erfolg schickte sie ein neues Team ins Rennen, die IHK Dresden. Es war hoch motiviert, aber marktwirtschaftlich untrainiert. Langsam warmlaufen? Nicht daran zu denken. Die Mannschaft musste gleich von null auf hundert beschleunigen.

Der Start glückte. Freier Markt und demokratische Gepflogenheiten wurden vertraut. IHK-Experten aus den alten Bundesländern coachten die Newcomer. Berufsausbildung, Weiterbildung und Prüfungswesen wurden neu aufgebaut, Reprivatisierer und Unternehmensgründer beraten und unterstützt, Rechtssystem und Außenhandel unter neuen Vorzeichen etabliert. Überall war Bewegung und Veränderung. Die neue IHK agierte, improvisierte, ermutigte. Im Wirbel der Ereignisse lernte sie, die Interessen ihrer Unternehmerschaft zu vertreten.

Aufbruchstimmung und Neubau

Wer dabei war, denkt gern an den Anfang zurück. Unter den damals rund 60 Mitarbeitern habe – so erinnern sich Mitstreiter der erste Stunde – „eine tolle Aufbruchstimmung" geherrscht. Dem Team, das selbst täglich dazulernte, machte es viel Freude, den Unternehmen in der Umbruchphase Hilfe zur Selbsthilfe zu geben. Die Wege waren kurz, auch nach „oben". So mancher Event wurde aus dem Bauch heraus organisiert, ohne viel Bürokratie. Die IHK-Mitarbeiter wuchsen hinein in den Neubeginn und gestalteten ihn zugleich mit.

Die IHK-Hauptgeschäftsstelle in Dresden hatte anfangs drei Standorte: eine Villa in der August-Bebel-Straße 48, Außenstellen in der Barlachstraße und am heutigen Straßburger Platz. 2002 fügte die Kammer der Architektur in Dresden ein modernes Gebäude hinzu. Der Neubau entstand im südöstlichen Stadtteil Niedersedlitz als Nachbar des IHK-Bildungszentrums Dresden. Das ist seit 1996 in einem rekonstruierten Gebäudekomplex zu Hause, der Traditionen der Kameraproduktion in Dresden seit 1897 verkörpert, verbunden mit den Namen Wünsche („Reicka"), Zeiss Ikon und Pentacon.

come to the fore. Concentration, ambition, determination, will power and endurance are the attributes that make entrepreneurs successful – all areas with quite apparent sporting parallels, thus giving birth to the idea for the CCI campaign.

From zero to one hundred

The 150-year old CCI signalises vitality, sporting spirit and trainer qualities. The Chamber fights for its members in the political ring. It helps them over the first hurdles at the start. The CCI professionals surge with them down the home straight with training, innovation and environmental protection, while daring to cross new terrain and get involved in (legal) disputes for fair play.

Developments in the year of reunification 1990 were no less athletic. The political and economic system in the east went through rapid transformation. Saxony's resurrected business sector picked up speed and sent a new team into the race for the sake of shared success – this was the CCI Dresden. Highly motivated, but lacking in training for the market economy. Gradual warm-up? No way! The team had to go from zero to one hundred in next-to-no time.

It all worked out well. Free market and democratic customs became familiar. CCI experts from the old German states coached the newcomers. Vocational training, advanced training and examination systems were set up, advice and support were provided for reprivatisers and new start-ups, while the legal system and foreign trade were re-established under new premises. Everything was moving and changing. The new CCI acted, improvised and encouraged. In the heat of the events, it learned to represent the interests of its business sector members.

New beginnings and new buildings

Those who had been part of it like looking back to the early days. The team of around 60 employees had worked in a "euphoric mood", says one who was there from the start. The team was learning more day by day and found great pleasure in helping companies to help themselves during all the initial upheaval. All distances were short, even those going "up". Events were organised on the spur of the moment with precious little red tape. The CCI members grew up with the new beginning which they helped to shape at the same time.

The CCI headquarters in Dresden initially had three sites: a villa in August-Bebel-Straße 48, a branch in Barlachstraße and today's site on Straßburger Platz. In 2002, the Chamber added a new modern building to Dresden's architecture. The new building was constructed in the south-eastern suburb of Nieder-

Unternehmertreffen in der
IHK Dresden

Meeting of entrepreneurs at the
CCI Dresden

Eine gemeinsame starke Stimme

Neben dem Hauptsitz verfügt die IHK Dresden über Geschäftsstellen in Bautzen, Görlitz, Kamenz und Zittau sowie das Regionalbüro Riesa. Für die Belange der Unternehmer setzen sich 160 Mitarbeiter ein. Als Hauptgeschäftsführer hält Dr. Detlef Hamann die Fäden in der Hand, ein gebürtiger Magdeburger, der an der früheren Hochschule für Verkehrswesen Dresden promoviert hat. Er folgte 2003 auf Elvira-Maria Horn, der IHK-Chefin seit 1990. Kurz nach der Wende war ihrem entschlossenen Handeln – getragen von der vorwärtsdrängenden Unternehmerschaft – ein Novum zu danken: die erste Satzung für eine neue Industrie- und Handelskammer in Ostdeutschland. Auf deren Grundlage konnte dann eine legitimiert gewählte Vollversammlung ihre Arbeit aufnehmen.

sedlitz right next door to the CCI Training Centre Dresden. Since 1996, this has been housed in a reconstructed building complex that embodies Dresden's camera production traditions since 1897, associated with the names of Wünsche ("Reicka"), Zeiss Ikon and Pentacon.

One strong joint voice

Together with its headquarters, the CCI Dresden also has branches in Bautzen, Görlitz, Kamenz and Zittau, as well as a regional office in Riesa. 160 employees are involved in protecting the members' interests. Chief Executive Dr. Detlef Hamann holds the reins; born in Magdeburg, he completed his doctorate at the former College of Transport in Dresden. He took office in 2003, following on from Elvira-Maria Horn who had

Was wäre die IHK Dresden als starke Stimme der regionalen Wirtschaft ohne Meinung und Mittun von mehr als 3000 selbstständigen Gewerbetreibenden, leitenden Angestellten und Mitarbeitern aus Unternehmen des Kammerbezirkes! Für Dr. Günter Bruntsch, den IHK-Präsidenten, steht und fällt die Selbstverwaltung der Wirtschaft letztlich mit den Ehrenamtlichen: „Ihr Wirken im Präsidium und in der Vollversammlung, in den verschiedenen Fach- und Prüfungsausschüssen sowie Arbeitskreisen ist eine tragende Säule der Arbeit und der Erfolge einer Kammer."

Ihr Engagement verschaffe den IHK-Mitarbeitern ständig neue Sach- und Problemkenntnis aus der unmittelbaren Unternehmenspraxis, die diese wiederum zugunsten der Mitgliedsunternehmen einbringen könnten, so Dr. Günter Bruntsch. Er kommt selbst aus der Praxis. Dem gebürtigen Dresdner, gelernter Werkzeugmacher und Experte des Chemieanlagenbaus, gehört die GB Consult Unternehmensberatung Dresden.

Das Abc der IHK-Leistungen

Sprachrohr nach innen und außen ist die Kammerzeitschrift „ihk.dresden". Zusammen mit dem hauseigenen Internetauftritt ist sie Orientierungshilfe und Ratgeber gleichermaßen. Zehn Ausgaben jährlich halten die Unternehmer mit dem Geschehen im Kammerbezirk auf dem Laufenden. Im ersten Heft 2012 stimmte Hauptgeschäftsführer Dr. Detlef Hamann die Mitglieder auf das Jubiläumsjahr ein. Es sei ein besonderes Jahr, auch weil im September die neue Vollversammlung bis 2017 gewählt und Dresden im November Gastgeber eines Kongresses mit allen 80 deutschen IHKs und dem DIHK sein werde.

„Bei aller Vorfreude und Spannung, die von diesen Ereignissen ausgehen, werden wir selbstverständlich die finanzpolitischen Turbulenzen, Europaszenarien, die Energiewende und viele weitere wirtschaftsrelevante Themen nicht aus den Augen verlieren", betonte er. Die Wirtschaft werde Stellung beziehen und ihren Sachverstand in die politischen Entscheidungsprozesse einbringen. Als Beispiel nannte er die Auswirkungen des demografischen Wandels auf die Belegschaftsstrukturen. Die IHK Dresden wolle angesichts eines historischen Tiefs bei der Schulabgängerzahl zukunftsfähige Lösungen aufzeigen, beispielsweise mit allen Beteiligten für die duale Berufsausbildung als attraktiven Einstieg ins Berufsleben werben und unbürokratische Weichen für die Beschäftigung ausländischer Fachkräfte stellen, so der Hauptgeschäftsführer.

Von Abwasser bis Zollauskünfte

Die IHK Dresden ist „immer in Bewegung", und sie sorgt für Bewegung. In den Köpfen und ganz praktisch. Einen aktuellen

run the CCI since 1990. Shortly after reunification, her resolve, driven forward by the whole business sector, was responsible for introducing the first statutes for a new Chamber of Commerce and Industry in East Germany, provided the basis for a legitimated, elected general assembly to take up its work.

How could the CCI Dresden be a strong voice for the regional economy, without the opinions and contributions of more than 3,000 self-employed business- and tradesmen, senior executives and employees from companies in the chamber district! For Dr. Günter Bruntsch, CCI President, self-administration of the business sector depends in the end on the honorary officials: "The effort they put in on the Executive Committee and in the General Assembly, in the various technical and auditing committees together with the working parties is one of the key pillars supporting the work and success of a Chamber."

Their commitment gives CCI members constant access to new know-how and problem solutions coming directly from business practice, which they in turn take with them into the everyday activities of the member companies, says Dr. Günter Bruntsch. He's a practical man himself. Born in Dresden, the trained toolmaker and chemical engineering expert is the proprietor of GB Consult Unternehmensberatung Dresden.

The ABC of CCI services

The CCI's internal and external mouthpiece is the Chamber newsletter "ihk.dresden". Together with the Chamber's own website, it acts as guide and advisor at the same time. Ten issues a year keep entrepreneurs up-to-date with what's happening in the chamber district. In the first issue of 2012, Chief Executive Dr. Detlef Hamann put the members in the mood for the jubilee year – a special year which includes elections to the new General Assembly in September which will remain in office until 2017, while in November Dresden acts as host for a congress with all 80 German CCIs and the DIHK.

"Despite all the anticipation and excitement generated by these events, we will naturally continue to keep our eyes on the financial turbulence, European scenarios, the energy turnaround and many other issues that are relevant to business and the economy", he emphasised. The business sector will take its stand and contribute its expert knowledge to the political decision-making process. As an example, he named the impacts of demographic change on workforce structures. Given the historically low number of school-leavers, the CCI Dresden will be illustrating future-oriented solutions, for example joining forces with all stakeholders to promote dual vocational training as an attractive career start, while pushing unbureacratic procedures for the recruitment of foreign skilled labour, says the Chief Executive.

Bildung baut Brücken in die Zukunft. Die IHK-Bildungszentrum Dresden gGmbH gehört zu den engagierten und fest im Bedarf des regionalen Arbeitsmarktes und der sächsischen Wirtschaft verankerten Bildungsdienstleistern.

Education builds bridges to the future. The education centre of Dresden's CCI is one of the most committed educational service providers in the Saxonian economy and a service provider that is firmly anchored in serving and satisfying the needs of the regional labour market.

Rekord kann sie etwa bei der Weiterbildung von Industriemeistern verkünden: 2011 schlossen 464 Männer und Frauen diese Fortbildung ab, so viele wie nie zuvor. Insgesamt nimmt die Kammer in der Berufsausbildung jährlich 17 000 Prüfungen und über 5000 Weiterbildungsprüfungen ab. Als versierter Coach beweist sie sich bei der Starthilfe, der Unternehmensförderung oder Außenwirtschaftsberatung. Dazu finden jährlich rund 130 Veranstaltungen, Gesprächsrunden und Seminare sowie mehr als 2300 individuelle Beratungen statt.

Von A wie Abfälle/Abwasser bis Z wie Zollauskünfte – das Infoheft „IHK kompakt" listet fast 140 Beratungs- und Leistungsangebote mit Kontakten auf. Bei diesem Spektrum wundert man sich fast, dass die IHK Dresden nicht auch noch Karten für die Semperoper, die Bautzner Domschatzkammer oder das Schlesische Museum zu Görlitz vermittelt. Für Kunstgenuss und Freude an Land und Leuten aber ist der Kammerbezirk selbst zuständig, von A wie Altenberg bis Z wie Zittau. Apropos Freude...

Gartenhaus, Freude und Freiheit

Dresden, November 1785: Im elbnahen Loschwitzer Sommerhäuschen des Oberkonsistorialrates Christian Gottfried Körner vollendet ein mittelloser Mittzwanziger ein Gedicht. Noch im selben Jahr erscheint es in einer Leipziger Zeitschrift: „Ode an die Freude". Von seinen Versen ist Friedrich Schiller – so heißt der junge Mann – allerdings nicht überzeugt. Sie hätten Wert „nur für uns und nicht für die Welt", schreibt er an Körner.

Das sahen nachfolgende Generationen anders. Beethoven vertonte die Ode mit dem berühmten Eingangsvers „Freude, schöner Götterfunken..." 1823 in seiner 9. Sinfonie. Ende 1989 erklang in Berlin der Chorsatz unter Leonard Bernstein mit der kleinen Textänderung: „Freiheit, schöner Götterfunken..." Seit 1985 ist die Instrumentalfassung offizielle Hymne der Europäischen Union. „Ohne Worte, in der universalen Sprache der Musik, ist die Hymne Ausdruck der idealistischen Werte Freiheit, Frieden und Solidarität, für die Europa steht", heißt es auf ihrer Webseite. Dresden, Weltkultur, Europa – ein schöner Dreiklang als Grundakkord für einen starken, fitten und sympathischen Wirtschaftsstandort.

Covering the whole range

The CCI Dresden is "always on the move" and keeps things moving – in people's heads and in quite practical terms. For example, it has recently set a new record in terms of advanced training for industrial master craftsmen: in 2011, 464 men and women completed this qualification, more than ever before. Altogether, 17,000 vocational examinations and more than 5,000 advance training examinations are taken before the Chamber. The CCI acts as an experienced coach in helping start-ups, fostering company development or providing foreign trade advice. To this end, around 130 events, round tables and seminars are held every year together with more than 2,300 individual counselling sessions.

The "IHK kompakt" information brochure provides information right across the board, listing nearly 140 advice and support services with all the contact details. Given the full range this covers, it's almost surprising that the CCI Dresden doesn't provide tickets for the Semperoper, the Bautzner Domschatzkammer or the Silesian Museum in Görlitz. But when it comes to art and enjoyment of the countryside and its people, this is where the Chamber district itself comes in, from A for Altenberg to Z for Zittau. By the way, as far as joy is concerned...

Summerhouse, joy and freedom

Dresden, November 1785: In the summerhouse of Senior Consistorial Councillor Christian Gottfried Körner in Loschwitz not far from the river Elbe, a destitute mid-twenty-year old completes a poem. Before the end of the year, it is published in a Leipzig magazine: "Ode to Joy". But the young man, whose name is Friedrich Schiller, is not convinced. His lines were of value "only for us and not for the world", he writes to Körner.

Future generations didn't agree. Beethoven put the Ode to music with the famous opening line "Joy, fair spark of the gods..." in his 9th Symphony in 1823. At the end of 1989, the symphony was performed in Berlin under conductor Leonard Bernstein with a slightly amended text: "Freedom, fair spark of the gods..." Since 1985, the instrumental version is the official anthem of the European Union. "Without words, in the universal language of music, this anthem expresses the ideals of freedom, peace and solidarity for which Europe stands", is the official explanation on the website. Dresden, world culture, Europe – a harmonious chord for a strong, fit and appealing business location.

Hat sich Friedrich Schiller in seiner „Ode an die Freude" von diesem Blick inspirieren lassen? Man möchte es gerne glauben...

In his "Ode to Joy", was Friedrich Schiller possibly inspired by this view? One would really like to believe this...

Verzeichnis der PR-Bildbeiträge

Die nachstehenden Firmen, Verwaltungen und Verbände haben mit ihren Public-Relations-Beiträgen das Zustandekommen dieses Buches in dankenswerter Weise gefördert.

List of illustrated contributions

We thank the following companies, administrations and associations which with their public relations contributions have made the production of this book possible.

ADZ NAGANO GmbH Gesellschaft für Sensortechnik,
  Ottendorf-Okrilla 62, 63
  www.adz.de / info@adz.de

Bergi-Plast GmbH, Berggießhübel 32, 33
  www.bergi-plast.de / info@bergi-plast.de

DIW Mechanical Engineering GmbH & Co. KG,
  Radebeul 108, 109
  www.voith.com / dresden@voith.com

Dresdner Wach- und Sicherungs-Institut GmbH,
  Dresden 57
  www.dwsi.de / info@dwsi.de

Elektro Zentrum Großenhain EZG eG, Großenhain 102
  www.e-z-g.de / post@e-z-g.de

fit GmbH, Zittau 100, 101
  www.fit.de / info@fit.de

Infineon Technologies Dresden GmbH, Dresden 67
  www.infineon.com

Kirchhoff & Lehr GmbH, Arnsdorf 71
  www.kirchhoffundlehr.de / info@kirchhoffundlehr.de

MFT Motoren und Fahrzeugtechnik GmbH,
  Cunewalde 97
  www.mft-cunewalde.de / info@mft-cunewalde.de

MICRO-EPSILON Optronic GmbH,
  Dresden-Langebrück 114
  www.micro-epsilon.com / info@micro-epsilon.de

Mitras Composites Systems GmbH, Radeburg 107
  www.mitras-composites.de / info@mitras-composites.de

Nehlsen-BWB Flugzeug-Galvanik Dresden
  GmbH & Co. KG, Dresden 110
  www.flugzeuggalvanik.de / info@flugzeuggalvanik.de

Ostsächsische Sparkasse Dresden 39
  www.ostsaechsische-sparkasse-dresden.de
  e-mail@ostsaechsische-sparkasse-dresden.de

PRETTL Electronics AG, Radeberg 68
  www.prettl-electronics.com / info@prettl-electronics.com

Pulverturm GmbH & Co. KG, Dresden 123
  www.pulverturm-dresden.de
  info@pulverturm-dresden.de

Schmiedewerke Gröditz GmbH, Gröditz 73
  www.stahl-groeditz.de / info@stahl-groeditz.de

SICK Engineering GmbH, Ottendorf-Okrilla 22, 23
  www.sick.com / info.pa@sick.de

slr-Elsterheide GmbH, Elsterheide 56
  www.slr-group.com / info@slr.de

SMT & HYBRID GmbH, Dresden 61
  www.smt-hybrid.de / info@smt-hybrid.de

Spedition Kunze GmbH & Co. KG, Dresden 35
  www.kunze.de / info.dd@kunze.de

Spezialtechnik Dresden GmbH, Dresden 24, 25
  www.spezialtechnik.de / info@spezialtechnik.de

STRABAG AG, Direktion Sachsen 29
  www.strabag.de / dir-sb-sachsen@strabag.com

VEM Sachsenwerk GmbH, Dresden 53
  www.vem-group.com / sachsenwerk@vem-group.com

Veritas Sachsen GmbH, Neustadt 106
  www.veritas-ag.de
  info.neustadt@veritas-ag.de / info.polenz@veritas-ag.de

VON ARDENNE Anlagentechnik GmbH, Dresden 55
  www.vonardenne.biz / office@vonardenne.biz

Bildquellen

Picture sources

Roland Schiffler, Bremen: S. 22, 32, 32/33, 33, 35, 39, 61 o., 62, 63 u. li. und u. re., 68, 71, 97, 100–102, 106–108, 109 o., 110, 114, 123.

Archiv (Werkaufnahmen): S. 22/23, 23–25, 53 o., 55, 56, 61 u., 67, 73, 109 u.

© Alexander Raths/fotolia.com: S. 81; © AlexCher/fotolia.com: S. 19; © Alterfalter/fotolia.com: S. 21 o.; Andreas Agne/pixelio.de: S. 9 u., 63 o. re.; © arsdigital/fotolia.com: S. 15; Jochen Balzer/SBO: S. 29 u.; © Bernd Jürgens/fotolia.com: S. 11 u. li.; Kai Burges: S. 89 o.; © c/fotolia.com: S. 27; © Daniel Fleck/fotolia.com: S. 119; © digi_dresden/fotolia.com: S. 130; Dresdner Verkehrsbetriebe AG: S. 94; © Erik Schumann/fotolia.com: S. 128; © farbeffekte/fotolia.com: S. 11 o.; © farbkombinat/fotolia.com: S. 7; Flughafen Dresden International: S. 40/41; Maik Förster, Riesa: S. 41 u.; Fraunhofer IWS Dresden: S 89 u.; René Gaens, Dresden: S. 53 u.; © Gina Sanders/fotolia.com: S. 43, 139; Glashütte Original, Glashütte (Sachsen): S. 116; Katharina Grottker, Dresden: S. 57; Joachim Grunwald/STRABAG: S. 29 o.; © Harald Lange/fotolia.com: S. 131; © heisedesign/fotolia.com: S. 16; © Horst Schmidt/fotolia.com: S. 31; IHK Dresden: S. 6, 79, 126 u., 135; Hagen Immel: S. 88; © Jeanette Dietl/fotolia.com: S 21 u.; © Karin Jähne/fotolia.com: S. 133; Andreas Keller/pixelio.de: S. 132/133; © krizz7/fotolia.com: S. 104; © LE image/fotolia.com: S. 47; © LianeM/fotolia.com: S. 3 Innentitel (1), 17, 126 o.; © lightpoet/fotolia.com: S. 45; © Lisa F. Young/fotolia.com: S. 11 u. re.; Eckhard Malcherek, Freital: S. 37; © Marina Lohrbach/fotolia.com: S. 77; © Mikhail Markovskiy/fotolia.com: S. 118; Novaled AG, Dresden: S. 66; © Olivier/fotolia.com: S. 99; © O.M./fotolia.com: S. 3 Innentitel (1), 51 li.; © oschatzpics/fotolia.com: S. 141; © osiris59/fotolia.com: S. 75; © Paulus Nugroho R/fotolia.com: S. 64; © Peter Eggermann/fotolia.com: S. 3 Innentitel (1); Porzellan-Manufaktur MEISSEN: S. 112; © racamani/fotolia.com: S. 105; © Raimundas/fotolia.com: S. 85; Holm Röhner, Dresden: S. 30; © Sabine Kipus/fotolia.com: S. 3 Innentitel (2); © Sandro Götze/fotolia.com: S. 122; Michaela Scharf, Pirna: S. 44; © Stefan Germer/fotolia.com: S. 3 Innentitel (1); © Stefan Gräf/fotolia.com: S. 49; Technische Universität Dresden: S. 80, 83, 87, 91; Thieme GmbH, Großröhrsdorf: S. 113; © ThKatz/fotolia.com: S. 51 re.; © Thorsten Schmitt/fotolia.com: S. 3 Innentitel (1), 59; © Tilo Grellmann/fotolia.com: S. 127; © Tryfonov/fotolia.com: S. 92; © U. Göbel/fotolia.com: S. 10; von Oheimb: S. 137; Web Gallery of Art: S. 9 o.; Weingut Schloss Proschwitz: S. 129; Wikimedia Commons: S. 121; Wirtschaftsförderung Sachsen GmbH: S. 42; © withGod/fotolia.com: S. 96; © World travel images/fotolia.com: S. 125.